When the Rains Come

When

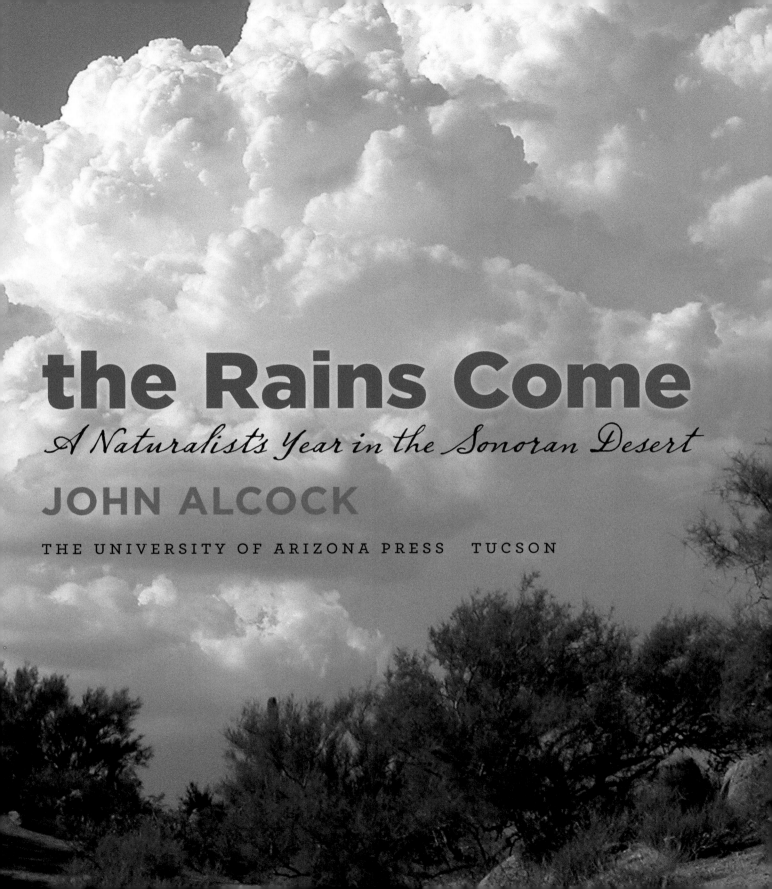

the Rains Come

A Naturalist's Year in the Sonoran Desert

JOHN ALCOCK

THE UNIVERSITY OF ARIZONA PRESS   TUCSON

The University of Arizona Press
© 2009 The Arizona Board of Regents
All rights reserved
www.uapress.arizona.edu

Library of Congress
Cataloging-in-Publication Data
Alcock, John, 1942–
When the rains come : a naturalist's year in
the Sonoran desert / John Alcock.
p. cm.
Includes bibliographical references.
ISBN 978-0-8165-2835-6 (hardcover : alk.
paper) —
ISBN 978-0-8165-2762-5 (pbk. : alk. paper)
1. Alcock, John, 1942– 2. Biologists—
Arizona—Biography. 3. Desert ecology—
Sonoran Desert. 4. Natural history—Sonoran
Desert. I. Title.
QH31.A37A3   2009
578.75409791'7—dc22   2008036823

Publication of this book was made possible
in part by a grant from Arizona State University with assistance from Rob Page (Director
of the School of Life Sciences), Sid Bacon
(Dean of Natural Sciences), and Quentin
Wheeler (Vice-President and Dean of the
College of Liberal Arts).

Manufactured in the United States of
America on acid-free, archival-quality paper
containing a minimum of 30% post-consumer
waste and processed chlorine free.

CONTENTS

When the Rains Come

INTRODUCTION

I have been fortunate to live in Arizona's Sonoran Desert for more than three decades. During this time, I have gone out again and again to certain desert locales, several of them not much more than a half hour's drive from my home in Tempe, a suburb of Phoenix. I have become especially familiar with one place in particular, the Usery Mountains, a perfectly ordinary, but utterly wonderful, collection of hills that are home to an assortment of desert insects. As an entomologist of sorts, I owe a lot to those insects, and this book gives me an opportunity to share my enthusiasm for them and for the equally interesting plants that are found in the Userys and in some other attractive parcels of desert that I have also visited repeatedly over the years.

By taking my camera with me when I travel to my favorite desert spots, I have been able to photograph certain objects and landscapes on many occasions. Although the desert looks pretty static at first, second, or even third glance, my photographs taught me that this is an illusion, even in areas untouched by urban sprawl and off-road vehicles. True, most desert plants grow very slowly, but grow they do, and in the process they change the desert around them. These changes are in turn superimposed on others that occur regularly on a seasonal basis. Indeed, despite the fact that some people think that the subtropical deserts of the Southwest are immune to the seasonal distinctions so characteristic of north temperate zones, the seasons of southern Arizona are real and full of significance for an appreciation of the place. Indeed, most naturalists accept the claim that the Sonoran Desert actually has more seasons (five, not four) than most places. So in central Arizona, spring (mid-February to April) is followed by the arid foresummer (May and June); then the monsoon summer (July to September) is capped by a two-month fall (October and November), topped off by winter (December to mid-February). In keeping with the importance of seasonal changes in the Sonoran Desert, I have structured this book about my experiences in the Userys and other nearby sites chronologically, over the course of one year, January to December 2006.

Many of the gradual changes that take place in the desert because of the shifting of the seasons would occur whether or not we humans were present. As such, they can be considered "natural" and therefore (perhaps) desirable and attractive, or at least not upsetting. The same claim is not usually made for most of the changes imposed on the desert by human beings and their livestock, their farms, and their cities. These changes do distress those of us who value any area with even a residual hint of the pristine.

Admittedly, remarkably few places in the entire world qualify as wilderness, if we apply that term only to areas that are truly free from human influence, a conclusion reached by a bevy of conservation biologists led by Eric Sanderson. His research team mapped the human "footprint" on the planet by using satellite pictures and the like to produce scores for such things as population density per hectare (one hectare equals about 2.5 acres), the degree of habitat transformation, the presence of roads, and the availability of electrical power. They then summed the scores, distributed them over the Earth's land surface, and then categorized all the regions of the world in terms of human influence, from very low to very high. Needless to say, the lowest-scoring regions were places like Greenland, the high arctic, and the Sahara, while the highest-scoring sites were the world's large cities: New York, Tokyo, London, and so on. But perhaps the most interesting and sobering figure is that not just cities, but more than 80 percent of the terrestrial surface of the planet can be classified as nonwilderness because the place contains one or more persons per hectare, or is being put to use by agriculturalists, or lies no more than fifteen kilometers (nine miles) from a road, major river, or coastline (insuring easy access by people), or has artificial lights that can be picked up at night by a satellite (74).*

I do not know what percentage of Arizona is free from the human footprint, but I bet that the percentage is low. People have been in Arizona for at least twelve thousand years, and currently there are more than five million of us, primarily in that part of the state where the Sonoran Desert once ruled supreme. Our species has generated all sorts of changes here over the past twelve thousand years, but especially over the last century. No book about our desert could therefore sensi-

* The numbers in parentheses refer to numbered references at the end of the book.

bly avoid an examination of how humans have altered where we live. Whether we like it or not, we are the major player in the desert now, a heavy-handed and heavy-footed player certainly, and what we have done here is therefore part of the story. Becoming aware of the entire spectrum of changes in our desert may give us a better sense of where we live and a greater appreciation for it. I would like to think that it is all worth knowing about, from the activities of a desert wasp to the rhythm of a desert year, from the establishment of a tiny saguaro to the death of a mature saguaro a century and a half later, from the deposition of a potsherd in the desert in 1430 to the re-creation of a desert wetland nearly six centuries later. One thing is certain: we do not live in a wasteland. Far from it. We Arizonans occupy a land with a glorious history, both natural and unnatural, a rocky, spartan, often bone-dry desert that happens to be one of the richest deserts in the world biologically speaking, a desert that still has the feeling of wilderness about it, even in mountains within sight of Greater Phoenix. For this I am grateful, even during a drought when the paloverdes, the desert insects, and I are anxiously waiting for rain.

January *Two Ravens*

The desert plain to the north of the trailhead has a sullen look to it in the early morning light. The winter sun is up but has yet to crest the line of black mountains to the east. Nearby in the gloom, an isolated saguaro cactus stolidly surveys its surroundings.

Silence saturates the cold air. Only my footsteps violate the quiet of the place as I crunch my way north toward a distant range of low mountains. The rhythm of walking ticks off the seconds as morning grayness gradually gives way to something a little more hopeful. Subdued light creeps over the mountains to the east, gradually illuminating the plain and coloring the nearer mountain slopes in pink.

I aim for what looks like an opening between two hills. The scruffy desert shrubs and trees, the creosotebushes and paloverdes, are so widely scattered that I rarely have to alter my course but instead can march straight toward my destination. Occasionally I take one step down into a little dry watercourse before taking one step up out of the wash on the other side, but otherwise the ground is largely free from obstacles of any sort.

My footsteps flatten tufts of brown grass, the still-abundant remains of the past spring, when desert plants grew and flowered with abandon, thanks to generous rains in the preceding months. Currently all is gray and brown, or brown and gray. The Sonoran Desert National Monument is usually austere at this time of year, but austerity has been taken to an extreme this winter. The last rain splashed down here in mid-October, nearly three months ago. Any seeds that germinated at that time produced plantlets that have long since died and disappeared. Now, nothing green remains, only the drab colors of desiccation and drought.

Desert droughts are common here. For every moderately wet win-

Two early spring seasons in the Sonoran Desert National Monument. The photo on the facing page was taken in February 2003, during a prolonged drought, and the photo above in February of 2005, after a much wetter winter.

ter, we have at least one very dry one. In some Januaries, the Sonoran Desert National Monument is devoid of anything green, except for the durable paloverdes, ironwoods, and saguaros. In other Januaries, you can almost imagine that you have stumbled on a verdant Shangri-la in golf course green dotted with early spring annuals. Among the first to flower is a diminutive mustard, the bladderpod, which grows so densely in places (in a good year) that the margins of dry washes are painted yellow.

After a wet winter, the local rodents and black-tailed jackrabbits must think that they have died and gone to heaven, such is the abundance of greenery at their disposal. Today, however, I feel for the few remaining survivors given the dreadful conditions they now face. Some small rodents are hanging on, judging from the handful of little burrows whose entrances show signs of the sort a pocket mouse or kangaroo rat might make in leaving or entering its home. A tail drag mark in the dust, a flurry of obscure footprints. Most burrows, however, have evidently been abandoned by their builders. A few of these may house a spider or two, perhaps a centipede, but nary a mouse or rat. If the brave or lucky rodents that managed to survive to this point are counting on a new crop of annual plants this spring, they appear to be in for a disappointment. The seeds of desert poppies and the like do best if several rains have fallen in the period from October to December, providing the water needed for germination and seedling survival. But the rains have failed thus far this winter, and no storms are forecast for the near future.

In the cold morning air, I zip up my jacket. The remains of four or five chain-fruit chollas lie scattered on the empty ground ahead. Portions of the elegant woody latticework of the cactuses' trunks and limbs are all that is left; the exterior of the plants has gone the way of all flesh.

I come to a broad wash that spills out onto the plain through an opening in the foothills. Behind the foothills, I find that the wash drains a valley bordered on both sides by low mountains. The fine gravel in the wash has been tumbled and cleaned by flowing water over and over again in the past, but today not a hint of moisture remains in the bone-dry streambed. By the edge of the wash, the skeleton of an ironwood holds what is left of its sun-blackened limbs in a twisted, rigid display.

Two ravens sail far overhead, one trailing the other. Neither bird moves a wing as they glide across the sky, looking straight ahead without a glance down toward the hard, dry land below.

January *A Dead Saguaro*

Today I make my first visit of the New Year to Michael Johnson's saguaro. This hike takes me to the Usery Mountains, which are much closer to my home than is the Sonoran Desert National Monument. Here, as elsewhere in the Sonoran Desert, dry washes make convenient hiking trails, and several such trails lead into the mountains. Today I have selected as my access route a big wash that drains much of the southwestern section of the Userys.

From my parking place just off the highway, the wash runs gradually uphill in an easterly direction before bending around to the north. The wash is bordered by creosotebushes, paloverdes, saguaros, ironwoods, teddy bear chollas, all standard Sonoran Desert shrubs and trees. I feel a certain empathy for these plants, which look stressed by the long and continuing drought.

Eventually the "trail" enters a narrow, rocky gorge composed largely of gray granite boulders. Here the walk becomes more demanding, especially when I come to a stretch where large boulders have tumbled into the streambed, forcing me to do a bit of scrambling. Soon, however, I am beyond the little canyon, and the wash, now just a narrow band of sand and gravel, levels out again. Continuing upstream, I come to a place where I climb up a small bank dotted with wizened bursage shrubs and coated with last spring's dead grasses. In a minute or two, I am standing by Michael Johnson's saguaro.

My first photographs of this distinctive saguaro were taken in June of 1990. These images reveal a big cactus with seven extremely long arms. The handsome specimen leaned noticeably to one side, perhaps because the cactus had tilted after a rainy period when its roots momentarily lost their grip on the softened soil.

Because of this saguaro's size and unusual posture, I checked it regularly, which is why I know that it crashed to the ground sometime in April 1992 following several heavy spring rains. After the rainfall, the saguaro added a great deal more water to its already top-heavy body, thereby apparently setting the stage for its ultimate collapse, perhaps when strong winds accompanying a storm pushed the saguaro over.

One of the things that saguaros do remarkably well is to harvest water from the soil, when it is available, for storage upstairs. According to the Saguaro National Park Information Page, a mature saguaro can take up as much as two hundred gallons of water after a good rain. Since a gallon of water weighs 8.33 pounds, a saguaro that took on this amount of water would gain 1,666 pounds. If this weight were unequally distributed, it could tip the balance in favor of a fall. Therefore, although the saguaro's ability to guzzle water helps the cactus make it through long dry spells, this benefit comes with a significant downside. The recently fallen leaning saguaro was full of water, but its liquid reserves can do it no good now.

I found the leaning cactus's death distressing in part because I had recently chosen this specimen as a living grave marker of sorts for my friend Michael Johnson. Michael had died from the slowly lethal complications arising from a combination of a brain tumor, chemotherapy, and valley fever, a fungal disease. He had acquired valley fever after having inhaled what is usually a harmless fungus abundant in the soil in the Phoenix area while he was on sabbatical leave from DePauw University. After his death, Michael was cremated and his ashes were transported from Indiana to Arizona by his wife, Kit, and their two sons, Bill and Christopher. Kit, the boys, and I then drove out to the mountains just north of Mesa, Arizona, where Michael and I had done fieldwork together during his sabbatical. During his visit, Michael had become enthusiastic about the desert, and so it seemed fitting to return his ashes to a place that he had grown to love. We emptied the box containing his remains onto the ground by the base of the leaning saguaro. I had picked this cactus to stand over Michael's remains because of its size and special character. I fully expected this individual to provide a durable living memorial for Michael, but I was wrong.

I now know that saguaros are not exceptionally long-lived, with most individuals checking out sometime between 125 and 175 years of age (65). The variation in estimated age at death stems in part from different methods of age determination and in part from variation in mortality patterns for different populations of saguaros. Desert plants far less imposing than the saguaro can actually live considerably longer. Thus, the scruffy, thin-stalked wolfberry, *Lycium berlandieri*, can top two hundred years despite its fragile appearance (15).

One cluster of saguaros that has provided especially good information on the population biology of the species occupies Tumamoc Hill, home of the University of Arizona's Desert Laboratory in Tucson. Raymond Turner and his colleagues took advantage of the fact that in 1908 all the saguaros growing on Tumamoc Hill were surveyed and their position precisely established on a map. This enabled the Turner team to count the number of saguaros alive in 1908 and to compare that number against counts made up to eighty-five years later. Because the death rate has often exceeded the rate at which new specimens were being recruited into the Tumamoc population, the number of saguaros at this site has fluctuated considerably, with long periods of decline interrupted by short intervals of increase. The population has definitely not stayed the same year after year on Tumamoc Hill (65).

Turner and his coworkers also had information on the heights of three thousand saguaros measured and tagged in 1964, measured again in 1970, and a third time in 1993. They used these data to establish the annual growth rate of saguaros, a key, as it turns out, to estimating the age of any given cactus. From this work, the cactologists learned that the growth rates of saguaro cacti are not constant. Baby saguaros start off very slowly, but as the cacti get taller, their growth accelerates a bit, reaching a maximum of about 0.14 meters per annum (an increment of roughly six inches) for saguaros that are four meters (thirteen feet) tall. Once saguaros get much past this height, their growth rate slows again and continues on a downward trajectory for the rest of their lives.

By incorporating the average annual growth rates for saguaros of different sizes in a mathematical model, the Turner team was able to estimate how old a saguaro was just by knowing its height. They concluded that a saguaro in the population they studied that was two meters (seven feet) tall would be about forty years old, whereas one that was four meters (fourteen feet) would be, not twice as old as a two-meter plant, but about sixty years old instead (because midsized cacti grow at an accelerated rate). Saguaros in the eight-meter (twenty-six feet) range were estimated to be about 100 years old, while those that came in at ten meters (thirty-three feet) were believed to be around 150 years of age, in keeping with the eventual decline in annual growth that occurs as tall saguaros add to their height ever more slowly. Turner's group speculates that the slowdown in growth occurs in older, taller saguaros because these individuals invest less in growth and more in flowers and fruit, whose energetic costs prevent the saguaro from putting nutrients and calories into the building of a bigger body (65). Support for this hypothesis comes from the finding that when flower buds were removed experimentally from a set of saguaros, these budless plants grew about a third more in the following year than a comparable group of saguaros whose flower buds were left to produce the large fruits of the cactus (86).

In Tumamoc Hill, as in most parts of the desert, only a handful of saguaros exceed ten meters in height, which means that few live much longer than 150 years. Even the leaning saguaro, a big one by local standards, probably did not make it much past this milestone. Admittedly this made its life span about three times as long as Michael's. The saguaro's death seemed to compound the uneasiness I felt about Michael's death, for which I considered myself at least partly responsible, having encouraged him to come out to Arizona and study the behavior of some desert wasps and bees in my company. Had I not done so, he would not have acquired the valley fever fungus, which lay latent before springing into action when his immune system was compromised by chemotherapy for his cancer. As an unwitting accomplice in his demise, I had hoped to identify a place for his ashes that would honor the man at least for those years that he had lost owing to his premature death. But the leaning saguaro joined the ranks of the deceased much too quickly for that. The body of the fallen cactus lay in a mound, the various arms and main trunk all roughly in place, except that the various parts lay on the ground instead of standing perpendicular to it.

The subsequent decay of Michael Johnson's saguaro took time. Even two years after the cactus had collapsed, an arm or two and elements of the lower trunk still retained their three-dimensionality, albeit in somewhat shrunken form. The ocotillo that had been crushed in the collapse of the plant disappeared long before the cactus, whose woody parts, thin and thick, were visible even eight years later. Now, however, some fifteen years after the death of the leaning saguaro, only the thickened lower trunk and part of the largest arm still serve as a marker for Michael's ashes, which have blended into the soil at the base of the presumably wind-thrown saguaro. When I visit the site now, I no longer find even a trace of Michael's remains, which disappeared years ago.

///// Michael Johnson's saguaro is not the only handsome big cactus to bite the dust in the Userys during my tenure as desert observer here. One of my favorites, and certainly the largest saguaro I have ever known, went down in August of 1983, during an unusually fierce storm that pounded the desert just to the east of Phoenix, Arizona. This cactus was so huge that its upright arms had sprouted a host of subsidiary arms, filling in the spaces between its limbs and trunk, and thereby creating an overwhelming mass of cactus, a benign Godzilla that towered over the ironwoods and paloverde trees nearby.

The storm that brought Godzilla to its knees was characteristic of those that occur when the monsoon comes to the desert Southwest, a period that usually begins sometime in July and carries on sporadically until the middle of September or thereabouts. Although the term "monsoon" is derived from an Arabic word and was first applied to condi-

tions in southeastern Asia, the phenomenon can be applied equally to the southwestern United States. As the Gulf of California and the Gulf of Mexico warm up, circulation increases, bringing seasonal winds up through Mexico and into Arizona, carrying moisture with them. Once in a while, these pulses of moisture translate into late afternoon and evening thunderstorms over Arizona, although early in the season the monsoon winds that blow into the Phoenix area generally supply far more dust than rain.

But whether a dust storm or a gullywasher, high winds are a defining part of the monsoon. They thrash the tall skinny palm trees that homeowners favor in this part of the world and send palm fragments and other botanical bits and pieces skittering down suburban streets until they are blown into shrubs, gutters, and entryways. Gritty hot air rushes frantically ahead of the temporarily cooling rains that sometimes spill out of the clouds, rewarding some residential areas while cruelly sidestepping neighborhoods right next door.

Out in the desert, a monsoon storm in August 1983 must have come with a microburst of truly violent winds, because when I happened to check the area a week or two later, I discovered dozens of saguaros lying flat on the ground, all laid out in a north-south orientation, organized rather neatly like a collection of corpses in a morgue. Perhaps all the downed saguaros collapsed at nearly the same moment, pushed over by an irresistible wall of wind that cut the top-heavy cacti off at their knees, flinging them facedown onto the gravelly desert soil.

I found the saguaro massacre upsetting, even though I recognized that the deaths were caused by a completely natural, albeit probably rare, event. I took comfort from the fact that the storm had left many saguaros untouched even within the several acres where wind-thrown cacti were common. The survivors tended to be smaller specimens with only one or two arms at most, which saved them from the fate of their many-armed, top-heavy companions.

Still, the scene had a Jonestown air about it, perhaps because saguaros look more like people than any other plant I know. Their typical upright posture, with arms thrown into the air, makes it all but impossible *not* to think anthropomorphically about saguaros, a tendency further encouraged by their great individuality. Saguaros differ in their height,

(facing page) The rapid death and slow decay of the leaning saguaro in the Usery Mountains. The photographs were taken in 1991 (top left), 1992 (top right), 1994 (bottom left), and 2006 (bottom right).

the number of arms they possess, and the orientation of their limbs. Although the arms of most older saguaros curl upward gracefully to parallel the main trunk, sometimes in more or less balanced arrays of four, five, or six limbs, many variations on this theme are on display in any saguaro forest. Some plants are symmetrical; others are lopsided. The arms of some saguaros are held up in the standard position, while others point outward at right angles to the main trunk, or droop downward, or form elaborate curlicues. Some arms are long cylinders of cactus flesh; others are short and stubby.

Because each large saguaro is unique, clearly different from all its fellows, one can easily learn to recognize them as individuals, as I have done in order to pay my occasional respects to the larger members of the local contingent. Because the big saguaros here appeared unchanged from one year to the next, I came to count on their staying the same even while I was doing some serious aging myself. I was grateful that at least a few things appeared to be constant, a modestly reassuring illusion as I moved into my sixties while Phoenix, a city that was once more or less manageable, metastasized into Los Angeles in the Desert.

But the notion that some things stay the same sadly does not apply to saguaros, as the storm-induced loss of so many seemingly invincible specimens made clear.

///// The farm that my parents owned in Virginia has a small family cemetery on a little knoll next to a pasture. One large oak and several dogwoods provide shade for the residents of the graveyard, which also sports a five-foot-tall granite obelisk with the names of twenty or so relatives who are buried close by. No one ever supplied professional individual gravestones for the deceased, although some very rough hewn rocks serve as informal headstones and footstones for some of the cemetery's inhabitants, whose names almost certainly do not appear on the obelisk. Indeed, my father, whose own ashes are now buried nearby, thought that some of those interred here were slaves who died in the service of my pre–Civil War ancestors. We (my father, brother, and I) discovered these crude grave markers during the many summers when we bravely attempted to rid the cemetery of the pokeberries, sumacs, young ailanthus trees, bull briars, blackberry vines, and the many other unwanted plants that grow here in abundance. The vast quantities of vegetation removed from the cemetery produced a memorable bonfire one summer after the debris had dried. The flames licked up the front of the woodlot on the western edge of the cemetery, but failed to set the standing trees on fire, much to our relief.

One year, after a particularly active period of cleaning up the cemetery, we put the nineteenth-century grave markers in rows in among the ornamental periwinkles and daylilies, which we hoped would flourish in the graveyard and hold down the weeds. Our hopes were in vain because the more undesirable a plant, the better it grows during the hot, humid summers of northern Virginia. Every year it was as if we had made almost no progress during the previous summer but instead were condemned to start afresh, chopping, cutting, yanking, and sweating, as we tried to give our ancestors a respectable final resting place. Even so, my father, brother, and I felt good about the hard work of cemetery cleanup. Although we knew that the task could never be finished, pulling weeds from the graveyard offered good exercise, a chance to work (briefly) like the unfortunate slaves that once labored on this land.

///// Just as I always visit the family cemetery when I am in Virginia, I have also made it a point over the years to keep in touch with what's left of Michael Johnson's saguaro and the giant saguaro as well. To reach Godzilla, I hike in from Usery Pass Road heading south until I pick up a trail on a low ridge that runs downhill to the west before merging with the plain that glides away to the distant Salt River. Before the low ridge disappears, I start to scan for a small ironwood directly ahead of me to the west, which I use as a landmark to march straight to the huge thrown saguaro lying on the ground near that tree.

When I first found the fallen giant saguaro a short time after the storm, many of its arms had separated from the central trunk, but they still lay more or less in place, the cactus seemingly having simply moved from the vertical to the horizontal plane. Nothing about the plant had deflated, nor was its color different from what it had been a

The remains of a particularly large saguaro that collapsed during a violent storm in August of 1983. The photograph was taken in March 2005 when only the main ribs remained. A packrat has built its nest mound on the lower portion of the trunk using fragments of cactus skeleton as building material.

couple of weeks earlier. I slowly walked about the cactus absorbing the reality of its death.

Even a year after the saguaro's demise, a few arms of the plant retained some semblance of their original volume and even a hint of greenness here and there. But much of the outer flesh had cracked, dried, and flaked off, exposing parts of the hard woody skeleton. These tan rib segments looked pale by comparison with the sun-dried crust of the saguaro that was still in place.

As the years passed, more and more of the outer cuticle of the plant oxidized and decayed. By March 1987 the internal tubular skeletons of the main trunk and some of the major arms were nearly all that was left of the saguaro. But inspection of the tip of the trunk revealed a filigree of thin mini-ribs that were still intact, lying in place on the ground where they had been for more than three years.

In some springs, the skeleton was outlined in green as brome grass grew up around the bleached ribs of the saguaro. By early summer, the grasses had died, turning from green to red to a brown more in keeping with the color of their fallen companion. Here and there tufts of red brome stems bearing clusters of seeds poked up through the openings in the ribs of the cactus.

As time went on, the saguaro skeleton completely lost its three-dimensional form. Even the thicker ribs of the arms flattened themselves against the desert, while the thick and woody main trunk gradually lost its upper ribs to become a hollowed-out half shell bleached by years of exposure to the sun, wind, and occasional rain. As the process of disintegration proceeded, the remaining ribs became disarticulated. A white-throated packrat took up residence in the end of what was left of the saguaro closest to the ironwood. The rat collected fragments of desiccated saguaro as well as fresher and more prickly segments from nearby staghorn cacti and teddy bear cholla. With these raw materials, it constructed a mound of unfriendly spines over the tunnels and chambers in which it lived hidden from coyotes and red-tailed hawks.

On my most recent visit to the giant saguaro's remains, I found the packrat's house to be its most conspicuous feature. Dried grass stalks, months old, stood in and around the cracked and tattered ribs, concealing parts of what had once been a giant among giants in its day. I like to think of the packrat's house as a temporary gravestone erected in honor of a plant that was exceptional in life and striking even in death.

January *Survivors*

Usery Mountain can be a delightful place to visit in January. The days are generally cool, like today, and the sunshine abundant. Some days, clouds come sailing in from the west, bringing with them parallel lines of shadows that sweep over the ground, forming a constantly shifting mosaic of darkness and light on the surface of the desert. From the ridgeline on Usery Peak, I can watch shadows climb to the top of Red Mountain several miles away on the other side of the Salt River, darkening the red sandstone but only for a little while before the clouds above move on and the sandstone regains its color in the bright sunshine.

To the south below my viewpoint on the peak, the mountainside forms a bowl tilted on its side, home to all the usual upland Sonoran Desert plants, a collection of scraggly paloverdes, small greenish-gray jojoba shrubs, and an assortment of cacti, including teddy bear cholla and saguaros galore. The bowl becomes an especially appealing landscape early in the morning when the sunlight streams over the ridge from the east. In this light, the saguaros stand out strongly against the

Usery Peak twenty-five years apart. Note that several large saguaros in the foreground of the upper photograph, taken in 1980, are missing in the lower photograph taken in 2005.

background of barren ground, or scattered weeds and green grasses, or golden Mexican poppies, depending on the season.

I took my first photograph of this part of the mountain in 1980. Three multiarmed saguaros dominate the 1980 image by virtue of their large size and pleasing shapes. Close inspection of the photograph reveals two other unusually tall saguaros growing off to the left, farther downhill than the central trio. The photographs I have taken in subsequent years document the changes that have occurred in this section of the saguaro forest. Today, four of the big five saguaros of 1980 are gone, presumably toppled by winds or eaten inside out by bacteria and fruit fly larvae. Only the big saguaro farthest from the camera in the 1980 photograph still holds court in 2006. However, one specimen that lacked arms in 1980 has survived to produce six substantial arms, four of which are clearly visible in the more recent photograph. Moreover, several other once armless saguaros have made the transition to the limbed state in the twenty-six years between photographs. I see, for example, that a pair of saguaros growing side by side on the far right of the two photographs have grown considerably, and one of the two even has a number of arms, admittedly modest ones, near its crown.

However, saguaros, both large and small, not only have the potential to get larger as the years pass, but counterintuitively they can shrink as well. A reduction in size can occur when a drought forces the saguaro to use up the water reserves stored in the pulpy material in its trunk and arms. As the saguaro's body loses mass, the pleats on the surface of the cactus come closer together, only to expand again after good rains as the cactus draws water out of the ground to replenish its internal supply. The current drought has been going on for nearly three months now, resulting in a significant loss of water for the saguaros standing in the Userys.

In addition to slowly losing water through transpiration, saguaros possess a much more dramatic means of losing body mass, which involves discarding entire arms or major portions of them. One specimen that I started watching in 1989 eventually lost most of two major arms as well as the top third or so of the main trunk, the bits and pieces falling off at intervals after our initial encounter. Despite the open wounds caused by these losses, saguaro-killing bacteria did not immediately kill this cactus after its various self-amputations. Indeed, the mutilated saguaro looked reasonably healthy for many years, probably because it quickly formed hard scar tissue over its wounds, stopping bacterial invaders at the door.

The saguaro amputee also illustrated another way in which these cacti can change over time. This individual possessed a down-curled arm that once was held well above the ground but over the years had drooped farther and farther until the arm tip practically touched the earth, presumably as a consequence of frost damage to the limb. As an arm partially freezes and weakens, it may not die but instead sag downward in response to gravity. Although in most cases the drooping arm subsequently turns away from the earth in the manner of a normal saguaro limb, this response may be thwarted by an additional freezing night or perhaps by the idiosyncrasies of its gravity-detecting mechanisms.

Thus, although it is tempting to look out at a stand of saguaros and think that the moment is forever, in reality the saguaros are part of a dynamic landscape. Although most of the alterations that take place in such a landscape happen so slowly that we barely notice them, we can, if we are patient and live long enough, become aware of these changes. The combined, if contradictory, effects of the establishment of seedlings and the deaths of adults, the growth of individuals and the loss of some of their limbs, add up to a considerable revision of the desert in the space of even a few decades.

My awareness of the reality of change in the saguaro-dominated Sonoran Desert was promoted by my casual efforts at repeat photography, a technique that others have employed in a far more professional manner. In particular, Raymond Turner and his colleagues have done wonderful things by tracking down photographs taken by surveyors and others working in southern Arizona and northern Mexico around the turn of the twentieth century (35, 91). Once these images were in hand, Turner and company located the exact spot where the photographer had stood in 1880 or 1892 or 1910 in order to photograph the exact same landscape in 1958 or 1962 and again in the 1980s or 1990s. By comparing three photographs taken over a century or so, the repeat photography team has been able to document in considerable detail the degree of stability, or lack thereof, in the vegetation growing at a particular site. Because Turner's group found three hundred historical photographs and produced a repeat series for each one, they were able to claim that they had a reasonable sample on which to base their conclusions about desert changes over a period of more than a century.

With respect to saguaro cacti, Turner and his associates found that in some areas the adult population of this species had plummeted. For example, photographs taken in the 1960s within what is now Saguaro National Park reveal the disappearance of anywhere from one-third to three-quarters of the saguaros visible in matched photographs from about twenty-five years previously. By the time the population was photographed again thirty years later, almost all of the really big specimens were gone, the very cacti that had provided the reason for protecting this place to begin with. In other places, however, the saguaro populations have been holding their own or even increasing, as in the Pinacate region of northwestern Sonora, Mexico, where saguaros are now far more numerous than they were in 1907.

By summing up the changes in the number of saguaros appearing in their complete set of photographs, Turner's team estimated an overall saguaro decline of about 40 percent during the last century or so. But remember this is an average value, not a universal result over the entire range of the saguaro. Inspired by Turner's example, I went back to my Usery Peak photos and did my best to count the specimens visible in the 1980 and the 2005 photos. I came up with about fifty-five in the 1980 image and approximately fifty-two in the later photo. I am not going to bet the house on those numbers, but they are more or less on target. Admittedly, some of those visible in the 2006 photograph were actually present on the mountainside twenty-six years earlier but were too small then to appear in the photograph taken of the area. As we speak, a small saguaro stands right at the base of the largest surviving specimen. This individual, a two-and-a-half-footer, cannot be detected in my most recent photograph of the top of Usery Peak, but it is there waiting to take over should the huge saguaro go to its reward (unless the big guy falls right on top of the junior cactus when its time is up).

The presence of an undetermined number of very small saguaros in both 1980 and 2005 makes it impossible to tell whether the population of this species has been going up or down in the Usery area over the last two and half decades. However, as best I can tell, my saguaro population seems to be doing fine, thanks to the recruitment of new youngsters to take the place of the disappearing oldsters. For the moment, I feel confident that in forty or fifty years, five or six really big saguaro cacti will be guarding the approaches to Usery Peak, just as they did in 1980. Even in the Saguaro National Park, where large saguaros are not nearly as abundant as they once were, many juvenile saguaros are now coming along nicely, which is encouraging for saguaro enthusiasts. And who isn't a devotee of these cacti? Perhaps some day a new generation of admirers will be able to look reverentially at a revived saguaro forest in Saguaro National Park. The new stand may well match the groves of giant saguaros that have come and gone an unknown number of times in the past several thousand years, the period in which saguaros have been part of the flora of Arizona.

That's right. Saguaros have been in what is now central Arizona for only a few thousand years, further evidence of the fundamentally ephemeral nature of almost everything given an appropriately expansive timescale. Needless to say, repeat photography has not supplied the data that have convinced paleobotanists of the very recent appearance (geologically speaking) of the cactus in Arizona. Instead, the saguaro time line is based on studies of the "fossil" pollen and plant debris contained in ancient packrat middens. These brown packets are composed of odds and ends that packrats, now long deceased, carted into the rocky alcoves that served as rat lavatories. The combination of botanical bits and pieces, masses of packrat feces, and dried packrat urine produces a highly durable aggregate, especially when stored in caves or under overhangs where rain almost never reaches the midden. These fossil bundles of waste can now be dated by radiocarbon techniques. When the botanical components are separated from dated middens, they provide a list of the plants in a packrat's neighborhood anywhere from today to as much as fifty thousand years ago, although most middens analyzed are less than twenty thousand years old. Because saguaro pollen and seeds are not part of dated Arizonan middens prior to eleven thousand years ago, we can say with some confidence that the plant was not widely distributed then in what is now Arizona. The detritus of saguaros has, however, been found in middens collected from far southern Arizona and dated to 10,500 years ago, indicating that the plant had begun to spread into this region by then. Subsequently, the climate became drier and drier in the Southwest, and as the size of the desert increased, the cactus gradually moved farther north into central Arizona (9).

Evidence of this sort has convinced Daniel Axelrod that the Sonoran Desert, in its current manifestation, is really a recent phenomenon despite its flora, which includes some ancient species and many that are beautifully adapted to a super-arid environment. Axelrod (5) and others (96) argue that the area in Arizona currently covered in desert has undergone a whole series of transformations over the last fifty million years. At times what is now Sonoran Desert was covered in either tropical deciduous forest or thornscrub forest, while at other times the vegetation has been similar to that found in modern Sonoran desertscrub environments.

The vegetative changes that have occurred over this period were driven by changes in temperature and rainfall, which in turn were affected by the volcanic uplift of the Sierra Madre Occidental in northwestern Mexico, which took place fifteen to thirty million years ago. These mountains blocked the flow of tropical moisture into large portions of southern North America, gradually drying out what is now Arizona and northern Mexico. Large regional deserts came into their own only in the last several million years as precipitation fell from about thirty inches per year to ten inches. However, the decline was not steady, with annual rainfall and temperatures fluctuating over the southwestern United States and northern Mexico as glaciers far to the north first spread and then retreated, only to advance again after warmer interglacial intervals of ten to twenty thousand years (95). Today's Sonoran Desert owes its existence to the last retreat of the glaciers, an event that took place a mere thirteen thousand years ago (5).

///// The current Sonoran Desert icon, the saguaro cactus, probably evolved from a now extinct columnar cactus that lived in a tropical deciduous forest in Mexico long ago. Many tall cacti occur today in the tropical deciduous forests currently found in the warm, relatively moist parts of western central Mexico, demonstrating that an ancestral species of the saguaro could have flourished in just such an ecosystem. As patches of tropical deciduous forests became cut off from one another with the rise of the Sierra Madre, some populations of cacti evolved into saguaros and the other large cacti of the modern Sonoran Desert. Their ancestors had already evolved a capacity for dealing with the prolonged spells of aridity associated with annual dry seasons. Therefore, a proto-saguaro that had evolved in the pre–Sonoran Desert era was in position to evolve adaptations that would enable it to cope with the even higher temperatures and drier conditions as thornscrub replaced tropical deciduous forests. These adaptations then enabled the saguaro to invade a growing regional desert some twelve or thirteen thousand years ago, a time of steadily increasing heat and aridity in what would become northern Mexico and southern Arizona.

The warming that occurred in Arizona about this time was also taking place throughout North America, leading to major changes in the geographic distribution of steppe grasslands, boreal forests, and other major ecosystems in the northern part of the continent. At the time these climatic and ecological changes were occurring, three-quarters of the North American megafauna, the mastodons, the mammoths, the giant ground sloths, and the like, went extinct. Not unreasonably, some researchers interested in the wave of extinction of the North American mammals around thirteen thousand years ago attributed the disappearance of these animals primarily to the environmental changes caused by warming of the climate.

This hypothesis, however, has some problems. Climate change and megafaunal extinction are closely linked *only* in North America but not in Australia, New Zealand, Madagascar, Hawaii, the West Indies, and elsewhere, all locations in which a great many large animal species also went extinct quite suddenly. In all these other places, waves of animal extinction always coincided with the arrival of the first human colonists. If, in the absence of climatic shifts, people were able to do in the giant kangaroos of Australia fifty thousand years ago and the moas of New Zealand twelve hundred years ago, then perhaps in North America as well human contact was the critical factor in the extinction of so many edible creatures (6).

The first person to make this argument was Paul Martin. In 1973, he put the onus of megafaunal extinction in North America on the human colonists who came from Siberia to the Americas about 13,500 years ago. Martin proposed that these Siberian hunters, the Clovis people, took advantage of the fact that they encountered extremely naïve, and thus vulnerable, large mammals, highly edible creatures who had not evolved adaptations against human killers. The Clovis hunters slaughtered and ate these big, vulnerable animals, which generated a human population explosion. Thereafter, each new generation of people moved farther and farther south and east, destroying the megafauna that they came across. If the Clovis people and their descendants were able to increase their populations just 4 percent per year, Martin estimated that they could have completely populated all of North America and South America in about a thousand years, eliminating many large animal species in the process.

Martin's "blitzkrieg hypothesis" quickly generated intense debate, and the arguments persist to this day (20, 99). Some critics of the idea have focused on a special prediction taken from the blitzkrieg hypothesis, which is that the larger mammals were most likely to go extinct since the first North American hunters would almost certainly have targeted the species that offered the greatest amount of meat per unit of hunting effort. However, recently gathered evidence suggests that a mammal's size is far less important than its probable rate of reproduction in determining its risk of extinction after human colonization of the Americas (and other places). Those species present some thousands of years ago that had very low rates of reproduction (assuming their similarity in this regard to closely related species that are still with us) were more likely to go extinct than those with higher rates of reproduction irrespective of body size (43). To the extent that the estimates of reproductive rates of now extinct species can be trusted, the data refute the blitzkrieg hypothesis, narrowly defined, although human hunters could still have played a major role in mammalian extinctions by killing species, large *and* small, that happened to lack the reproductive potential to replace their losses quickly.

///// Whatever the reason for the loss of so many interesting and impressive North American animals, there is no question that they are extinct. Although it is sad that we will never have the opportunity to see a band of mastodons marching along an Arizonan riverbank or a giant ground sloth munching its way through a creosotebush, at least we in Arizona today can enjoy a megacactus, the saguaro, which the first Clovis hunters here knew nothing about. The saguaro story tells us that it doesn't matter what timescale we use: change is inevitable when one examines a given locale, over periods ranging from a few days to many thousands of years. An awareness of this point enables me to look at the saguaros growing on Usery Peak from several angles. On the one hand, I know I am looking at the descendants of what paleobotanists would say are relatively recent cactus colonists. On the other hand, saguaros have been around the mountain for a very long time by human standards, creating a strikingly different kind of landscape from that which preceded the current Sonoran Desert. Many of the particular individuals I have come to know and appreciate will outlive me by a substantial margin. During their time on the planet, however, they will not remain forever in their current form but will grow, some will lose a limb or two, and all will eventually die, at each step in their life journey changing their environment, generally subtly, sometimes dramatically. I plan to keep tabs on this band of saguaros as we proceed together through life.

February *Urban Changes*

From the ridge on Usery Peak, I not only can scan the southern slope, checking on the condition of the major saguaros present, I can also see all the way to downtown Phoenix. Today the view is particularly good, thanks to a winter cold front that has happily removed much of the smog and haze that normally fills the Valley of the Sun during winter, summer, spring, and fall. In the clear, dry air that pushed away the smoky haze, skyscrapers, houses, and highways stand out clearly in a geometric pattern that runs from horizon to horizon, a pattern produced by a huge metropolis filling a flat plain rimmed with dark mountains. The Userys supply one small component of the rim.

From the top of the mountain I also have an excellent view of the Granite Reef Diversion Dam just below the Userys. This dam steers the Salt River into the concrete-lined canals that direct the river to destinations where it can be put to good use by Phoenicians. By the time the Salt River reaches this point, it has made an epic trip, starting in far eastern Arizona before surging rapidly down the impressive Salt River Canyon only to pause behind the Lake Roosevelt dam, the first and largest of four artificial impoundments that slow the Salt River on its odyssey. The last of the four big dams on the Salt River, Stewart Mountain Dam, creates Saguaro Lake, just a few miles upstream from the much smaller Granite Reef Dam. I can glimpse the lower end of Saguaro Lake from Usery Peak.

The Usery Mountains themselves are part of the Tonto National Forest, land that was set aside by the federal government in 1905 to protect the Salt River watershed. This river originally provided much of the water that farmers used when most of the exceptionally hot desert that is now Greater Phoenix was agricultural land. Now the water that once flowed from the Salt River into a maze of irrigation canals before flooding a cotton field or alfalfa farm goes instead to one or another water purification plant before magically reappearing in the kitchens and bathrooms of single-family residences in thirty-five municipalities ranging from Apache Junction to Youngtown, which combine to form metropolitan Phoenix. We are fortunate not to have to rely on local rainfall for our dishwashers, because even in a normal year only seven or eight inches of rain falls directly on us. This year to date, the total is still nil, a fat zero. Fortunately for Phoenix, it has rained and snowed in the mountains of western New Mexico, providing us with New Mexican drinking water.

Between the two dams at Stewart Mountain and Granite Reef, the river flows lazily through a band of mesquites and salt cedar. Because this portion is protected under federal regulations, no housing developments have sprung up in the desert here, even though building would be relatively easy and surely profitable, with access offered by the Bush Highway as it parallels the river. Instead of Riverbrook Estates and Saguaro Vista Homes, we have only a handful of parking lots built by the U.S. Forest Service to promote river recreation, of which floating down the Salt River in an inner tube in July is the quintessential example.

One of these recreation sites, the Coon Bluff picnic area, is home to a substantial forest of mesquites on the old sandy floodplain of the Salt River. In among the mesquites, bird-watchers have a good chance of seeing a vermilion flycatcher even during the winter months. Gorgeous creatures, the bloodred males twitch their tails nervously while clinging to the lower branches of the trees. Bird-watchers can also see much that is not attractive at Coon Bluff—namely, the dirty paper plates and empty beer cans left by retreating picnickers as well as the chopped limbs on almost every mesquite within a quarter of a mile of the parking area, the trees having been vigorously pruned by woodcutters seeking fuel for their smoky campfires. The understory of the mesquite bosque also lacks appeal, consisting as it does of an ugly European mustard, inadvertently brought to this location, perhaps by picnickers or perhaps on the hooves of horses wandering in from the nearby Indian reservation. During a recent visit, I observed a dead horse lying swollen and half-submerged in the shallows a few feet from a riverbank where plastic bottles were lined up shoulder to shoulder. This tableaux led to my quick departure, but I am grateful nonetheless that at least some semblance of the natural world persists at Coon Bluff.

If one goes downstream below the Granite Reef Diversion Dam, public desert lands give way to privately owned real estate lying within the city of Mesa, one of the many cities that have coalesced into Greater Phoenix during the thirty-four years that I have been coming out to the Userys, a period of riotous suburban expansion.

Mesa was not always on the go. The first Anglo settlement here occurred in 1878 when a handful of Mormon colonists put down roots and turned to the long-abandoned Hohokam irrigation canals to water their agricultural fields. (Hohokam is the name given to the native people who occupied central Arizona from about AD 200 to about AD 1450. We will have more to say about them later.) The first expansion of Mesa began in 1908 when the Granite Reef Diversion Dam was built, increasing the reliability of water for the local farmers. But prior to the construction of Roosevelt Dam in 1911, the farmers in Mesa and Phoenix had to contend with natural fluctuations in Salt River flow. After 1911, when President Theodore Roosevelt personally pushed a button that began the controlled release of water from a full Lake Roosevelt, farmers far downstream were guaranteed a steady supply of water for their crops. Agriculture in Mesa flourished, with a boom in cotton production followed by a period when citrus orchards became all the rage.

Growth in agriculture provided the wherewithal for a continuously expanding population. At the start of World War II, seven thousand people lived in the town, a figure that rose to seventeen thousand by

1950. As air-conditioning became standard practice, Mesa's population took off; by 1970, town boosters could and did boast of having sixty thousand residents, a total that skyrocketed to nearly four hundred thousand by 2000, with another fifty thousand inhabitants added during the next five years. During the time I have been coming to the Userys, Mesa has tripled in size. The city, no longer even remotely a town, now covers 125 square miles, up 125-fold from the original settlement.

What happened in Mesa has taken place in Phoenix as well. From fewer than thirty thousand inhabitants in 1920, Phoenix (narrowly defined) grew to a city of one hundred thousand or so by 1950. From that time forward, the city has not looked back on its way to becoming a vast megalopolis of about 1.4 million people occupying some five hundred square miles (an area "larger than Los Angeles" gloats the Phoenix city Web site). An additional 2.1 million inhabitants, including those who live in Mesa, call Greater Phoenix home.

From my perch in the Userys, the most conspicuous evidence of development in Mesa is very close indeed, in the form of two subdivisions visible to the southwest of the mountain, one on either side of the Bush Highway. In 1985 developers erected a chain-link fence along the western side of the highway. Behind the fence they put up a billboard announcing the coming of the Red Mountain Ranch development, named after the conspicuous red sandstone mountain just across the Salt River on an Indian reservation. Shortly thereafter backhoes and bulldozers rumbled into the desert. The developer's employees dug trenches around some of the larger saguaros, paloverdes, and ironwoods, which were subsequently moved into huge wooden containers for replanting later. Then the bulldozers scraped the remaining desert bare in preparation for street layout and house building. The crisp stucco houses with their pale red tile roofs soon lined up cheek by jowl along East Trailridge Circle and East Raftriver Street and others like them. The shrunken front yards associated with these houses were mostly xeriscaped, with big pink gravel strewn around a handful of lantanas and bougainvilleas. A thoroughly nonxeriscaped golf course designed by Pete Dye, built in 1986 and operated by the Red Mountain Ranch Country Club, provided the one amenity that is all but essential for any modern development in Greater Phoenix.

Construction was somewhat slower to get under way on the other side of the highway, but by the early 1990s, work had begun on Las Sendas, a master-planned community covering twenty-four hundred acres with, of course, a centerpiece golf course, this one designed by Robert Trent Jones, another big name in the golfing world. You could hit the links by 1995. Ever since then, the developers have been filling in the surrounding terrain with row upon row of houses. What was left of the desert landscape has been subjected to the double-barreled approach of "salvage" and bulldoze. The many desert cacti and other plants that have been rescued in the salvage phase have, according to the Las Sendas promotional material, been replanted within the community in keeping with their self-proclaimed enthusiasm for a green approach to development. Before then, while the saguaros and paloverdes cooled their heels in their containers, the land was smoothed and graded, after which building crews moved into high gear, creating one subdivision after another with names like Eaglefeather and Canyon Creek. The earlier clusters of houses to be built had gray tile roofs; the more recent subdivisions feature homes with red tile roofs.

Blandford Homes, one of the builders at Las Sendas, offers a full range of house sizes from fifteen hundred square feet to more than four thousand in the Ironwood Pass, Desert Vista, and Sonoran Heights series. The owners of these houses belong to the Las Sendas Association, which claims that the guiding vision of the development has always been "Celebrating the Community of Nature and Man." From Usery Peak, Las Sendas appears to be celebrating man somewhat more vigorously than nature, but I have no doubt that proximity to the Tonto National Forest is a plus for many of the persons living in this award-winning town within a town. Evidence on this front comes from the multimillion-dollar custom homes, which are just now going in at the very end of the building phase. These mansions with their circular driveways back up onto the Tonto National Forest boundary, guaranteeing their owners easy access to the genuine desert fortunate enough to lie outside the borders of Las Sendas.

From Usery Peak, I can sometimes hear the construction crews pounding away far below me. I wonder where they will go to work once Las Sendas is completed. Mesa and Apache Junction must be on the

Sonoran Desert urban sprawl. The Las Sendas development was underway in 1997 (facing page, top). By 2002 (facing page, bottom) the initial phase of house building had been completed; the spread of the development continued through 2004 (above). The bulldozed and flattened area visible in the 2004 photograph was filled with housing by mid-2005 (bottom).

verge of running out of room for the really big developments that the really big developers favor these days. So the crews may have to head well out of town, taking their bulldozers and truckloads of red roofing tiles with them. If the creosotebushes and paloverdes far from Mesa could tremble at the thought, they would.

February *The Long History of Littering*

When I first went out to the western edge of what is now the Sonoran Desert National Monument, the developers had just begun to flatten the creosote plains to the north and put up houses by the hundreds. At that time, even finding my way into the reserve was a challenge, so much so that I missed the ranch lane turnoff despite having a detailed and reasonably complete set of directions to my destination. But when I doubled back and took what I guessed had to be the right way, I was gratified to find a track running off into the desert. A gate needed to be opened and closed and residual uncertainty overcome, given the absence of any reassuring sign, but after the first half mile or so, I could see that I was at least headed in the right direction, even though the "road" consisted of two shallow ruts that sometimes entered and followed a dry wash to the east. In one section of the wash, our approaching car flushed a group of four mule deer, which dashed past the paloverdes and saguaros and disappeared so quickly as to make me wonder whether the animals were a special kind of desert mirage.

After several miles of bumping along this half-road, a Bureau of Land Management sign finally appeared that steered us to the south and into one end of a sweeping flatland that separated two low mountain ranges. There the road dead-ended at a little campground with four or five campsites. I had not expected to find a camping facility here and was not surprised to find that the campground was deserted. Once out of the car, glad to be at our destination rather than lurching along a dusty road, we visited the outhouse, one that had obviously been only recently erected and so had not yet been vandalized. On the interior wall, a plaque contained the customary plea to users, begging us not to put trash or other camp debris in the toilet on the grounds that these materials were very difficult to remove once deposited, a reasonable request as far as I was concerned. May those who visit this isolated outhouse follow the rules of bathroom etiquette outlined there.

From the trailhead, we enjoyed the expansive views afforded by the big valley with its northern and southern mountainous borders. Running down the middle of it all was an east-west oriented wash, lined all along the way with big ironwoods and paloverdes. The riparian forest here seemed unusually dense and was all the more striking because of the otherwise desolate nature of the surrounding desert.

Not only were there relatively few large plants away from the wash, but those that had managed to stake out a patch of desert as their own looked as if they were barely holding on. The creosotes in particular had a parched look, their dry leaves more brown than green as a result of the relentless drought. But even in good times this region receives far less rain than the uplands on the northern and eastern sides of Phoenix, and the condition of the vegetation here reflects this fact of life.

The trail, and there was one despite the isolated nature of the site, ran more or less in a straight line across the valley with only a small bend here and a dip there. A lone turkey vulture drifted overhead heading nowhere. Once a rock wren flitted from one small rock to a larger one, where it bobbed several times before flying silently to yet another perch on the ground, only to dart away again, this time disappearing for good.

At the very end of this first long flat section of the trail, I finally had a chance to enter the big wash. The quiet of the day continued in an almost oppressive manner. If I could have silenced my footsteps, I would have done so.

Moving up the wash, which had become the trail, judging from the occasional rock cairns that had been erected here and there, I came at last to a narrow side canyon that seemed to invite investigation. I took the hint and turned into this canyon along a minor dry streambed whose gravel was coarser and more tossed about. Away from this wash, a considerable number of creosotebushes had claimed the adjacent alluvial deposits as their own. No creosote flat can be said to be luxuriant, but this plot of *Larrea divaricata* (sometimes labeled *Larrea tridentata*) looked especially beat-up and at wit's end. Many of the plants had lost most or all of their leaves. Those that had retained some leaves still looked more like a collection of twigs than a viable photosynthesizing machine. Clearly these plants were in shutdown mode, trying only to survive to the next rain, whose arrival was uncertain. The skeletal nature of the creosote permitted me to see the structure of the individuals in this forgotten side canyon more clearly. Quite a few of the plants formed rings or donuts, with a circle of upright stems surrounding a barren patch of soil. The diameter of these circles rarely exceeded a few feet, although I know that in other parts of the Southwest, especially in California's Mojave Desert, these creosote "fairy rings" can be as much as fifteen meters (fifty feet) across.

Thanks to the work of plant ecologists (97), I believe I know how to interpret the circles of creosote that occur in the Maricopas and many other places as well. These rings are creosote clones, the descendants of an original pioneer that took root in the coarse alluvial gravel favored by the species. As the mother creosote grew, she sent out new stems around the central main stem. Over time, branches in the center of the bush began to die, while new stems of the same genetic makeup appeared on the outer part of the plant; these in turn sent propagules outward in a process of clonal reproduction, forming a circle of genetically identical bushes around a barren central ring.

If the process of ring expansion occurs very, very slowly, then large creosote rings would be very old indeed. One of the pioneer students of the age of creosote clones, Frank Vasek, found one particularly large creosote ring, the so-called King Clone, that had a diameter of twenty-two meters (more than seventy feet). He dug out some creosote bits from the center of the clone, dated them via the radiocarbon technique, and from that date concluded that the clone had been growing for about thirteen thousand years. He checked this estimate by measuring the annual amount added to the radius of the upright stems of creosotes of various sorts. He found that the stems grew outward less than a millimeter per year. Assuming that the same outward growth rate applied over the life of clones, a clone with a radius of 7.5 meters (7,500 mm) and an annual radial increment of 0.75 millimeter would have been growing outward for eleven thousand years. Since the annual increment is actually a little less than 0.75 millimeters, his growth rate estimate came close to matching the radiocarbon dating estimate of eleven thousand years plus. Because bristlecone pines, once believed to be the champion in the plant old-age derby, do not exceed five thousand years of age, creosotebush could claim to be the oldest plant in the world.

Vasek's claim, although appealing, has generated some controversy. For one thing, the particular chromosomal variant of creosotebush found in the area in which Vasek worked does not appear in packrat middens older than nine thousand years (based on carbon-14 dating of fossil creosotebush fragments found in these middens) (41). This finding suggests that the King Clone cannot be more than ten thousand years old. Moreover, the largest clones are not found in desert sites with the oldest, most stable soils but instead are concentrated in areas where the soil has been deposited fairly recently by the wind and water. This finding too would seem to contradict the claim of ancient origin of the larger clones. However, a team led by Joe McAuliffe concluded that the large clones did establish themselves on older soils that were then covered by the more recent deposits, rescuing (to some extent) the assertion that big clones are the immediate descendants of very ancient pioneers (53).

If we accept that the oldest living creosotebush clones are thousands of years old, although not necessarily thirteen thousand years of age, then they would have been here during a period of spectacular changes in the desert Southwest. As mentioned already, over the last thirteen thousand years or so the Sonoran Desert has become significantly warmer and drier, with the slow replacement of pinyons, junipers, and oaks in favor of the quintessential Sonoran Desert plants: saguaros, foothill paloverdes, and ironwoods (9, 55).

This gradual but ultimately dramatic transition was taking place when another event of huge ecological importance was also occurring, the peopling of the Americas by immigrants from Siberia. Just when the very first American pioneers marched into what is now Alaska continues to be debated, with some persons believing that humans were in the Americas by roughly thirty thousand years ago. Even if true, the major settlement of the American continents must have taken place later, with a wave of humans starting from Alaska about 13,500 years ago and reaching the tip of South America in a couple of thousand years, or maybe less. By twelve thousand years ago, when the oldest currently surviving creosotebush clones might have been getting started, people were filling up the continents, moving into even the most challenging of arid environments.

Among the most famous of the early occupants of Arizona are descendants of one lineage of Siberians, the Clovis people, whom we have met already. These hunters came with gorgeous fluted spear points designed for insertion into the bodies of the mammoths and other big-game animals that were their contemporaries. Much later there were the desert-dwelling Hohokam, an agricultural people, irrigation specialists whose canals crisscrossed what is now Greater Phoenix and whose rather abrupt apparent disappearance in the mid- to late 1400s has stimulated considerable speculation. In northern Arizona, the Anasazi and Salado cultures built cliff dwellings of remarkable attractiveness and appeal; the durable remains of these villages in sandstone cliff alcoves attract millions of tourists to the Southwest. A great many people preceded the modern Indian groups, the Hopis, the Navajos, the Tohono O'odham, and the Apaches, all of whom have had the great misfortune to overlap in time with settlers of European descent.

The long history of occupation of the Southwest means that for centuries large numbers of people here have been abandoning their buildings, their broken pottery, their stone tools, and other durable artifacts. Wherever I go into the Sonoran Desert, scattered remnants of one or another pre-European culture are often on display, provided I keep my eyes sufficiently focused on the ground in front of my feet. The virtues of this policy were brought home during a hike long ago in the Maricopas when, to my great delight, I saw a pale whitish projectile point only slightly more than an inch in length lying fully exposed on the equally pale gravel of the wash that doubles as a trail.

Finding an intact "arrowhead" is cause for personal celebration given that in more than thirty years of hiking in the West, I have found three such artifacts, which calculates to roughly one per decade. The first of these was a gorgeous specimen, a classic arrowhead, composed of a cleanly fractured, largely white stone, lying on ground composed of red Navajo sandstone in Coral Pink Sand Dunes State Park in southern Utah. I am embarrassed to say that I could not resist collecting this gorgeous artifact, although even then in 1975 I must have known that it was more than merely poor form to do so, especially in a park. Back in suburban Tempe, I put the arrowhead in a drawer somewhere, and at some point this illegally removed object simply disappeared. I have not seen it in twenty or so years. But even before my find somehow evaporated, it had lost all its relevance and appeal as a result of its removal from the place where it had been made, used, and presumably lost. As a result, I have been an obedient servant of the law ever since when it comes to leaving Indian artifacts and other archeological items where I find them.

Therefore, when I saw that arrowhead in the wash in the Maricopas, I photographed it in place from several angles, feeling the thrill of discovery and possession without walking off with the piece. I did pick it up, a technical violation of the law I suppose, but I did not pocket the point. Instead, I placed it underneath a flat rock by the side of the wash rather than leave it exposed to view (until the next major storm rearranged the gravel in the streambed and buried the point for years or decades or millennia). My thinking was twofold. First, I guessed that the next casual hiker who found the arrowhead, should it remain in view, would not be able to resist the temptation to remove it from the area. Second, I selfishly wanted to have the pleasure of relocating the arrowhead myself on a subsequent visit to the wash. Indeed, some months later I came back to the site and after a considerable amount of hunting, found the concealing rock, which I lifted up to expose the artifact in question. Seeing the point again in its proper environment did please me, although not nearly as much as the original discovery. I then replaced the rock over the arrowhead.

Now in February of 2006, I am back again to try to relocate the arrowhead for a second time. The abundant rains of the preceding February, which was part of an unusually wet winter overall, have left their mark in the form of all sorts of dried grasses and annuals. This relatively dense vegetative cover has remained more or less upright, hardened by the sun and still largely frozen in place because after the winter of 2005–6, little rain fell here. Without follow-on rains to moisten and flatten the dead plants, fungi have not been able to degrade the plant material. Nor have termites swarmed over the months-old detritus because they like to have damp earth with which to fashion mud tubes around plant stems. When the protective shelters are in place, termite workers labor within them, stripping cellulose from the dead stems.

Subterranean desert termites are enormously important recyclers; they normally digest huge amounts of dead plant matter every year with the invaluable assistance of their symbiotic gut flora. In so doing, they move great quantities of dirt up to the surface and add valuable nitrogen to the soil (36, 61). But in a drought year, the termite removal squad cannot function effectively. The bottom line for February 2006—the desert still sports a dense coat of dried plant material, a tangle of foot-long grass stems and upright annuals frozen in attitudes they adopted nine or ten months previously. Under these conditions, I cannot find any flat rocks by the edge of the wash, which probably lie beneath a concealing layer of old plants. No thrill of rediscovery for me on this trip.

Most of the aboriginal material that I find constitutes little more than junk, stuff that a Hohokam man or woman just didn't need or want any more. These people understandably chucked the worthless fragments of broken pots, and they often dropped the easily made small stone scrapers, little serrated stone knives, and microliths (very small sharp-edged flakes that were presumably attached to small wooden handles) when they were finished with them. Still, one Hohokam's trash is another man's delight, and so I invest some effort in finding this debris of the past.

Indian artifacts found in the Sonoran Desert to the southwest of Phoenix, Arizona. The broken pot was found lying on a hillside in the Barry M. Goldwater Range, the projectile point on the surface of a dry wash in the Sonoran Desert National Monument.

Detecting aboriginal discards poses some challenges. In my experience, potsherds rarely exceed two inches by two inches, and may be partly buried in soil to boot. Just once, I found the better part of a pot in one piece, to my delight. The numerous stone flakes that I have discovered are generally smaller than potsherds and therefore well concealed by other unworked fragments of rock on the ground. Thus, it often requires some attention to detail to see an aboriginal potsherd or stone artifact and recognize it for what it is. Indeed, some skeptical friends of mine have been known to cast cold water on my claims that such and such was a micro-knife or scraper used by an aboriginal person hundreds, if not thousands, of years ago. Stung by the accusation of an overactive imagination by persons who flatly refused to admire my "finds," I have on occasion sent photographs of presumptive stone tools that I have found to anthropological colleagues here at Arizona State. These academics have verified my conclusions, with the gratifying (to me) result that I can hold my head high when dealing with those skeptical of my amateur anthropology.

Of course, the Hohokam and Anasazi have not been the only ones to engage in casual littering in the Southwest. Modern Arizonans are wonderfully adept at this practice as I have seen firsthand in the Usery Mountains and their surrounds. Recently deposited trash litters the lower portions of the wash that snakes past Michael Johnson's saguaro and heads down toward the Bush Highway. In recent years, the Forest Service has installed a heavy-duty wire fence along the edge of the Bush Highway so that ATVs, dune buggies, SUVs, and other motorized vehicles cannot now turn from the road to travel up the wash. Prior to this operation, a great many such vehicles had, over the years, maneuvered into the desert via the wash, bringing with them drivers often armed with rifles or pistols or both and targets of one sort or another. When these motorized vandals departed, they invariably left their targets behind, so it used to be that a hike along the wash was rather like taking a walk in a dispersed landfill.

I have tried to change the ambience along the wash by carting out the debris discarded by past visitors. To this end, I bring with me a plastic garbage bag or two whenever I walk, not drive, up this wash. During the twenty or so years that I have been playing at sanitary engineer, I have removed many, but not all, of the smaller items that accumulated along this route into the Userys. In so doing, I believe that I have demonstrated my moral superiority to the litterers who came before me. Admittedly I have not even tried to move the rusted frame of an old car that lies next to a big creosotebush, nor have I touched something that looks like a primitive hot-water heater lying three-quarters buried in the middle of a side wash, although recently someone with a similar civic-minded sense of duty has somehow managed to carry or drag this quite dreadful piece of junk out to a resting place near the Bush Highway.

In my role as human Hoover, I have wisely concentrated on the aluminum beer cans, some intact, others bullet-shredded, and the larger fragments of beer bottles, the rest shattered into small pieces of green or brown glass, which emerge from the fine gravel of the wash whenever a surge of water rearranges the usually dry streambed. In places on the borders of the wash, the quantity of glass bits and pieces is so great that the whole area sparkles in the sunshine. I do not find it profitable to deal with these tiny fragments. Instead, my garbage runs focus on the bullet-riddled plywood sheets, wrinkled old cardboard boxes, fragile, half-decayed Styrofoam coffee cups, deflated plastic balloons, shotgun shells in black, red, and yellow, chunks of cheap carpet, large paper cups that once held Pepsi or Coke but are mostly filled with sand and dirt when I find them, small metal clips and rods that are I believe to be automotive odds and ends, the remnants of a small refrigerator compressor, the refrigerator having been dragged out to the wash for target practice, and much, much more. Did I mention golf balls, bullet casings, gentlemen's magazines, newspaper sheets, plastic bottles of every conceivable size and shape, empty Pennzoil containers, and the occasional old shoe, the sole separated from the curled upper? I draw the line at collecting used condoms. There is only so much moral superiority that one can acquire by picking up after others.

Sometimes, persons accompanying me on a wash walk have been good enough to lend a hand in the practice of garbology. They and I have been surprised to learn how much a medium-sized garbage bag weighs when filled with the artifacts abandoned by our fellow men. Carting a full bag a half mile or so back to the car requires repeated transfers from one hand to the other. But my companions and I have made progress, so that now it takes considerably longer to load up a bag than it did at the outset. However, in some sense the task is truly Sisyphean. Even though motor vehicles have been completely blocked from entering the wash into the Userys, the job of garbage pickup may never end because many of those who have used their two hind legs to hike the wash continue to come with trash but without the means or willingness to pack it out. Thus, many walkers resemble their motorized predecessors in that they regularly leave behind an assortment of items to commemorate their presence in this small corner of the desert.

For example, just the other day I found a large number of heavy particleboard sheets lying at the narrow opening through the fence where walkers can access the wash. I was astonished to find that an undetermined number of individuals had dragged or carried these bulky four-by-six-foot sheets down the trail and well up the wash. There they had been propped up with medium-sized rocks and gravel, apparently for use as ramps by dirt bike users who wished to launch themselves in flight. The group that had troubled themselves to bring this impressive collection of materials with them into the wash had not troubled themselves to carry the stuff out on their departure. I examined the sheets morosely, calculating the time and number of trips that would be required to do what the team of master litterbugs had not done. I found the calculations depressing.

In the Maricopas, which lie considerably farther from Greater Phoenix than the Userys, the amount of recent litter is correspondingly less. But here too I can almost always find a few aluminum cans, hiding under creosotebushes or half buried in a wash, partly filled with sand and gravel. Even after I have shaken the dirt from a can, it still manages to deposit some more inside my backpack where I store trash of this sort when I have forgotten to bring a plastic bag along. Later, I have to scrub the inside of the pack to remove the fine silt clinging to the interior. Very rarely I encounter a completely oxidized sardine tin or an old thoroughly rusted can that might have held baked beans or the like. I typically remove these items as well, although if they are more than fifty years old they apparently are considered archeological in nature and should in theory be left in place. As far as I am concerned, however, the Sonoran Desert National Monument deserves to be utterly exempt from trash less than a century old. No matter how well rusted the modern artifact, it still reminds me of just how heavy-handed and numerous we are these days. It's "out with the new and in with the old" for me.

February *Drought*

Litterbugs reduce the aesthetic value of the desert, while construction crews just plain reduce the desert, making life hard or impossible for Sonoran Desert plants unfortunate enough to have to interact with people. But there are also some long-standing natural challenges for desert plants, among which droughts are especially prominent. A really lengthy dry spell can reduce even the toughest creosotebush or paloverde to a collection of cracked pale brown bits. In some parts of Arizona, many creosotebushes have succumbed to the current southwestern drought, which began in the mid-1990s and has continued for a decade. However, during this period, the extent and severity of the dry spell has varied greatly from place to place and year to year.

So long-term droughts have their ups and downs rather than supplying the same relatively low rainfall amount from one year to the next. But in order to know when a drought is on, one has to compare the current average against an overall average rainfall amount for a given period. Figuring out what constitutes normal precipitation requires a long-term perspective, which commonly involves calculating the average annual rainfall for the twentieth century, the only time for which good weather station records are available. One can, however, go much farther back in reconstructing the climate of the past with the aid of tree-ring analyses. This technique is based on the familiar principle that during hot, dry years trees add very little woody material to their trunks, creating narrow annual rings of growth, whereas during cooler, wetter years, trees grow more vigorously, with a corresponding increase in the size of the annual ring for that year. Periods with slow tree-ring growth can be considered episodes of drought; periods in which the annual rings are relatively large can be categorized as nondroughts.

Having established the pattern of tree-ring widths over a known block of years, one can then cross-match distinctive elements of the pattern with tree-ring samples from other older trees, living and dead, thereby extending the record backward in time. Bristlecone pines have been instrumental in this regard because still-living specimens provide thousands of tree rings' worth of annual data and because even older deceased trees are beautifully preserved in the cold high mountains in which they occur. A "fossil" tree trunk can provide banding patterns that overlap with other dead and living specimens, providing the data needed to construct a tree-ring chronology for the last nine thousand years.

Between the twentieth-century rainfall information and the tree-ring data, we have the basis for comparing the current drought against other periods in the past. Thus, 2002 was the driest year on record for Arizona over the last fifteen hundred years. In contrast, the years from 1905 to 1917 constituted one of the wettest periods in Arizona and eight other western states over the past twelve hundred years (108). "Normal" or "average" years or decades are actually in the minority given the sharp ups and emphatic downs that extend back as far as climate can be reconstructed via tree-ring analyses and other methods. Indeed, radiocarbon dating of vegetative fossils in Sonoran Desert packrat middens reveals an unusually wet period about a thousand years ago (9), a time when the Hohokam of central Arizona were flourishing.

The climate records also tell us that many droughts lasting anywhere from twenty to four hundred years have occurred in the West during the past three thousand years (24). A prolonged dry spell around AD 1450 has long been suggested as the cause of the great collapse of several major Indian cultures, notably the Hohokam as well as the Anasazi of northern Arizona and Utah. All these peoples appear to have abandoned their homes and cornfields to go somewhere else at roughly the same time, leaving behind their often monumental buildings, which had required so much effort to build. However, although tree-ring analyses of the juniper and pine logs contained in buildings abandoned by the Anasazi indicate that they were indeed left behind in the mid-1400s during a substantial drought, many archaeologists advocate other causes for the disappearance of several ancient cultural groups at this time (7).

For example, it is possible that in the mid-1400s a shift occurred from more gentle rains to severe thunderstorms. Rapid runoff from gully-washers would have cut deeply into canyon bottoms and river channels alike, disrupting the irrigation of cornfields along streams and rivers. The Hohokam living on the Salt and Gila Rivers had constructed an especially complex network of irrigation canals. If river channels dropped or shifted because of downcutting, many Hohokam canals would have lost their utility, requiring repair projects so massive that the social system may not have been able to cope.

However, although geologists have indeed documented substantial channel downcutting in the Gila River, these changes took place between AD 1050 and 1150, long before the demise of the Hohokam. During the downcutting phase, Hohokam society made a number of adjustments, including a consolidation of the population into larger towns, which may have enabled these groups to assemble a large workforce whenever dealing with a major irrigation problem (101). Severe damage to the Hohokam irrigation system may also have occurred when several major floods swept down the Salt River between 1350 and 1400 (52). Even so, another two or three generations passed before the final disappearance of the Hohokam from their riverside communities.

The search for explanations for the Hohokam mystery has led some archeologists to discount the negative effects of drought, channel downcutting, and floods and to propose that hundreds of years of farming had caused the Indian farm fields to become less productive, perhaps in part through salt accumulations in the soil. Food shortages could have generated conflict among groups and a reduction in village populations, so much so that the remaining communities were too small to sustain traditional Hohokam culture, which depended on communal efforts to maintain their vast network of irrigation canals. There is little doubt that ancient cultures sometimes have managed to destroy the land on which they depended, leading to agricultural collapse and forcing the people to go elsewhere. A group living in central Mexico about nine hundred years ago abandoned their cultivated hillsides after their farming practices caused severe soil erosion, the effects of which are still visible on these hills centuries later (54). Closer to home, as Julio Betancourt and his colleagues have documented, the inhabitants of Chaco Canyon removed all the large trees, including the pines that yielded valuable pinyon nuts, for miles around their monumental buildings, surely contributing to the eventual collapse of their culture (25).

However, no clear and simple lesson can be taken from the past and applied with any confidence to the situation in the Southwest today. Yes, drought conditions now apply and we have no idea how long they may persist. Yes, irrigated farmland in western Arizona has become degraded by salinization. Yes, people have left the rural West in droves to live in our rapidly growing urbanopolises. But are we nearing the point when things might suddenly fall apart? No one seems to think so. Water conservation is discussed from time to time in Arizona, but the powers that be offer few incentives for conservation in Phoenix, nor have they passed laws demanding that we reduce our water use. And heaven forbid that anyone should even mention putting a brake on the growth of our cities. Arizona's economy is built around the prospect of there being an ever-increasing number of Arizonans, and to consider setting a ceiling on population size would be viewed as downright un-American by almost everyone in our state today, especially our political leaders. Most of us do not want to think about the effects of a really prolonged drought at a time when there will be ten million Arizonans here instead of the current five million or so. According to the U.S. Census Bureau, we will hit the ten million people mark by 2030, so we may not have long to wait before we test the proposition that never-ending population growth is inherently good, even in a desert environment prone to lengthy droughts.

February *What a Difference a Year Makes*

Meanwhile, the current drought continues, so that on this bright February day the Userys are looking anything but cheerful. The desert, mountains, and plains alike seem drained of color and life. In all directions, I see only brown stalks, gray limbs, and desiccated shrubs. Only the paloverdes and assorted cacti seem to be gritting their teeth and hanging tough in the face of extreme adversity.

A great deal can change in a year. On this day last February, the Userys were awash in moisture, thanks to a soaking storm that produced a gentle but persistent rain lasting the better part of a day and night. The storm was one of a long series that came in from the Pacific at nicely spaced intervals of a week or so starting in October 2004 and continuing through February 2005. During this period, almost eight inches of rain fell on the desert, about double the historical average, enough to interrupt the drought that had been going off and on for the better part of a decade.

Almost three inches of that welcome eight inches of rain fell in February, far more than the modest 0.7-inch average for the month in Phoe-

nix. Thanks to this largesse and the relatively ample rains in the preceding months, the soil became saturated. Excess water dripped down hillsides and entered gullies of all dimensions, forming little rivulets in places. Here and there you could watch thin streams of water two inches wide and two yards long slipping over an underlying platform of solid rock before disappearing underground again when rock gave way to gravel and sand. The water went along hidden from view for a time before reemerging well downstream after joining forces with a number of other underground streamlets.

The bursages that lined the depression and gullies became as radiant as this self-effacing little shrub can ever get. Their leaves actually looked green, smooth and fresh, totally unlike the few gray, dehydrated wisps found on the bursages in February 2006. On the ledge above the side channel, the wetted skeleton of the fallen saguaro that stood guard over the ashes of Michael Johnson appeared to have been dyed dark brown, almost black in fact.

In rainy February 2005, desert annuals, like Mexican poppies, were already growing vigorously; some were on the verge of blooming late in the month. These annuals would create a floral fiesta in March of that year. The perennials also seemed to know that conditions for growth and reproduction were excellent. The brittlebushes sent up a profusion of thin stalks above their winter green leaves; these stalks would soon support masses of bright yellow daisylike flowers. At the peak of brittlebush season, what had been hillsides dotted with blue-green shrubs and granite boulders in February were transformed in a few weeks into mosaics of yellow and green accented with splashes of orange (Mexican poppies), purple (lupines), and blue (chia).

When I climbed to the peak in February 2005, I found the paloverde there surrounded by an absurdly dense vegetative ruff composed of fiddleneck, Mediterranean grass (an introduced species), and filaree (an introduced annual weed). Some of the fiddlenecks were nearly two feet tall, and the grasses and weeds that would normally be three inches high were at least twice that height. This was a spring of botanical riot.

Although readers of *Arizona Highways* may well get the impression that floral exuberance is guaranteed during spring in southern Arizona, in reality over-the-top displays constitute the exceptions to the rule.

The wet winter of 2004–5 was a blip in a decade-long drought, which reasserted itself after February 2005. The summer monsoon winds that followed carried only enough moisture for a couple of decent rains. In fact, if it were not for one fierce gullywasher in August, the summer rainy season would have been a total bust in Phoenix. After that August storm, it turned dry again, with only one shower in October to interrupt the drought. Since then, we have had a steady diet of week after week without rain. When will it end?

February *Fire in the Desert*

Although the spring of 2005 was exceptionally beautiful thanks to the frequent and well-spaced winter rains, the glorious spring was superseded by a much less attractive summer of seemingly endless wildfires. In late June, the attention of everyone in Phoenix was riveted on the Cave Creek Complex fire, which eventually burned on the order of a quarter of a million acres to the north of the city at a firefighting cost of more than $16 million. At the peak of the conflagration, I could see the smoke from this fire while standing on Usery Peak, a good thirty miles from the disaster.

Most of the Cave Creek fire occurred outside the boundaries of the Sonoran Desert at higher elevations covered by the woody shrubs and small trees that constitute the chaparral ecosystem. Other major wildfires this season, however, took place wholly within desert limits where they were fueled by desert plants. Indeed, most of seven-hundred-thousand-plus acres of Arizona that went up in smoke in 2005 were located in the relatively sparsely vegetated Sonoran Desert rather than in the more heavily forested regions of the state (67). At the same time that the Cave Creek fire was attracting intense news coverage because of its size and threats to communities near Phoenix, another fire was also flaring out of control in the 2.7-million-acre Barry M. Goldwater Range, south of Gila Bend in an area far from any populated area, which is why this fire received little attention even though it eventually burned over fifty thousand acres of more or less pristine desert.

I had seen a line or two about the Goldwater fire in the *Arizona Republic*, and it alarmed me because in recent years my wife and I had grown fond of that portion of the range set aside for outdoor recreation. Although the main mission of this huge military reservation is the training of air force and marine fighter pilots, the range on the eastern side of Route 85 provides potential entertainment for campers, hikers, hunters, and the like. This part of the range is fenced off and the gates are locked, but the combination is available to those of us willing to apply for a permit to enter the prosaically named Area B.

When I asked for my most recent annual permit in February of 2006, I did so at the Gila Bend Air Force Auxiliary Field, a quiet little airfield with a World War II–vintage plane perched in the middle of a lawn and a number of no-nonsense khaki-colored buildings. One of these buildings houses the base's security staff. There a young woman armed with an extremely large revolver gave me a number of forms to sign while urging me to watch a thirty-minute video. I followed orders. The film tells potential visitors to the range to exercise a modicum of common sense: bring drinking water, stay strictly on established tracks (which require a four-wheel-drive vehicle), keep your hands off Indian artifacts, and do not play around with unexploded ordnance dropped by bombers on past training runs. These regulations made as much sense to me on this third viewing as they had on two previous occasions. So I was happy to indicate my acceptance of the range's rules in return for two small paper permits and information on the lock combination that would open the gates into Area B.

After securing what I needed, I returned to my vehicle and drove down the road, slowing briefly for an immigration checkpoint staffed by U.S. Customs officials at mile 18 on Route 85. When I reached gate #9, an entryway to Area B, I turned off the highway and entered the correct code in the gate lock. Soon I was bumping down the narrow track toward the Sauceda Mountains, a line of stony hills up ahead on my left. As I drove slowly forward, I scanned in all directions, looking nervously for fire damage, not knowing whether the Goldwater fire had consumed this part of the range. To my relief, the desert looked intact, albeit bone-dry without any signs of winter plant growth. But at least the place had not been reduced to charcoal and ash.

Things stayed that way until I had driven about five miles in, lurching across small washes and tilting to one side or the other on the occasionally uneven roadway. Then—horrors. Just as I was about to turn off the main track to enter the lovely valley that we had especially enjoyed in the past, the desert turned gray in front of me. The low yellow grasses, greenish creosotes, and living paloverdes in the unburned section gave way abruptly to a great sweep of gravel interrupted only by the occasional upright skeleton of a plant.

Here and there, a saguaro stood forlornly in the scalped plain; some were definitely deceased, while others were clearly headed in that direction. Almost no barrel cactus remained upright, let alone alive, and although some chain-fruit chollas were still standing, their thin trunks were blackened at the base, making their long-term chances of survival doubtful. Nearly all the paloverdes, including those lining the washes, had become pale beige skeletons, with cracked bark, broken limbs, and no hope of recovery. The creosotebushes in the scorched zone consisted of a cluster of charcoaled stems rising out of the gray gravel of the sterilized desert floor; among the fricasseed specimens, a few sported a fistful of fresh green leafy twigs, either a pathetic attempt at resurrection or a truly hopeful note for the future, depending on the mood of an observer.

Given the complete absence of winter rains, I was not surprised by the total absence of desert annuals in either the burned or unburned portions of the desert. At almost exactly this time last year, the floor of the then intact desert had been painted with flowering poppies by the acre. A year later, flowers of any sort are nowhere to be seen except, ironically, in small patches within the burned desert. Here and there, one semiperennial species, desert senna, had somehow found enough moisture to exploit the open space and the soil nutrients once contained in the bodies of other, now incinerated, plants. Thousands of

seeds of desert senna must have germinated after last summer's monsoon, feeble though it was, and in clusters of dozens to thousands, modest little sennas faced the sunshine. The little yellow flowers of the plant looked out of place in the Hiroshima-like desert.

The Goldwater fire had its origins in the abundant plant growth in the spring, which led to mass displays of poppies as early as January and later an unusually heavy production of the little native grasses that usually grow sparsely in the Sonoran Desert. These plants, when thoroughly dried in the scorching days of May and June, were just waiting to go up in flames when lightning struck during thunderstorms early

The devastating effects of fire in the desert. The plains in front of Hat Mountain in the Barry M. Goldwater Range provided a poppy festival in January 2005 (on facing page). In January 2006, (above) following a severe summer wildfire the previous year and no winter rains, the poppy-covered plains of the preceding year were reduced to barren gravel.

in the summer, or when a careless smoker discarded a lit cigarette, or when a group of illegal immigrants left a campfire unattended while they headed north.

Elsewhere in the Sonoran Desert, nonnative plants supplied much of the fuel for the devastating wildfires that raced through southern Arizona in 2005. These exotics, introduced from Europe and Africa, had also taken advantage of the unusually heavy and evenly distributed winter rains. They grew heartily at first, then died and dried out in the heat of late spring. Foremost among these nonnative combustibles was red brome grass, a native of the Mediterranean region but now well estab-

lished in the desert. The species pretty clearly first took root in North America in the mid-nineteenth century in California, possibly by way of Chile. The grass spread into Arizona in the early 1900s, thanks to its intentional introduction near Tucson by persons interested in its potential as livestock forage. Elsewhere, the grass managed to spread on its own and is now established throughout the West from New Mexico to British Columbia (72).

By May 2006, the red brome in southern Arizona had taken advantage of the high levels of soil moisture in the spring and formed ragged blankets of tinder-dry stems that were practically begging to be set afire. Once their wish had been granted, these dried grasses carried flames across the desert, forming a line of fire that moved steadily forward, consuming not just the dead brome but also the living cacti, shrubs, and small trees.

In addition to red brome, another flammable nonnative, African buffelgrass, is now widely distributed in Arizona. Like red brome, buffelgrass appears to be rapidly expanding its Sonoran Desert range during recent decades in part perhaps because its seeds germinate successfully in response to as little as a quarter inch of rain. With its ability to get started on so little, buffelgrass does as well as or better than almost all plant species that occur naturally in the Sonoran Desert (100) and the Mojave Desert of Nevada, California, and western Arizona. Even if the new competitors do not kill the native plants, they take water and nutrients from them, stunting their growth, a point that has been shown to be true of the interactions between red brome and true desert animals (73).

Buffelgrass, like red brome, has been given a helping hand on the way to becoming a major component of Sonoran Desert vegetation. In northern Mexico, for example, a government-subsidized program for cattle growers has resulted in the conversion of desert scrub into a buffelgrass savannah, a program so "successful" that by now fifty million acres or so of desert has been lost forever in that country (21). In Arizona, buffelgrass was first planted in the Tucson area in the 1930s, apparently as part of a soil conservation program, but for years it was a very minor component of the desert vegetation there and elsewhere in the state. Recently, however, the grass has taken off in some places. It

(facing page) The conditions in the wet winter of 2004 were perfect for the germination and growth of Mexican poppies in the Barry M. Goldwater Range, judging from the number of plants flowering there in January of 2005.

now covers four times as many acres in the Saguaro National Park as it did four years previously. Disturbed areas along roadsides are particularly prone to colonization by this invasive grass.

The extraordinary ability of some exotic grasses to thrive in new environments, including the American West, is also illustrated by a relative of red brome (*Bromus madritensis*, also known as *Bromus rubens*) called cheatgrass (*Bromus tectorum*). This grass has made its way from its home in Eurasia and North Africa to a host of far-flung destinations, such as New Zealand, Australia, Argentina, Hawaii, and multiple locations in North America. At least some of the populations that now occupy the western United States can be traced back to the Mediterranean region or to central Europe. The plant was collected by a botanist in Provo, Utah, as early as 1894 and since that time has expanded its range dramatically in the Great Basin Desert of Utah and Idaho (60).

Some have wondered if cheatgrass, red brome, buffelgrass, and the like are able to change the chemical makeup of the soil in ways that are especially favorable for their descendants rather than for the native species that they displace. As any gardener knows, soil nitrogen is extremely important to plants, with different species best able to deal with different concentrations of this key substance. Some plants do especially well when soil nitrogen levels are relatively high; other species prefer lower levels. Introduced species may alter the amount of soil nitrogen around them by increasing or decreasing the kinds of ammonia-oxidizing bacteria in the soil around them. These microorganisms have the ability to convert ammonia, a substance that plants cannot readily use, to different nitrogen-containing substances that plants can metabolize as they grow and reproduce. An experimental study of a Californian grassland revealed that introduced grasses do alter the bacterial community in the soil, a change that did indeed modify the kinds of nitrogenous compounds in the soil. Modifications of this sort could conceivably tilt the balance in favor of the very exotics that initiated the soil changes (37).

The possibility that exotic plants gain an advantage from their ability to change nitrogen cycling in invaded ecosystems is plausible but speculative. We can be more certain, however, that some exotic invaders have benefited from increased levels of carbon dioxide in the Earth's atmosphere, a phenomenon for which we humans are responsible thanks to our land clearing and fossil fuel burning. Higher carbon dioxide concentrations in the air stimulate photosynthesis and thus the production of plant material, judging from the known effects of experimentally boosting the amount of carbon dioxide available to some plants. In experiments of this sort, machines pump extra carbon dioxide into the air over plots of vegetation while other plots are left as is. In an experiment of this sort done by Stanley Smith's team of researchers in the Mojave Desert, the plots with elevated carbon dioxide were exposed to roughly 50 percent more CO_2 than the controls. In the "enriched" plots, native plants like creosotebush responded positively to the extra carbon dioxide, but only in a good (i.e., relatively rainy) year. With sufficient water available, the creosotes in enriched areas put out about twice as many new shoots as the creosotes growing under normal concentrations of CO_2. Likewise, in the good year, native annuals became much larger and produced many more seeds when exposed to extra CO_2 (85). But exotic grasses, like cheatgrass and red brome, did even better than the native annuals in a wet year under higher levels of carbon dioxide.

In not too many years, we Americans (with help from the Chinese and Europeans) will have raised the level of atmospheric carbon dioxide to that used in the Mojave Desert experiments. In so doing, we will be helping exotic grasses outcompete the native annuals in our southwestern deserts by making the exotics larger, more fertile, and more combustible (in years with decent winter rainfall). When stands of red brome, cheatgrass, and buffelgrass catch on fire, which they do readily, the flames spread, rather than quickly running out of steam as desert fires have usually done in the past when the desert floor was populated by the sparser native grasses and annuals (29). In the distant past a lightning strike in June might have incinerated an especially dense patch of dried chia and lupines, but the destruction would have been confined to that one small patch, surrounded as it would have been by a gravel firebreak. No longer. Now a fire can expand freely, running on dried grasses that were not present in the past. Once barbecued in a grass fire, the native bursages and brittlebushes are reduced to circles of crisp papery charcoal.

The first wildfire known to have been fueled by buffelgrass in southern Arizona occurred in 2004, with several more documented the following year. If we are now entering an era when buffelgrass fires become ever more frequent, desert enthusiasts are probably in for much unhappiness. Wildfires do special damage in the Sonoran Desert because the native plants lack special adaptations to deal with fire (51). In forest and savannah ecosystems where fires do occur commonly, resilient plant species that quickly rebound after being burned come to dominate. The diversity of plant life in these areas may even be increased by the occasional wildfire, so much so that fire is now considered a positive tool in habitat management in many places (4). In Australia, for example, foresters regularly set low-intensity fires in eucalyptus forests, thereby creating ideal habitat for a variety of fire-adapted plants, which even include some of the delicate little terrestrial orchids found in this part of the world. The seeds of some orchids have evolved the capacity to detect smoke, which acts as a signal for germination, enabling the baby orchids to exploit the nutrients added to the soil after a fire. Other plants, including many eucalypti, are adapted to withstand even intense fires, as is evident when one sees a thoroughly scorched and blackened tree sporting clusters of fresh green leaves. Some eucalypti can even be burned right down to the ground, only to resurrect themselves from their tough woody root balls, which survive the heat of intense wildfires (68).

In contrast, if a saguaro gets even slightly burned so that its lower trunk turns brown and cracked, it may remain upright for a time, but sooner or later (usually sooner) that cactus will be flat on its back, finished, with no chance of resprouting from the root system of the plant. The same holds for the other desert cacti as well as for the thin-skinned larger trees, the paloverdes and ironwoods, which have little or no bark protection at all against fire, since fire has never played much of a role in their evolution.

Unlike saguaros, red brome and buffelgrass have evolved under pressure from fires, and they actually thrive in the aftermath of a wildfire (51). The nutrients from burned plants, both native and exotic, feed the exotics when they germinate the next season. A thicker coat of red brome, then, not only provides unwelcome competition for the seedlings of native annuals and any perennials that may have survived the fire, but the invigorated grasses will become a still more incendiary resource should lightning strike or a glowing cigarette butt get tossed in their general direction. The odds are that many parts of the Sonoran Desert are destined to become buffelgrass savannah (8), a duller-than-dishwater environment when compared to the gloriously diverse and wonderfully distinctive plant communities that it will replace.

People are beginning to recognize that invading alien species are dreadful things and not purely because of their negative effects on natural biodiversity. The damages caused by outsiders sometimes can be measured in dollars and cents as well. Indeed, a team led by David Pimentel of Cornell University calculated that the roughly fifty thousand foreign species that have been visited upon us have left us with an annual bill of $120 billion (as of 2004). Much of the economic damage is done by foreign pathogens, like the AIDS virus and assorted microbes that attack our agricultural plants, but weed pests cause many headaches as well (66). Although red brome and buffelgrass create relatively minor *economic* disruption at this moment, and so do not rate direct mention by Pimentel and company, they nevertheless deserve our disapproval.

Practically the only good news on the buffelgrass front comes from the formation of an organization called the Sonoran Desert Weedwackers, whose volunteers have effectively removed by hand great quantities of buffelgrass, plant by plant, from places like the Tucson Mountains. Activity of this sort has received an official stamp of approval from the Arizona Department of Agriculture, which, as of 2005, put buffelgrass on a list of "regulated and restricted noxious weeds." The species is clearly noxious; whether it will ever be successfully regulated and restricted remains to be seen. But should the plant's spread be brought under control, every remaining saguaro in the state would have reason to rejoice and so would I.

March *Paloverde #10*

Fortunately, buffelgrass is not as well established in the Phoenix area as it is around Tucson, although here one can sometimes find clumps of a closely related exotic, fountain grass (another member of the genus *Pennisetum*), along roadsides and in dry washes in our part of Arizona. Although fountain grass is far more attractive than the decidedly ugly buffelgrass, it too is a nonnative escapee, an unwanted addition to the plant list for the Sonoran Desert. In this drought-stricken March, fountain grass is not doing well in Greater Phoenix and environs, but then again this rule applies to all plant life in central Arizona. I have begun to think that this could be a year when the winter-spring rains will fail completely, which would yield a death sentence for this year's spring flowering season and a good many desert perennials as well. In fact, since the desert plants have already been hammered by four months of drought, I wonder whether they will be able or willing to respond even if it should finally rain sometime in 2006.

But at least there's no need to bring a poncho today as I climb one of the lower ridges that leads up and into the Usery Mountains. The shrubs are barren and the annuals absent. Even the green limbs of the paloverdes seem bleached today, thanks to the combined action of sun and drought.

Puffing my way higher and higher along the ascending ridge, I pass any number of foothill paloverdes, most of which are not much taller than I am. But as I come onto a more level portion of the ridge, I encounter a fairly tall specimen that is particularly good-looking as well. I pause to catch my breath near a favorite of mine, paloverde #10.

I first saw paloverde #10 on a spring day in 1978 when I decided more or less on a whim to wander up into the Usery Mountains. At the time, I regularly visited the broad floodplain of the Salt River nearby where a population of native bees kept me gainfully employed as a recorder of their mating and nesting activities. Getting to the bee site involved a drive along the Bush Highway heading north out of Mesa, with the river on one side and the Userys on the other. So I had known for some time that there was more to the local desert than the riparian stands of mesquite surrounded by open clearings dotted with sand verbena and desert primroses. However, I had never bothered to explore the Userys until, as I say, I did so on the spur of the moment.

In order to satisfy my exploratory urge, I drove up Usery Pass Road from the Bush Highway and headed toward the northern edge of the Userys. Since these "mountains" are more hill than Himalaya, I knew that my ascent would be relatively easy. The prospect of a simple climb put me in a good mood as I turned onto a dirt track that seemed to head toward the long north-south running ridge that I intended to use as my stairway into the mountains.

My happy face disappeared at the end of the track where the way forward was blocked by a shallow but extensive gravel pit used in the past for the excavation of materials needed for assorted roadworks. By the late 1970s, the spot had been taken over by target shooters and desert plinkers, every one of whom left their spent shell casings and blasted targets behind after their half hour or so of explosive entertainment. The quantity of debris carpeting the old pit had to be seen to be believed and included everything from rusted washing machines to splintered plywood rectangles to broken beer bottles. All these items and more had been riddled with gunfire and then abandoned. Magazine fragments, newspapers, cardboard strips, and old propane gas cylinders littered the gravel scrape and beyond, many of the lighter items having been blown into the desert proper before getting trapped under a jojoba or snagged on the limb of a staghorn cactus. The place looked more like a landfill than a desert.

Nearly thirty years later, I can report that this entryway to the Userys has been substantially changed—and all for the good. In the late 1990s, the Forest Service decided to put an end to the use of the gravel pit as a shooting range, probably largely for safety reasons given the proximity of the site to Usery Pass Road but also perhaps because of the incidental damage done to the desert by those persons eager to exercise their Second Amendment rights without exercising any corresponding quotient of common sense. To control these yahoos, the Forest Service installed a fence that now runs the length of Usery Pass Road on either side of the highway. This barrier prevents drivers from using the side track to reach the shooting pit. Forest Service employees also put up a large sign stating that the whole area was now closed to shooting for safety's sake, "pursuant to special order 12–146 and 12–181 (revised), title 16 USC, sec. 156." Over the years, this sign has regularly been vandalized by persons upset at learning that the old gravel pit is now off-limits to those of their persuasion. But the Forest Service has patiently replaced signs that have been shredded by shotguns, ripped in two by irate gun owners, or knocked flat by those upset by the sign's message. Special order 12–146 has worked in that almost no plinkers ignore the restrictions against free-wheeling gunfire in the desert proper. Instead, the heavily armed gentry of Mesa and Apache Junction take themselves to the Usery Mountain Gun Range, a noisy but carefully controlled outdoor shooting gallery just up the road from the old gravel pit. Although when I am in the Userys, I can hear the high-powered rifles blasting away at the gun range, I take comfort in the fact that while the shooters are at the range, they are far less likely to despoil the desert proper. Moreover, and I find this especially reassuring, suburban gunners confined to the range are much less likely to produce stray bullets, any one of which could conceivably end my career as a desert hiker.

After the USFS took action to restrict casual shooting along Usery Pass Road, a group of volunteers from a local corporation organized a pickup day at the old gravel pit. The Forest Service provided a full-sized garbage truck, and the volunteers raked and shoveled and lifted like troopers. Their hard work had the gratifying effect of greatly improving the appearance of the scarred landscape, although to this day shards of plastic bottles and tin cans abound in the fringe of desert surrounding the largely barren gravel pit. Although here and there desert broom and some desert marigolds infused with pioneer spirit have insinuated their roots into the lead-filled ground, I suspect that it will take a great many decades, if not centuries, before this thoroughly abused area recovers from the combined effect of bulldozers and bullets.

On my very first venture into the Userys, I was alarmed and depressed by what I encountered at the base of the ridge. Nevertheless, I skirted the gravel pit and cut over to the toe of the ridge and began my ascent, glad to be leaving the trashed desert behind. As I climbed, I was reminded again of the pleasure of being among jojobas, creosotes, teddy bear chollas, and the like rather than being surrounded by shooters' debris. When I paused, I could look out across the distant bajada that sloped down to the Salt River, a descending plain covered in foothill paloverdes and ironwoods. In due course, the paloverdes' canopies would turn yellow with flowers, while the ironwoods' puffs of magenta blossoms would come later. The traffic on the Bush Highway and Usery Pass Road was light, and I was not bothered by the faint sound of cars scurrying this way and that on their various missions. A red-tailed hawk screamed as it circled far out over another ridge that climbed up from the bajada to join the ridge that I had selected for my expedition into the Userys.

As I made my way uphill, I eventually came to the paloverde that I would later label #10. I was instantly taken by its good looks and attractive setting. The tree was, as I say, a fairly substantial specimen with an array of smooth green-barked trunks fanning out from a short stocky base. In the background, far off across the distant Salt River, Red Mountain loomed large, adding its color and weight to the landscape. Just to the left of the paloverde, an upright cluster of ocotillo branches provided a kind of botanical exclamation point to the scene.

The attractions of the tree included not only its appearance and surroundings, but also its inhabitant. A conspicuously large black wasp with reddish wings had made itself at home on the crown of the paloverde. I spotted the wasp when it looped out from a perch high in the tree, only to return to land near this same spot. When I continued my walk uphill, I kept an eye open for other paloverde perchers and was rewarded when I reached what could fairly be said to be the end of the ridge I had been ascending. Here too was a larger-than-average paloverde, one generously supplied with limbs, branches, and twigs, which made the tree seem greener than the other paloverdes nearby. The tips of the branches of this paloverde drooped to touch the ground. I could position myself here so that Red Mountain provided part of the backdrop for this handsome tree as well. The paloverde, which would become #17, had also attracted a tarantula hawk wasp, about two inches long and full of vim and vigor, which it demonstrated by circling the tree confidently and then swerving off to chase another male that dared to approach.

And so I was introduced in 1978 to *Hemipepsis ustulata*, one of several species of tarantula hawk wasps found in central Arizona, a group noted for the ability of the females to hunt down and paralyze large burrow-occupying spiders, including tarantulas. The unfortunate spiders are then dragged into a burrow where they are left with a wasp egg attached to their abdomen. The egg becomes a wasp grub that is free to feast on its helpless prey.

The individuals I had found perched in paloverdes #10 and #17 did not appear to be hunting for spiders, which are not found in the tops of paloverdes in any case. Instead, the perching wasps appeared to be defending "their" particular tree. Whenever another tarantula hawk flew up to the tree, the resident launched itself out to meet the newcomer and to escort it a short distance away from the plant before returning to the paloverde. Landing clumsily on the outer twigs of a branch, the returning wasp often struggled to pull itself up onto a twig before turning around to look out across the great vista available to it.

Based on the behavior of the first few tarantula hawks I met, I guessed that I must be looking at males, a point that I confirmed eventually by catching a tree-perching specimen in my insect net and pulling it cautiously out of the net by hand. The fact that I was not stung by this captive told me that I was definitely dealing with a male, since male wasps

Males of a territorial hilltopping insect, *Hemipepsis ustulata*, a tarantula hawk wasp. The males are scanning the area from their perches on top of plants they have chosen as landmark territories, a paloverde (top) and a creosotebush (below).

lack the stinger so effectively utilized by the females of their species. I concluded that I had discovered an insect that would surely repay careful study, one that would not sting me either.

Believing that I had found a wasp with territorial males, and a large and attractive insect to boot, I immediately began to try to get to know more about this handsome creature in the Userys. My simple research strategy required only that I capture the males I wished to study in order to measure their size and to give them identifying dots of colored paint or typewriting correction fluid. Thereafter I revisited the spots along a ridge where I had marked a sample of males, checking to see which individuals were where, and capturing and decorating any unmarked wasps located during my censuses. This approach enabled me to learn, among other things, how long male blue-yellow spent on his perch each day and how many days male red-two-dots showed up at his tree. As it turned out, some males manage to return faithfully to the same paloverde for as many as forty mornings for five or so hours of territory defense each day.

Because my tarantula hawk research demands that I keep tabs on where given males are found, I have become familiar not only with individual wasps, but also with the landmark perches they favor. In order to keep track of these plants, I numbered seventeen prominent paloverdes that eventually attracted territory-holding tarantula hawks in the first year of study.

I have continued to monitor the behavior of new generations of male tarantula hawks one spring after another for nearly thirty years. Over the years I have come to expect the first tarantula hawk of the spring to appear sometime between early March and early April, at which time I will find the pioneer wasp perched proprietarily on either paloverde #10 or paloverde #17. As the season progresses, other perch sites are claimed by males willing to defend them, but #10 and #17 are continuously occupied by a progression of males long after most of the secondary perches have been taken and then abandoned.

As springs have come and gone, I have grown especially fond of paloverdes #10 and #17, and I have celebrated our friendship by taking a long series of photographs of both trees. When I examine these photographs side by side, one conclusion stands out: neither tree appears to have grown appreciably, if at all, since the early 1980s when my photographic project began. Unlike saguaros, which continue to become ever taller and more massive throughout their lives, albeit at a slower and slower rate as they get older, the growth pattern of paloverdes seems much more static. Once they reach a height of twelve to fifteen feet, that is pretty much that.

Paloverde #17 in 1981 (top) and 2006 (below). Note that the little tree is, if anything, somewhat smaller after twenty-five years of "growth."

So, how many years does it take for a paloverde to reach its upper limit and call it a day? And then for how many additional years does the tree remain stuck in neutral at least with respect to additional growth? These questions have not been answered to everyone's satisfaction, but no one doubts that paloverdes can achieve a ripe old age. Many suppliers of botanical information for gardeners and desert yard installers note that the foothill paloverde is a particularly slow-growing tree, which suggests that relatively large specimens are likely to be quite old. Indeed, Forrest Shreve, the first great botanist of the Sonoran Desert, used tree-ring analyses to claim that many foothill paloverdes that he studied were two hundred years old, with some possibly four hundred years of age. Shreve also reported extremely low annual mortality rates for the paloverde, another finding consistent with the long-life hypothesis. If his estimates were correct, paloverdes live for more years on average than saguaros.

Other plant ecologists have questioned whether Shreve was on target with his four-hundred-year figure, given that he did not realize that paloverdes can put down two growth rings per year, not just one (13). Moreover, mortality rates of this species may be significantly higher than Shreve realized. For example, at one recently studied site, about 7 percent of the paloverde population died in less than a decade, probably due to the intense drought occurring during this period.

If paloverdes are subject to occasional die-offs during particularly difficult times, then populations of this species need to be followed for a great many years in order to get a truly accurate estimate of the average annual risk of dying. If a life history study of paloverdes encompassed one or more periods when relatively many trees died, the data would lead to a different conclusion about the plant's average life span than if the study happened to be done during a long interval between die-offs when almost no trees went to their reward.

In the Userys, I have numbered seventeen paloverdes on the lower ridge and twenty more on the peak itself. Of these thirty-seven numbered trees, four died during a twenty-five-year period; in other words, more than 10 percent of this population has expired in a relatively short spell. However, two of the deceased trees died at the hands of my fellow man. One tree, paloverde #16 on Usery Peak, was literally hacked to pieces by a crazed maniac who for some reason brought an axe to the peak while leaving behind whatever sense of decency he may have possessed. Another tree, paloverde #1, which grew on the knoll at the base of the lower ridge, was shot to bits by gunners who began in the 1980s to place their plastic milk bottles, empty gas cylinders, and cardboard boxes near the tree rather than limit themselves to blasting away in the gravel pit. Among the hail of bullets that struck this assortment of targets, some may have ricocheted into the unlucky paloverde, while others may have been fired directly into the tree by shooters using the plant as a bull's-eye. In either case, being drilled time and again, whether inadvertently or advertently, was lethal for this paloverde, whose wounds began to ooze a bubbly yellowish sap. The tree's bark then turned yellow brown. Shortly thereafter, the paloverde died.

If we remove the two unnatural deaths from the list, we can say that foothill paloverdes in the Userys have had a fairly low probability of dying per annum during the period when I have been visiting these hills. If this rate has been consistent over previous centuries, some of my numbered paloverdes may be quite ancient. However, odds are that even the oldest trees on the ridge do not exceed 180 years old, the maximum age estimated for the foothill paloverde by Elizabeth Pierson and Raymond Turner (65). By plotting the diameter of paloverde trunks against the known age of a subset of trees, they produced a graph that could be used to convert trunk diameter into the age of a paloverde. (These botanists secured a sample of trees of known age by a variety of means, including finding trees growing in areas that had been completely bulldozed on a recorded date.) According to Pierson and Turner, most paloverdes on Tumamoc Hill in Tucson are less than one hundred years old. Probably the same is true for the trees in the Userys, unromantic though this conclusion may be.

Although I may have given the impression that the paloverdes of the Userys have barely changed over the years, their trunks presumably have become at least a little bit bigger each year. Moreover, a good many of the larger specimens in particular, including paloverdes #10 and #17 from the lower ridge, have lost some substantial branches in recent years. This capacity for self-amputation is something paloverdes share with saguaros. Both species may respond to a lack of soil moisture or some other stressor by sacrificing a limb or two and thereby reducing their water demands. When times are tough, it is probably adaptive to lose a portion of one's body rather than one's life.

Limb autotomy helps explain why the paloverdes on my transects generally appear no larger now than they did a decade or two previously. Mature trees may undergo cycles of limb loss followed by times of limb addition (up to a point) in reaction to long-term fluctuations in climatic conditions or some other factors that affect growth and maintenance.

Further evidence that even the older trees are not completely static but instead react to their environment comes from watching the trees change from season to season. As I mentioned, by the time the trees flower in spring they have exchanged their mini-leaves for small yellow flowers from which delicate orange-tipped stamens protrude. In some years, almost every tree is a solid mass of yellow; in others, most trees have just a handful of blooms or none at all. It seems likely that the paloverdes are responding to things like rainfall and its timing, but I have not been able to find a definitive statement on what triggers mass flowering in populations of this plant.

The consequences of variation in paloverde reproduction have been analyzed to some extent. When a banner year for flowering comes along, the trees may (or may not) convert a majority of their flowers into seed pods. Thus, on occasion a great many paloverdes more or less simultaneously undergo a transformation in which masses of yellow flowers give way to masses of dangling green seed pods. These pods start out as thin two- or three-inch strips and then gradually grow longer and expand and bulge with one to four seeds. The maturation process coincides with a change in pod color from dark green to pale tan. Shortly after the seeds have reached full size and hardened, the trees shed their pods en masse, littering the ground beneath them with thousands upon thousands of mature fruits. By dropping their pods, the trees prevent a small bruchid beetle from attacking the seeds within; bruchid larvae burrow their way into hanging seed pods and destroy the plant's offspring. On the ground, the intact seeds are extracted from the pods by an army of collectors and consumers, especially small burrowing mammals, like packrats and pocket mice, which stuff their cheeks with seeds

Mass flowering by foothill paloverdes in the Usery Mountains in May 2005. In some years, individual paloverdes produce huge numbers of flowers in synchrony with their neighbors.

and dash off to bury them in caches for later excavation and consumption (50).

By providing such quantities of seed simultaneously with their fellow paloverdes, any one tree makes it difficult or impossible for the local seed predators to destroy its entire crop of offspring. Moreover, having been inundated by so many seeds at once, pocket mice and the like have an incentive to bury a good fraction of the annual crop. Buried seeds have a reasonable chance of never being found again and so survive for months (or even years) after the cache was constructed. Having been planted in the soil, these forgotten seeds then can germinate and

The seed pods of a foothill paloverde. In some years, these trees convert very large numbers of flowers to fruits that contain one to four seeds.

grow in the event that the rains come along at the right time, namely July or August.

A summer storm that drops something over a half inch of rain is required if buried paloverde seeds are to germinate, and the seeds must also have been nicked or scratched. Such nicks and scratches must be common, however, given that one often sees pods of three, four, or five seedling paloverdes poking up out of the soil in a tight cluster. These seeds almost certainly were buried together by a small mammal in the course of which the cache maker presumably nipped or scratched several of the seeds it was storing.

Although a great many hopeful seedlings can appear when conditions are just right, the late summer provides a reality check for juvenile paloverdes, the vast majority of which succumb to heat exposure or to the depredations of small but hungry herbivores. Thus, a seasonal pulse of flowers followed by a burst of seed production leading to the later appearance of goodly numbers of seedlings usually is followed by the death of these small plants, leaving only those paloverdes that reached adulthood long ago.

Of course, before we can have paloverde seedlings, we have to have paloverde seeds, which are preceded by paloverde flowers. This year's unending drought seems more and more likely to short-circuit the whole process. Even if it does rain now, I have no idea whether the currently rain-starved trees will opt for a late spring dash to reproduce. There certainly have been years when the local paloverdes have in effect folded, deciding instead to conserve whatever energy reserves they might still possess for a more propitious year when a costly investment in flowers and seeds could lead to a return in offspring. For the moment, we all are on hold, waiting for a rain that might not come. It has been a long wait.

March *A Wonderful Rain*

Oh how quickly pessimism can fade. The long-awaited rain came yesterday, March 11, a date to be remembered, a glorious day, a day for celebration. The interval between the last rain in 2005 and this first storm of 2006 was 143 days. In between, no measurable rain at all. Zero, nada, zilch. During this long dusty dry spell, the weathermen tantalized us on the local news with occasional forecasts that featured a 10 or 20 percent chance of showers, but we became increasingly aware that a 20 percent chance of rain equals an 80 percent chance of no rain at all. Even when the forecast for March 11 spoke of 60 percent odds in favor of showers, I had become conditioned to expect disappointment. So when early in the morning I heard the distinctive light pattering of raindrops on the roof, I hardly dared believe my ears. Hurrying out to the kitchen, I saw in the dawn light that our endless dry spell had really come to an end. The back patio was wet, and water dripped encouragingly from the roof. The lesser goldfinches ignored the drizzle to hang from the thistle sock from which they plucked their breakfast.

The rain came in spurts throughout the day, ranging from the lightest drizzle to brief spells of real rain. My jury-rigged rain-catching system involving a gutter along the front of the house, a gutter spout, and a heavy duty plastic garbage can worked like a charm. Several times during the day, during lulls between showers, I hurried out to cart buckets of water from the overflowing container to my garden out front or to the citrus tree in a container in the back. My plants respond far more enthusiastically to rainwater than to the salt-laden local water piped in from the Colorado River or the aptly named Salt River. In between water delivery runs, I found myself staring out the sliding door window in the kitchen, luxuriating in the novelty of seeing raindrops. Even though I was dry and comfortable indoors, I felt the thrill that I imagined the desert would feel if only it could sense the salvation offered by this late-arriving, but oh so welcome, winter storm.

By the time the slow-moving front slid wetly off to the east, Phoenix had been bathed in nearly one and a half inches of water, a large amount considering that in an average *year* the city receives less than eight inches of rain. Still, the rain had come so late in the winter rainy season that I guessed that it would have little or no botanical effect, especially with respect to triggering germination and the growth of annual plants, like desert poppies and lupines. Surely at this late date the seeds of these plants would remain quiescent, given that too little time is left for them to grow, mature, flower, and set seed before the killing heat of late spring and summer. Only time will tell.

March *Another Paloverde*

For those of us living in the Sonoran Desert, the month of March typically provides many glorious sunny days, and today illustrates this principle to a T. Just four days after the all-day rain, what we have on tap is a pleasantly cool early morning with light winds that will give way to a delightful midday and a warmer, breezier afternoon in which rows of puffy white clouds will sail serenely across the sky from west to east. Sunshine will be abundant on a day when the many golf courses in Greater Phoenix will be aswarm with aged winter visitors trying to get their money's worth in a subtropical environment before returning to frigid Kansas, Ontario, or Minnesota in a week or two. Phoenix is said to have the highest ratio of golf courses to residents of any western city.

Although golf holds little appeal for me, I too am eager to get outdoors today. My destination is the Usery Mountains because I know that I have a nearly perfect day to accomplish my goal, which is to document the arrival times of insect visitors to the peak over the course of one spring day. Because of the relatively cool early morning tempera-

The view west from Usery Peak on a
glorious day in March 2006.

tures, I am in no rush to get out to the Userys. Only when temperatures
get into the fifties will any insects show up at the top of the mountain.
So it is about eight-thirty when I park my car just off the dead-end road
to the local collection of microwave towers and begin my twenty-five-
minute ascent to the top of the ridge. The first part involves squeezing
past a gate on the road above my parking spot and continuing higher
on the asphalt. Then it's up a little bank and into the desert proper for
a slow but steady climb up the hillside. I am in no rush, and since the
ascent is fairly steep, I pause now and then to regain my breath and my
enthusiasm for this venture.

Once I reach the saddle between the two main peaks in the Usery Mountains, I take yet another opportunity to reduce my heart rate, during which time I often look westward where downtown Phoenix shows up on a smog-smudged horizon. Should I choose instead to gaze to the south, I am rewarded with the vision of a classic case of suburban sprawl, which ends below me at the foothills of the Userys. Far off to the east, I can see the magnificent front range of the Superstition Mountains as it towers over Apache Junction, while to the north one mountain range follows another: the Goldfield Mountains, Four Peaks, the Mazatzals, and others lost in haze.

But on most days I am on the mountain not to secure an elevated pulse or to revel in the scenery but instead to collect data of one sort or another from the insects that perch on plants growing along the roller-coaster ridge that constitutes Usery Peak. I walk up to the western high point of the ridge and then turn around for a stroll back along the ridge to the eastern high point, a distance of about two hundred yards, with a terminal high point occupied by a scraggly creosotebush. As I walk the transect, if I am in the midst of an insect study, I busy myself by capturing individuals of whatever species is of interest at the moment. Typically this involves using an insect net to sweep my subjects off their perches in paloverdes, creosotebushes, or jojoba bushes. If a captured male has been previously marked, usually with a paint pen or dab of liquid paper, I record his identity (e.g., blue 123) in my notebook; if the male of the moment has not been marked, I remedy this deficit by giving him a set of identifying paint marks on his thorax. Once he has been released, if I see him again that day or on another visit in, say, paloverde A or paloverde B, I will record the time and place where he happens to be, all part of a program designed to help me describe the lives of whatever creatures have caught my interest on the hilltop.

When hiking back from the easternmost creosotebush, there are several places where I can look over to paloverde B, which occupies the highest part of the transect and so is outlined conspicuously against the sky. It does not matter whether I am studying tachinid flies or bot flies or pipevine swallowtails, paloverde B is *the* place to be for male insects intent on meeting a female of their species in the Usery Mountains.

Today I sit down next to paloverde B using a small boulder as a rather

uncomfortable seat where I can wait for hilltopping hexapods to appear. A gentle southerly wind comes and goes, chilling me slightly when little gusts of cold air sweep over the ridge. But the sun compensates by beating down from a sky without a cloud, supplying the solar radiation that warms my bones as well as heating the much smaller bodies of an assortment of flies intent on something more serious than golf.

The gravelly slope that runs up to paloverde B has many bare spots and openings among the scattered brittlebushes and goldeneyes growing here. Soon these patches have attracted perhaps ten or twelve or twenty hover flies or flower flies, depending on what you prefer to call members of the family Syrphidae. These small honey-bee-sized flies hover above their stations for a few seconds before rocketing off in apparent pursuit of a companion, which is chasing something else, perhaps yet another member of its species. When I flip a pebble down the slope, flies converge on the object, flashing after the stimulus and catching up to it just as it dives to earth. Each swirl of activity, whether naturally or experimentally induced, is followed by a few moments of stationary hovering, which gives way once again to another mad rush in a different direction. From time to time, individual flies take a break, dropping ever so slowly closer and closer to the ground before coming to rest on the gravel in the sunshine where they doubtless absorb the heat that is available to them this morning.

This species, whose scientific name I have yet to learn, is always one of the very first to make an appearance on sunny days at the high points along Usery Ridge and elsewhere in the neighborhood. Their early arrival time suggests that this fly must be among the most cold tolerant of those that gather at hilltops to compete for mates. I suspect that the fly's rapid wingbeats, which require a high level of muscular activity, generate metabolic heat that helps the insect keep active even when it is cool outside. In any event, this syrphid fly provides a moderately lively start to the day on the peak near paloverde B.

At 9:15, the point of the males' frenetic activity becomes evident as a pair of flies *in copula*, to use the delicate jargon of entomology, settles gently on the whitish gravel in the midst of the "swarm." One member of the pair, the female, perches upright on the ground; the other fly, the male, lies upside down on his back while firmly attached to his

(facing page) A view along a portion of the ridgeline at the top of Usery Peak. On this day, male insects of various species occupied some of the prominent trees and shrubs growing along the ridge, especially at the higher points. One such tree, paloverde B, is outlined against the horizon in this photograph.

partner via his inserted genitalia. I am quite certain that the female came to the peak specifically to enter the swarm and secure a sexual partner. I approach the pair cautiously, but not cautiously enough, since the female suddenly takes off with her partner dangling behind her as the pair travels to safety somewhere amid the tangle of shrubs below paloverde B. This couple is the only one I will see this morning in the Usery Mountains and indeed will be the only mating pair of this species I will encounter during my many visits to the Userys this spring and early summer.

Although the male syrphids get things going at the peak, other kinds of insects are not far behind in joining the show around paloverde B. One of these fairly early-arriving species is the large and conspicuous tarantula hawk wasp, one of the first to select paloverde B as its perch site this year. Up here, this is the tree that is almost always first occupied and last abandoned over the long spring flight season of the wasp. Because the wasps have just started to show up at Usery Peak this spring, only paloverde B and a couple of other ridgeline trees will attract resident males today.

Paloverde B is really two trees growing so closely together that they appear to have merged into one plant. Because both specimens have united to form a single landmark, "paloverde B" is larger and denser than the average foothill paloverde in the Userys. The position of paloverde B on the very top of the peak also means that it is visible from a great distance, outlined by the blue sky in spring, summer, and fall and in season made all the more handsome with the production of its own flowers or the surrounding decorations supplied by annuals and shrubs in the months when they are in bloom.

The first male tarantula hawk wasp of the day sailed in at 10:17 to land on paloverde B. Right now the male is perching awkwardly on an outer twig of a branch high up on the side of the tree out of the breeze. After nearly falling off this twig, the wasp, like a green army recruit trying to get over a training course obstacle, struggles to pull himself up and into a position where he can scan for others of his species as they approach the landmark.

Just a few minutes later, the perched male detects another wasp and jumps off his perch to circle sedately with this larger newcomer just

Paloverde B, the favored mating rendez-vous site for a diverse set of hilltopping insects, including the tarantula hawk wasp, *Hemipepsis ustulata*. The photographs were taken in March 2005 (left), May 2005 (center), and August 2006 (right).

over the prickly crown of the paloverde. As the wasps maneuver about, the trailing male closes the gap with the leader, which then climbs into the sky above the paloverde at an initially modest angle that soon becomes nearly vertical. His companion matches his ascent precisely, the two wasps seeming to accelerate as they go higher, almost in contact with one another, until they have reached a spot perhaps fifty or sixty feet above their starting point. Then one wasp breaks away from his companion and dives straight back down almost to the ground before cruising back to the paloverde. Rising up over the crown, this wasp is soon joined by the other male. They circle the tree, lining up again so as to make a nearly side-by-side ascent once more, this time flying even higher than on the first round. But when the two males hurtle downward, only one comes back to paloverde B while the other turns to fly away to the east in parallel with the ridgeline.

The "winner" of this oddly ritualized form of combat is the larger male, red 50, an individual that I had marked the previous day at this very same paloverde. Evidently this male has returned to reclaim his tree from an earlier-arriving interloper. I am able to identify red 50 with my binoculars when he finally settles onto a perch close to the one chosen by his predecessor. The wasp sports two red marks from a fine-point paint pen, the ornamentation courtesy of me. One red spot lies on the upper surface of the left wing near its base (the "5" position), while the other is placed on the upper surface of the right wing near its outer edge (the "0" position in my idiosyncratic numbering system).

Today red 50 will remain on paloverde B for slightly more than six hours, providing me with nearly continuous companionship until 3:53 in the afternoon. The wasp does take a number of brief breaks, sometimes sailing off for no apparent reason, only to return in a few minutes to take up his post again. Once, however, red 50 leaves his perch in order to pursue another wasp far along the ridgeline. I lose sight of the duo when they curl behind paloverde D, some 160 feet away. Racing down the ridge, I am unable to locate them again, although I suspect that red 50 was chasing a female, which it may have captured in flight for a tumble onto the ground and a roughly minute-long copulation. But since I cannot find the pair, my speculation on the outcome of the chase remains only speculation. Disappointed, I walk back to monitor paloverde B again, and so am there to record the return of red 50 about three minutes after his abrupt departure. He has been gone long enough to have chased, captured, and mated with a female before returning to his territory. But did he?

The possible male-female interaction is the only excitement provided by red 50 and his fellow tarantula hawk wasps on March 15. For the vast majority of the time that red 50 is under observation, the wasp sits stoically on paloverde B waiting, waiting, and waiting, with only an occasional brief chase of an intruder tarantula hawk to keep him (and me) awake.

Some days later on an unseasonably warm March morning, I have the pleasure of seeing why male tarantula hawks exhibit such patience. The male resident at paloverde B is now white V, this male having replaced red 50 on March 24. White V appeared again in the morning of March 25 at about eight-thirty to take up his post high on the crown of the paloverde, and there he stayed, living the life of a territory defender. This life requires long spells of alert inactivity interrupted from time to time by a short flight around the tree and back to his perch or, more rarely, by a brief chase of a transient male. But shortly after ten o'clock, at a time when my own alertness had faded somewhat, a very large tarantula hawk wasp came over the top of paloverde B and crash-landed on the gravel clearing near my observation post. On the back of this female, for it was a female wasp, rode two males, white V, of course, and blue 450, the much smaller male from paloverde A, a single tree that is actually taller than paloverde B but located eighty feet away from the top of the peak at a slightly lower elevation on the ridge. I believe that the female was flying up toward paloverde B along the ridgeline, going west to east so that she first passed near paloverde A. Blue 450 was up to the challenge of detecting the passing female, which he probably followed very closely and may even have "captured." However, he lacked the weight to bring the female to the ground. But when the much larger white V grasped the flying female, she no longer could remain airborne, and down they went with blue 450 also riding the female or perhaps grabbing on during her descent.

I normally would have been eager to see which male actually succeeded in copulating with the giant female, because I have long been interested in the effects of body size on mating success in this and other insect species. Given that white V weighed at least twice as much as blue 450, I would have placed a substantial wager on him rather than his pipsqueak rival who had, after all, been unable to force the female to the ground during her journey from paloverde A to paloverde B. But because of another research project of mine that required some captured females, I decided to put my curiosity on hold about who would get to mate with whom in favor of doing the safe thing, which was to net the female immediately. Which I did. After letting the two perhaps disappointed males escape from the confines of the net and return to their lonely perches in the two paloverdes, I turned my attention to the female in order to force her into a small vial before capping it. While trying to encourage the female to crawl into the vial, however, I managed to let the wasp slip down a fold in the net on her way to the ground, a maneuver that she accomplished with surprising speed. Once on the ground, she squeezed out beneath the metal ring on which the net was hung and took flight while I flailed futilely at her. The female wasp climbed steadily higher into the sky and then descended slowly as she traveled far, far from the point of capture. I could have wept.

I have no such traumatic experiences on March 15, when only male tarantula hawks are around to keep me company during the day. On this date, however, some other insects do come to the peak to enhance its biodiversity, for which I am grateful. One is a bot fly, *Cuterebra austeni*, a member of the Cuterebridae, not the Syrphidae, the first male of the day cruising in at 9:56 to settle its big black body on the gravel apron just to the east of paloverde B. The other is *Leschenaultia adusta*, a member of yet another family of flies, the Tachinidae, the first male of which lands directly in paloverde B at 10:23. This fly too is largely black but considerably smaller than the bot. The tachinid's abdomen sports the large curved hairs that constitute one of the distinctive features of this group, whereas the abdomen of the bot fly is smooth, hairless, and blotched with small unhealthy looking patches of gray on black.

The male bots and tachinids that come to the hilltop do so to compete for mates, as is true for the syrphid flies, tarantula hawks, and other insects as well. But whereas male syrphid flies seem to be trying to outrace one another to females that enter their diffuse swarm, the bots and tachinids closely resemble the tarantula hawks in aggressively encouraging rivals to depart from a perching area that residents try to monopolize. Male bots, tachinids, and tarantula hawks engage in speedy chases with opponents that appear to be energetically demanding. The effect of these chases is to send one of the contestants off in defeat, leaving the other to perch in an area without the aggravation of a competitor, although sometimes several male bots find space in which to perch some distance from one another at sites scattered about paloverde B. Today the resident bot pretty much has the peak to himself, although later in the morning two males race back and forth over the clearing by the paloverde for a couple of minutes. They are capable of generating the Doppler effect as they zoom past me first in one direction and then in another like miniature race cars on an oval track. After darting around paloverde B for a while, one male disappears while the other drops down to perch again on the gravel by the tree.

The aerial contests of the tachinid take a different form: often two opponents simply fly at high speed together about the paloverde, generally for only a few seconds, before one leaves and the other remains. But these chases occasionally become far more complex, with the two flies intercalating their pursuits with periods in which they appear almost to spin about one another for ten or fifteen seconds at a time. Instead of ascending into the sky during these bouts, the flies drop lower and lower, so that sometimes one fly actually lands on the ground before darting away, leaving his whirling dervish of an opponent in command of the paloverde.

I capture two flies in midcombat with a single sweep of my net, an accomplishment that fills me with pride. I extract one fly and give him a set of red paint dots (red 1-2) and then remove and gussy the other male up with a red paint "V" on his thorax. Both males return quickly to paloverde B, as if only mildly annoyed by my interference with their affairs. The spinning fight-flights then resume but end about eight minutes later, after which I see only the victorious red V perching on a green outer stem here and there in the paloverde for forty minutes or so. Then, around eleven forty-five in the morning, a new spell of spinning flights occurs after which an unmarked male takes the tree over after apparently dismissing red V.

The day wears on. The sun creeps slowly across the sky. High thin clouds form overhead, interposing themselves between the sun and earth. The resident tarantula hawk, red 50, lifts off his perch in paloverde B and sails lazily down to paloverde A where he interacts in a half-hearted way with the male wasp there before looping back to his home tree.

A violet-green swallow hurries south, passing over the saddle that connects two peaks on the ridge. On the slope below the swallow, one black-throated sparrow sings a tinkling song, and then a rival answers back with exactly this same song, one of many song types in the two birds' repertoires. The birds take turns to repeat themselves for several minutes before each falls silent again.

By early afternoon, the syrphids and bot flies have all disappeared, probably gone to resting places, perhaps on the slopes just below paloverde B. There's one exception, a single bot fly with tattered wings that appears literally and figuratively to be on his last legs. The old boy in front of me stumbles forward a few steps, pauses, and then in slow motion flies across the open gravel patch by paloverde B. This species of bot does not feed after it becomes an adult and instead relies on energy stores acquired during the larval stage when the bot grub feasts

Three hilltopping flies found on Usery Peak. (top) A paint-marked male of the tachinid fly *Leschenaultia adusta*, (center) the cuterebrid bot fly *Cuterebra austeni*, and (below) an oestrid bot fly belonging to the genus *Cephenemyia*.

on the flesh of an unlucky white-throated packrat. After reaching full size, the larva exits from within the body of the packrat and drops into the litter of the packrat house or environs, where it pupates. When the adult bot emerges from a pupa, it has a fixed amount of fat to burn, and by the time the fly is four or five days old, it can be down to the last drops in its tank, scarcely able to move.

A Say's phoebe halfway up an arm of an ocotillo watches the last bot of the morning with great interest. His head tilts toward the fly before the bird dives from its perch and arrows directly toward the bot some thirty yards distant. With a last flurry of wingbeats, the bird reaches the big fly and snatches it up in its beak. Bird and prey return to the ocotillo, where the phoebe whacks the doomed bot emphatically against an ocotillo limb. The bird then positions the now insensate insect so that it can be swallowed headfirst. With a toss of its head, the phoebe gulps down the last of the bots to visit paloverde B on March 15.

The afternoon proceeds in an unhurried manner. Tachinids continue to come and go from paloverde B. They are now the only remaining representatives of the contingent of hilltopping fly species. I catch an unmarked male and give him two blue dots in paint on his thorax at 2:40 p.m. Once released, he quickly returns to his beat within the paloverde. Occasionally this new fly, when on territorial patrol, buzzes close to the wasp, and red 50 sometimes briefly chases this pale imitation of an intruder male of its own species, only to settle back down again. In the middle of the afternoon, a turkey vulture drifts unsteadily past paloverde B. Red 50 obviously sees the bird because it dashes off in a short and fruitless chase, demonstrating its hair-trigger reaction to any dark moving object in its visual field.

Shortly after 3:00 p.m., a gray hairstreak darts directly in to land on paloverde B. This is the first hilltopping butterfly today, although in other springs following decent winter rains, a parade of butterfly species comes to the hilltop starting in midmorning and continuing through to the late afternoon. The drought of the past winter may explain the general absence of butterflies this spring. (Ten days later, a single pipevine swallowtail and one black swallowtail approach paloverde B for short spells of circling flight from around ten to noon. They have no luck in finding a female, receptive or otherwise, and soon both males leave, perhaps to inspect one of the many other hilltop paloverdes in the neighborhood where a freshly emerged female might possibly be waiting for them.)

Gray hairstreaks often stay put, perching on a paloverde of their choice, such as paloverde B, for an hour or two in the afternoon. Individuals marked with little dabs of paint or liquid typewriter correction fluid have been known to return repeatedly to a favorite paloverde. In these cases, the interval between first marking and last sighting can be as much as twenty-seven days (2). Resident males are so keen to stick to "their" tree that they will often permit a human admirer to approach them closely, which you need to do to fully appreciate just how good-looking these little butterflies are. Although admittedly small and mostly pale gray, the gray hairstreak's superficial drabness conceals some especially attractive features: the orange spots on the upper and lower surfaces of the hindwings, the delicate white and black scalloping on the underside of the forewings and hindwings, and, especially, the thin black and white projections off the trailing edge of the hindwings. Hairstreaks must get their common name from these little hairlike additions to their wings, devices that appear to mimic a butterfly's antennae. The fact that the pseudoantennae are positioned close to the relatively conspicuous orange spots on the hindwings helps create a pseudohead on the rear of the butterfly. The faux-head is actually more conspicuous than the real McCoy on the anterior part of the butterfly, where a head should be.

Speculation and some research suggest that the false head has evolved to distract small predators, such as insectivorous birds, from the true head. A Wilson's warbler that grabs the false head of the hairstreak is likely to wind up with a beakful of inedible wing rather than a mouthful of butterfly head, giving the hairstreak a greater chance of survival. In keeping with the predator-distraction hypothesis, gray hairstreaks, like others of this large group, often keep their hindwings moving so that the pseudoantennae appear to be twitching, in the manner of the real antennae of many butterflies. These movements presumably enhance the overall effect of the false head color pattern, further encouraging predators to mistakenly attack the hairstreak's rear end so that the insect can fly off to live and reproduce another day.

In any event, one has to wait for the midafternoon to add the gray hairstreak to the list of visitors to the hilltop paloverdes, as the array of hilltopping insect species runs through its daily schedule in March. Nor is the gray hairstreak the last butterfly species to grace the highest elevations in the Usery Mountains. The painted ladies, a cluster of several very similar species, and the red admiral, all members of the genus *Vanessa*, send their representatives uphill in the late afternoon where some remain until the sun sets and evening arrives. And between the gray hairstreak and the vanessas, one other species completes the hilltopping contingent for the day, the great purple hairstreak, a great insect indeed. In the spring months, males of this species generally flutter into paloverde B around three o'clock and are gone before dusk, so that they overlap with their much smaller and less showy fellow hairstreak in the midafternoon but remain long enough to oversee the arrival of the vanessas that perch on the ground by the tree in the late afternoon.

The great purple hairstreak is a stunner, twice the size of the gray hairstreak and far more conspicuous thanks to its wings, which appear intensely black when folded together while the hairstreak perches. But the wings have colorful patches of brilliant blue, not purple, that are hidden when the butterfly is stationary. These patches are revealed stroboscopically when the butterfly takes wing to shift its perch or to pursue a newcomer, almost invariably a rival male. The interactions among males follow the familiar pattern for territorial hilltopping insects: the resident pursues the incoming male, which generally leaves as quickly as it came, but if it does decide to make a contest of it, then the two butterflies engage in a rapid ascending flight that takes them far above paloverde B (or its equivalent elsewhere) before they break off to dive back to the tree, perhaps to repeat their performance again, and again, until one male gives up and dashes off downhill.

Between their highly infrequent clashes with rivals, male great purple hairstreaks sit and wait with the same dedication to duty shown by the other insects that defend paloverde B and other hilltop plants as rendezvous sites for meeting females. As a result, one can approach male great purple hairstreaks and peer at their exceptional colors at close range. The fore- and hindwings, when closely inspected, reveal several strategically placed dots of white and bloodred, along with some smears of baby blue in a sea of black. The ventral abdomen adds deep orange to the mix. Like the gray hairstreak, the great purple hairstreak possesses false antennae on its hindwings that draw attention away from the true antennae on the anterior part of its body. I have on several occasions found specimens of this species with V-shaped chunks missing from the hindwings, sections that once sported the false antennae. Damage of this sort seems certain to have been done by a bird that misdirected its attack to the rear of the hairstreak, which lost its pseudoantennae but not its life.

Three hilltopping butterflies found on Usery Peak. (left) A mating pair of the pipevine swallowtail, *Battus philenor*, that met at a hilltop paloverde; (top right) a male gray hairstreak, *Strymon mellinus*; and (below right) a great purple hairstreak, *Atlides halesus*.

At 5:12, the great purple hairstreak that had been on the lookout in paloverde B darts out from its perch and instead of returning at once, as has been its custom, flickers off along the ridge and out of view, his day's work done, unrewarded as usual. As he flies over the open gravel by the tree, a painted lady leaps up to chase after the departing hairstreak, a case of mistaken identity reflecting the readiness of males of most hilltopping species, including the vanessas, to err on the side of inclusiveness when making decisions about what to pursue. Rather than restrict their inspection of possible mates or rivals only to those that clearly and unequivocally belong to their own species, hilltopping male insects are prepared to chase almost anything that moves if it is approximately the same size. Thus, syrphids chase pebbles thrown their way, tarantula hawk wasps pursue turkey vultures passing overhead, tachinid flies chase flying tarantula hawk wasps, and red admirals charge after hairstreaks. Better to respond indiscriminately than to miss an opportunity to investigate something that could be a receptive female of one's own species, a potential mother of a batch of offspring that will carry the genes of a less discriminating male to the next generation.

Dusk slips over the mountain. The last male painted lady of the day drifts off the peak, dropping quickly out of view. The temperature has already begun to fall and by tomorrow's dawn will be in the high forties before rising again, warming the large cast of arthropods waiting to take their turn at mate-locating on Usery Peak.

I wonder why syrphid flies are prepared to start their day's work at the hilltops before tarantula hawk wasps, which in turn precede the pipevine swallowtail, which are followed by the gray hairstreak and then the great purple hairstreak, each of which has its own block of time reserved on or near paloverde B during that species' mating season. The result is a highly predictable sequence of perch defenders at the peak over the course of a day. We might explain these changes by reference to the different physiological mechanisms that each insect possesses, mechanisms that control such things as its tolerance for lower (or higher) temperatures and willingness to seek out hilltop perching sites at particular times of the day. But we may also ask why male (and female) tarantula hawks that tended to go to hilltops between nine and eleven-thirty left more descendants than those that showed up to find a mate between, say, two-thirty and five. If the earlier-arriving hilltoppers had inherited timing devices that consistently enhanced their chances of reproducing relative to other members of their species, then these devices would spread over time and gradually become standard for their species. But why should receptive female tarantula hawks come to hilltops at midmorning, while female great purple hairstreaks choose to meet up with their males in the late afternoon?

No one has ever attempted to answer this question rigorously, which leaves me free to speculate on the subject. One could imagine that if two closely related, similar-looking species both used the hilltop rendezvous strategy as a means of finding mates, then selection might favor females of species A that happened to avoid overlapping the time slot used by females of species B. Why? Because *males* of species B would tend to gain descendants by focusing on the period when females of their species were most likely to appear. The absence of B males at other times would increase the odds that females of species A that used these other open periods would not be sexually harassed by undiscriminating males of the other species. Females of species A that avoid having to deal with males of another species save time and energy that they can use more profitably for other activities. Moreover, if females stay away from males of the "wrong" species, they will not mate with these males with the attendant risk of producing infertile or defective hybrid offspring, which could cost them their chance of having viable descendants. The result should be selection that drives the mating periods apart for close relatives.

The trouble with this explanation for the time partitioning of hilltopping insects on Usery Peak is that relatively few combinations of close relatives are present in the set that visit paloverde B during the spring bacchanalia. Among the butterflies, the two hairstreaks and the two swallowtails are actually not that closely related, as indicated by their placement in different genera. And in the one instance involving several members of the same genus (*Vanessa*), all these butterfly species appear during much the same block of time. So I believe we can discard both the "avoidance of harassment by males of the wrong species" hypothesis and the "avoidance of hybridization" hypothesis for why males and females of different species get together at desert hilltops at different times of the day.

Perhaps the key to understanding the phenomenon lies in understanding what factors regulate the timing of metamorphosis from the pupal to the adult stage in females of hilltopping insects. I think we can be certain that hilltopping males are attempting to maximize their contacts with receptive females. In the hilltopping cohort, receptive females generally seem to be virgin females that need to mate just once in order to secure sperm that they will store internally and use over their lifetime. Because virgin females are likely to have emerged recently, the timing of their visits to hilltops should be related to when they have made the transition to adulthood. One could imagine the timing of this transition to be affected by female body size, metabolic rate, and color among other things, because all these variables presumably affect how quickly female pupae would warm up on a spring day. A pupa's body temperature ought to affect when the creature undergoes the changes associated with metamorphosis.

If this hypothesis were correct, however, one would expect to see some sort of connection, for example, between female body mass and the scheduling of male visitors at hilltops. No such pattern exists, with small syrphids followed by large wasps followed by intermediate-sized flies followed by large butterflies, then the small hairstreak before the larger hairstreak, and so on.

So my speculations on this matter have not taken us very far toward a possible answer to the question of why different species show up at different times at paloverde B and the hilltop on which it grows. Perhaps it is just enough to be aware that a daily schedule of species' activity does exist, a pattern that remains unexplained, a modest challenge for entomologists and natural historians of the future.

March *The Saguaro Recruit*

Over the years, I must have walked along the ridge between the two highest points on Usery Peak hundreds of times in order to record which marked tarantula hawk or tachinid fly is in which paloverde tree. Of late, I have also begun to check on the modest baby saguaro that grows just off the ridgeline trail in the shade of an unnumbered paloverde. Although I walked past this paloverde over and over again between 1980 and 2000, I never spotted the saguaro, presumably because of its small size, which helped it hide in the shadows cast by the paloverde. When I finally did notice the cactus in the spring of 2001, it was already the size and shape of a baseball. By March of 2005, it had become as big as a softball on steroids. Now in the spring of 2006, the juvenile saguaro appears to be undergoing a growth spurt of sorts that has started it on the path to becoming rather more elongate than round. (Later in the year, I can see that it is not only stretching out, it is beginning to bend a little, perhaps in response to differences in sunlight reaching its two sides.)

The growth of a young saguaro cactus. (left) Photograph taken in the spring of 2001; (center) the same cactus in spring 2005; and (right) the now noticeably elongated specimen in the fall of 2006.

(facing page) Many Arizonan populations of the saguaro cactus are stable or growing, as seems to be the case in this area along the Ballantine Trail northeast of Phoenix.

So here is one of the youngsters coming along to replace the giants that have had their day (or perhaps we should say, their 150 years) in the sun on Usery Peak. The saguaro population here appears in no immediate danger of winking out soon. Nor is this group of cacti unusual in this regard. Although saguaro populations may decline for decades, a series of milder, wetter-than-average winters can lead to a surge in recruitment that makes up for the losses in a preceding period characterized by drought, long freezes, or intense cattle grazing (63). It is not too surprising therefore that, in a study of thirty populations of saguaros scattered all over southern Arizona, Taly Drezner discovered that every one possessed a large contingent of small, young specimens, indicating that all these populations had an excellent chance of long-term persistence (28).

I do have one nagging worry about the future of saguaros, a worry that stems from another of Drezner's discoveries, which is that the survival of baby saguaros is largely a function of the *highest* temperature recorded in the month of July in any given year. When Drezner developed a statistical means to analyze the effects of a host of variables on recruitment of young saguaros into established populations, she found

that the higher the maximum July temperature, the less likely juvenile saguaros were to survive to the next year (28).

Even under the best of circumstances, July features some really hot days. The worrying thing is that the hottest days in July are likely to get even hotter, if global warming occurs or is occurring, as so many climatologists believe. Maximum temperatures steadily increased worldwide in the period from 1950 to 2004 (98), and warming has also been detected in the Sonoran Desert itself in the form of a decrease in the frequency with which winter temperatures drop below freezing (102). If the warming trend continues, it seems highly probable that the maximum temperatures during July in our part of the world will continue to rise, increasing the annual mortality in those little saguaros upon which future populations depend. (When July 2006 came round, it roasted the Phoenix area with brutally high temperatures, including one day at 118 degrees Fahrenheit, the fourth highest temperature ever recorded for the city. Not a good sign.) With fewer young survivors, fewer will make it to adulthood, and the more likely a saguaro population is to decline. I don't want to think about it.

Happily, the small saguaro beneath the ridgeline paloverde on Usery Peak appears to have made it through its really vulnerable phase thanks in part to the sheltering microenvironment unwittingly supplied by the paloverde. If Pierson and Turner are correct, the cactus will begin to grow more vigorously in the next few decades, and if all goes well, it will eventually stick its head through the canopy of the paloverde (65). It can then take its place among the truly substantial saguaros in its neighborhood as it prepares to reproduce for the first time, perhaps a mere forty years or thereabouts down the road. I will not witness this landmark year in its life, having run out of years myself, but I can imagine the plump baby saguaro as it may appear in the future, part of an always-changing landscape on Usery Peak.

April *A Symmetrical Saguaro*

Many mature saguaros grow in the Userys, and most are visually appealing in one way or another. But when I saw the symmetrical saguaro for the first time in 1990, I was delighted to have found such an exceptionally handsome individual. Here was a big, unblemished specimen with no bullet scars, not even a woodpecker burrow to disturb its good looks. This saguaro had a thick, tall central trunk with eight arms distributed evenly about the middle of the trunk. The arms were all about the same size, perhaps a third as long as the trunk, growing upward, not one drooping or listing to one side. The result: a superbly balanced specimen.

True, in order to appreciate the symmetrical saguaro, I did have to climb down the precariously steep slope that forms the south side of Usery Peak. An abundance of loose gravel and spiny cacti encouraged me to proceed with great caution. Once I made the descent, I had to climb up the hill, which seems even steeper on the way back than on the way down. But the reward was real, the chance to admire an extraordinary saguaro at close range.

Growth in a saguaro is evident in these photographs taken in 1991 (left) and 2005 (right) of an especially symmetrical specimen growing on the southern slope of Usery Peak.

Over the years, I have photographed this cactus quite often, with the result that I have more images of it than of any other plant in the Userys. My photographic record reveals that the symmetrical saguaro has retained its good looks over the years from 1990 to 2006, and if anything is even more handsome now than it was when I first stumbled across it. Based on images taken over the past sixteen years, I can see that the arms have become considerably longer, while the main trunk has also elongated, not by a huge amount but nevertheless an amount that I can detect. Today the saguaro looks more iconic than ever.

My photographs tell me that the symmetrical saguaro has not only grown with the passage of time, it has also changed in another way. A shot of the icon in June 2002 shows a tall, imposing saguaro but one that is obviously thinner, less plumped out, than the same individual in May 2005. The winter and spring of 2001-2 were seasons of drought; the winter and spring of 2004-5 featured unusually heavy rains. Although the ability of the pleated saguaro to expand or contract, depending on the availability of moisture in the soil, is common knowledge, actually observing this response requires comparison photographs. My obsessive desire to photograph this (and other) saguaros repeatedly has enabled me to see drought-induced changes in the cactus.

Even when somewhat depleted, the symmetrical saguaro maintains its classic shape and, thus, my admiration. However, just a short distance to the west of the handsome saguaro stands a remarkably asymmetric specimen, a so-called cristate, or crested, saguaro. One of its limbs developed in an extremely abnormal fashion, with its growing tip spreading out into a squat fan rather than forming an elongate cylinder, although a small normal-looking arm is attached to the fan on one side. The fan-shaped element is heavily pleated, with far more ridges per inch of circumference than an ordinary arm or trunk. The upper surface of the fan is more or less flat and is divided down the middle by a shallow groove. During the early summer, the cristate arm produces flowers on its upper ridge, although most are concentrated on the top of the little arm attached to the crest like a Siamese twin.

Cristate saguaros have their own enthusiasts, who are attracted by the unusual shapes of the abnormal arms and trunktops and by the relative rarity of this kind of saguaro. According to the *Tucson Daily Star*, two lovers of cristate saguaros, Bob Cardell and Pat Hammes, have assembled a photo presentation of some of the four hundred or so they have tracked down over the years. These dedicated saguaro hunters appreciate cristate cacti because they are scarce and therefore a challenge to find. Others, namely cactus rustlers, consider them attractive targets because they bring a premium price from homeowners who want a rare and unusual cactus in their front yard. I, however, would not want the Usery cristate cactus moved to my front yard, even if the yard were large enough to accommodate a saguaro. For one thing, I do not find the antisymmetry of the cristate cactus appealing. Strange, odd, unusual, rare, yes, but pleasing to the eye, no. Better that "my" crested saguaro holds its position on the slope below Usery Peak, providing a counterpoint to its elegantly symmetrical neighbor, an illustration of the extreme individuality of saguaro cacti.

April *The Responsive Desert*

Although less than one month has passed since the big March rain, the effects of that single storm have been nothing less than spectacular. For one thing, the saguaros in the Usery Mountains have become pleasingly plump once again. The rain also stimulated both annuals and perennial plants to grow, contrary to my pessimistic guess that the storm had come too late in the year to make the desert green again. In fact, even two weeks ago I could already see patches of tiny green plantlets arising from what had been utterly barren gravel just a short time before. Up came some filaree, a smattering of red brome, a little of this and a little of that. No great carpets of annuals but enough to take the edge off the pale brown and gray emptinesses between the paloverdes. Although the greenery is less than overwhelming, the scene is more lively than it would be otherwise.

Not only plants but animals too appear to have been rejuvenated by the rain. After the storm, a mourning dove quickly constructed a flimsy nest on the supporting struts of an exceedingly spiny chain-fruit cholla (all chain-fruit cholla warrant this description). The bird now sits tight

A mourning dove on its nest protected by the spiny limbs of a chain-fruit cholla.

(facing page) Spring-flowering plants that occur widely in the Sonoran Desert include (clockwise from the top left) the scorpionweed (*Phacelia ambigua*), white ratany (*Krameria grayi*), desert chicory (*Rafinesquia neomexicana*), and Mexican poppy (*Eschscholtzia californica* ssp. *mexicana*).

on its clean white eggs, a clutch of three, nestled in among the long white spines of its host plant. The dove appears to believe that its prickly environment confers complete protection on him or her because he or she (both sexes incubate) refuses to budge even as I creep up almost close enough to touch the bird.

Not far from the stoic dove, I find a few, a very few, desert poppies and lupines in the early stages of their development. These classic desert annuals will go on to rush themselves through their life cycle, so that by late April both poppies and lupines will be in flower. Admittedly they achieve this reproductive goal by producing their flowers when the plants are still diminutive, a mere three or four inches in height. These dwarves are miniaturized in every respect, with flowers a fraction of their normal size. But the poppy's flowers are as cheerfully orange as ever, a testament to the ability of this species to endure months of drought and then respond with alacrity to even a small opportunity to reproduce.

The perennial plant species also reacted with surprising speed to the drought's interruption. Three weeks after the storm, I found a handful of three-inch-long leaves of the desert larkspur, one of my favorites because of the mature plant's pale blue delphiniumlike flowers, which typically ornament stalks one to two feet tall. This year, alas, the plants never reached the flowering stage. When I checked several weeks after first discovering the larkspurs' dark green basal leaves, I was disappointed to find that the plants had disappeared. Apparently the young larkspurs had been eaten by an industrious herbivore that had found all five clusters of the plant along my homemade trail up Usery Peak. But the larkspur had at least tried to bloom, sending leafy shoots up from its perennial roots immediately after the big rain.

Likewise, a host of shrubs wasted no time in making the most of the 1.5 inches of precious rainwater they had received on March 11. Ocotillo are well known for their ability to rapidly clothe their skinny gray limbs in green after a rain, and the local specimens did not disappoint in this regard. Within a few weeks following the big storm, all of the many ocotillos in the Userys had sprouted rows of yellow-green leaves along their spiky limbs. By early April, the leaves, now darker and larger, had

A desert tortoise feeding on green spring annuals in the Usery Mountains.

more or less hidden the plant's notable spines, creating a superficially far friendlier looking version of this drought-adapted species.

The wolfberries that had been leafless on March 10 also treated the rain as a godsend, hurrying to manufacture thousands of little green teardrop leaves and equal numbers of small trumpetlike flowers. The transformation from a collection of lifeless gray sticks and twigs to a demonstrable shrub covered in pale green foliage and white flowers seemed almost instantaneous.

Almost every perennial shrub reacted similarly. Fairy dusters that had looked on death's door on March 10 had completely resurrected themselves in less than a month, at which time they were thickly coated in handsome feathery little leaves and dotted with the pinkish filamentous flowers of this species. By late April the goldeneyes had generated large numbers of deep yellow daisylike flowers, while the paloverdes added a vast quantity of paler yellow ornaments of their own, providing further evidence that the March rain did not come too late. The hedgehog cacti certainly found it profitable to invest in a set of substantial buds, which are destined to become the glorious magenta flowers of this species. Not to be left behind, brittlebush got into the act as well. Normally this species flowers primarily in mid-March, but in the spring of 2006 the plant responded to the rain in stages, first leafing out and then letting flower stalks grow to full size. Only then could buds form at the tips of the foot-long stalks, and so it was early May before many specimens managed to come into flower. But flower they did.

Admittedly, not every single brittlebush or paloverde put out the maximum number of flowers. Indeed, many individuals of various desert perennials in the Userys gave spring 2006 a complete pass, while others flowered in what can only be described as a half-hearted manner in favor of investing in plant growth rather than reproduction. But still, the contrast between early March and, say, mid-April was stunning, a demonstration of the ability of desert plants to make something out of nearly nothing.

When desert plants grow, desert herbivores show up. One of my favorite plant consumers, the desert tortoise, generally puts in an appearance in the Userys in spring when the winter rains have been average or better. (In desert grasslands, the tortoise evidently waits for the summer rainy season before becoming active [48].) Last year I saw several specimens in my study site over the course of the spring, but in 2006 only one hardened individual showed up to pull at the greenery produced by the March rain. I spotted the animal next to the trail at a sufficient distance so as not to alarm the beast, which would have pulled its head into its shell had it seen or heard me. Instead, the tortoise stretched forward, grasped a small clump of filaree, jerked its head hard to one side, tearing off a mouthful that it then methodically swallowed before repeating the maneuver. With each mouthful, the tortoise was consuming a little bit of the rain that fell on March 11, a life-sustaining rain indeed.

May *A National Monument*

The afterglow of the good rain has begun to fade now in early May as temperatures have climbed with the passing of spring. On a day when we are promised 105 degrees Fahrenheit in metropolitan Phoenix, I make it a point to get an early start on the drive to the North Maricopa Mountains. After rushing down several busy freeways and major highways in the predawn, I finally reach a right turn onto a far less crowded road that eventually leads me to yet another right turn, this one a dirt track. An aesthetically crafted sign near the dusty turnoff announces that I have entered the Sonoran Desert National Monument. Sunrise happened on the way to the Monument, and by now the sun has already topped the line of mountains on my right, the better to warm the desert and get the day rolling. On the way to my ultimate destination, I pass a couple of recreational vehicles the size of tractor trailers. Their owners have towed their massive homes-away-from-home off the dirt road into the Monument where they tower above the creosotebush flats. Here the occupants of the RVs spent the night, and here they remain tucked within their steel cocoons at this early hour.

Early spring morning in the Sonoran Desert National Monument.

I reach the trailhead well before seven o'clock. I am now and will continue to be the only person to park a car on this small circle of dirt. Even though dawn has come and gone not so long ago, I am fully aware that summer is upon us when I get out of the car. Not only is the temperature already well on its way toward ninety, but the sky is cloudless and the air without moisture, signs of late May, a month when the forces of evaporation take command. As I stand by my car getting my daypack in order, I hear no bird singing nor any other sounds of life. The desert seems to be holding its breath, steeling itself for another day of trials. A transitory breeze briefly stirs the twiggy paloverdes, almost all of which have finished flowering.

Judging from the quantity of bleached yellow petals lying beneath some of the paloverdes, many individuals of this species did manage to flower fairly profusely in the weeks just past. However, the trees that covered themselves in flowers do not seem to have converted the flowers to fruits, the seed-containing peapods that paloverdes sometimes generate in vast quantities. The nearly universal failure of the trees to reproduce raises some questions. Is the absence of seed pods dangling from the branch tips the result of an active decision by the plants to cut their losses? In other words, did the local paloverdes "voluntarily" opt out of pod production given that there were no follow-on rains after March 11, rains that might have facilitated the making of fruits and seeds? Perhaps without the extra rain, trees that tried to manufacture large quantities of fruit would have paid dearly in terms of depleted water and energy reserves, even to the point of endangering their own survival. If so, better to cut seed production this year in order to live to reproduce another year.

On the other hand, maybe the local paloverdes actually did try to set fruit but failed, thanks to herbivorous consumers, which destroyed many flowers before they could be converted into seed pods. On occasion, I have found the flowers on some trees festooned with filaments of silk, the handiwork of moth larvae that nibble on the flowers. These flower eaters may have simply short-circuited the process of making pods, perhaps to the detriment of the paloverdes, which could not create the potential descendants that they were trying to produce.

Reproduction in desert plants certainly can be affected by flower-destroying consumers (16). In one study of the foothill paloverde conducted outside of metropolitan Phoenix, small gelechiid moth larvae were found living in flower buds, which they ate inside out. These caterpillars eventually metamorphose into drab little moths, but during their juvenile stages they can eat enough flowers to reduce the number of paloverde offspring by up to 80 percent (84), a figure that does not seem out of line based on my own observations of paloverdes in years when the trees have become moth-infested in the spring. The botanist David Siemens, who documented the massive destruction of paloverde flowers by moth larvae, made another interesting discovery by protecting a sample of flowers from the ravages of these caterpillars and other herbivores. He found that in the year of his study, most of these apparently perfectly good, undamaged flowers were subsequently aborted by the paloverdes. In other words, paloverdes can stop trying to reproduce even after having committed themselves to the production of flowers, presumably because they can in some way sense that conditions are not conducive to successful fruit assembly. So, for example, if the trees flower in response to winter rains only to have drought take over, then it could pay the paloverdes to give up on potential fruits. But even in good years, when attempts by the trees to reproduce would have positive payoffs for them, moth larvae may show up in numbers to destroy many flowers before they can get pollinated and grow into seed-containing fruits.

Whatever the reason, the scattered foothill paloverdes of the Maricopa Mountains have produced very few fruits this year. They have reverted to their customarily ascetic green twiggy look now that they have neither flowers nor leaves. It remains to the neighboring ironwoods to generate a certain floral exuberance, although by late May the representatives of this species in the National Monument have clearly lost much of the color they had just a short time before. But even in their slightly faded state, the Maricopa ironwoods still add a splash of life to their surroundings in the form of masses of pale magenta, pinkish, or purplish flowers that festoon their leafless outer branches. In anticipation of the flowering season in late spring, the ironwoods shed many or all of their dark green leaves some time ago, replacing these with large numbers of flower buds. When the flowers themselves appeared, they transformed the ironwoods from more or less standard trees to something resembling a pastel starburst.

The nature and depth of a tree's color is partly dependent on the individual, the age of its flowers, and the time of day, richer colors being produced by the light of early morning and early evening. As I walk a wash in midmorning under the bleaching sun, I encounter a pair of near-white ironwood neighbors, each of which is completely blanketed with blossoms. The pale mound of ironwood flowers glows against the dark background provided by a mountain slope composed of boulders coated with desert varnish.

A pale-flowered ironwood at the edge of a large wash in the Sonoran Desert National Monument. (below left) A cluster of more typically colored ironwood flowers. Note the bee, *Centris pallida,* extracting nectar from a flower in the center of the photograph. (below right) The tan seed pods of ironwood on a tree that produced many such fruits in the late spring of 2006.

The flowering ironwoods hum with the wingbeats of flower-visiting bees, most of which belong to the species *Centris pallida*, a longtime favorite of mine because of its intriguing natural history. Among other things, males of this bee can find and dig down to fresh adult females that are burrowing upward through the hard soil in anticipation of mating, which they usually do immediately after climbing out of their emergence tunnel. The males' ability to detect potential mates is not based on X-ray vision but an extreme olfactory acuity, which permits them to smell potential mates concealed beneath a blanket of dirt. On the blossom-rich ironwoods, I see both mated females collecting provisions for their brood and males topping off their energy reserves so that they can continue their demanding search for new sexual partners. Given that flowering ironwoods are one of a very few energy sources available to bees at this time of year, their attractiveness to native bees is not surprising. The pale gray males and the gray, brown, and black females of *Centris pallida* are perfectly color coordinated with the life-sustaining mauve ironwood flowers.

Ironwoods generally schedule their flowering season to coincide with that of saguaros, and this is the case in the Monument this year. So today my viewing pleasure is regularly magnified when I come across a saguaro in full bloom standing next to a pastel ironwood. The glossy white trumpets of the saguaros do not attract digger bees, although other native bees, including several tiny ones, forage in the waxy flowers in the company of the introduced honey bee, which clearly relishes the rewards offered by the cactus. During the saguaro flowering season, some honey bee colonies specialize in gathering the abundant pollen of this species (77). But although honey bees are capable of exploiting a huge range of flowering plants, including ironwoods, here they seem outnumbered by the energetic *Centris* bees.

The many flowering saguaros that I encounter today are also attracting animals other than bees. White-winged doves clatter off saguaro tops where they have been dipping into the open flowers crowning the cacti. Over the course of the morning, I also see at intervals three Scott's orioles probing saguaro flowers with their sharp beaks, presumably drinking the nectar contained within. Well before I see any of the orioles, I hear the bird's song. To a human, the male oriole's clear whistled song seems remarkably cheerful and confident, a delightful signal of this time of year when only a few other birds are still singing frequently. To a male oriole, however, hearing the song of another male may stimulate quite different emotions, perhaps anger or fear, almost certainly not pleasure. I am glad that I hear the oriole's song through my anthropomorphic filter, knowing that the pure whistles in the distance mean that I may soon see a male in his crisp black and yellow outfit. A male oriole flees a saguaro on my approach and dives into a large ironwood whose remaining foliage is sufficient to conceal this brilliant bird.

Change takes place quickly at this time of year. In a week or so, the ironwoods will have finished flowering, casting dry gray petals by the thousands on the ground beneath them. Shortly thereafter male orioles will cease to announce their territorial and sexual eagerness, either having attracted a mate, which has begun nesting, or having accepted failure for the year. Already the mating season of the digger bees is all but over. Only a handful of mate-searching males remain active today; when I find them, they are patrolling low to the ground in the shade under a handful of big ironwoods, looking for the very last females of the spring. These females, once they have emerged and mated, will join others of their species in a race to remove whatever nectar and pollen still remain within the dwindling supply of ironwood flowers in the Monument.

Summer is bearing down on the desert. Better hurry, finish up, get things done.

May *Urban Sprawl and Urban Wildlife*

On my recent trip to the Sonoran Desert National Monument, I was forced to pass through the town of Maricopa about twenty miles to the southwest of Phoenix and some twenty-five miles to the east of the mountains I wanted to visit. Once a dusty farming community, Maricopa was until recently notable only for one of the ugliest cattle feedlots in the nation, a grim rectangle of barren ground that was home to hundreds, and at times thousands, of cows, standing about next to their feeding troughs or out in trampled "pastures" devoid of all living things. After a rainstorm, the cows often had to stand up to their knees in a singularly unappealing greenish liquid apparently composed of equal parts water, mud, cow urine, and cow dung.

The feedlot is now on its way out, which cannot upset the newcomers to Maricopa, of which there are many. A portion of the wasteland with dead mesquite stumps and cowpies has already been converted to tightly packed residential housing, one of several brand-new developments in the area. ("The home of your dreams comes to life at Desert Springs in Maricopa Meadows. From the high 200's.") This kind of massive housing project has become commonplace in the areas within forty or fifty miles of Phoenix, as developers build new cities from scratch on relatively inexpensive rural land. The lower-than-average prices of the homes in these places attract price-conscious home buyers. These newcomers are then forced to commute to Phoenix, which is where the jobs are. The taxpayers of Arizona pick up the tab for the highway expansions and general infrastructure needed to sustain these satellite cities ringing Phoenix.

A CVS pharmacy, a Bashas' supermarket, and the host of other institutions characteristic of suburban living are now available for those who have recently purchased a home in what were never meadows in Maricopa. These arrivals have lifted the population of the town from 1,040 in the year 2000 to around 24,000 people in 2005. By 2025 one projection puts Maricopa's population at a staggering 185,000. Even if this figure only represents one realtor's fantasy, there is no question that Maricopa is not finished growing.

What will be the consequences of having 24,000 people, let alone 185,000, less than twenty miles from the Sonoran Desert National Monument? This magnificent chunk of Sonoran Desert, which lies just to the west of Maricopa, received monument status in 1999 during the waning moments of Bill Clinton's presidency over the objections of many Arizonans of the Republican persuasion. Although Clinton ignored these complaints, he could not insure that the budget of this new monument would expand to meet its growing needs. The fiscal 2005 budget for the Monument was not much more than a million dollars, with most of this amount set aside for the development of an administrative plan for this new federal entity. The feds have sprung for a few new signs at the boundaries of the Monument, some of which urge visitors to exercise restraint with campfires and their off-road vehicles, requests that are regularly ignored. On my visits to the Monument, I have seen motorcyclists and all-terrain vehicle owners racing across the creosote flats, cutting ugly new trails through the desert, the riders confident that they will not be brought to justice by stern-faced, pistol-toting rangers. Their confidence is justified, since in 2005 at least, the Monument had exactly one park ranger, although several members of the Bureau of Land Management's law enforcement staff also chip in, patrolling parts of the Monument on occasion. The combination of urban sprawl, affordable off-road vehicles, and a shortage of Monument protectors seems certain to generate additional changes to this wonderful desert parcel that won't please the cactus-huggers in Arizona, who admittedly never constitute more than a small minority of this state's ever-expanding population.

Anyone driving through Maricopa or Phoenix (which most of us do as quickly as the traffic permits) will note that city building requires a great deal of land. The construction of these two communities has largely involved the conversion of agricultural fields to residential and commercial neighborhoods. The now-vanished crops of cotton and alfalfa were in the past grown on land that had once been a desert sparsely vegetated with creosotebush and foothill paloverdes. In just a hundred years or so, we have traded natural areas of this sort for cropland, only to later exchange these agricultural systems for an urban environment of asphalt, houses, automobiles, grassy lawns, and the tall trees that people like to have around their houses and in their parks.

What we have then is a massive unplanned, unregulated experiment in ecological change. Identifying some of the consequences of this experiment does not require an advanced degree in biology. Anyone can see, for example, that uniform rectangles of nonnative Bermuda grass make up a considerable part of the cityscape, whereas in relatively undisturbed desert, native grasses of any sort are usually scarce or nonexistent. Instead, shrubs and open gravel rule supreme in the desert (or rather, they did before introduced nonnative grasses invaded the Southwest). In the city, sprinklers and hoses work overtime to keep exotic grasses and ornamental vegetation alive. In contrast, creosotebush is hard to find within city limits, having been essentially extinguished in the agricultural interim between the desert period and the city development phase. Today many species of Australian eucalyptus and South American palms have supplanted cotton fields and citrus orchards, which in their day displaced the saguaro and the paloverde.

Some other effects of urban conversion are not so apparent. For example, has the temperature in town gone up, stayed the same, or decreased? One might think that temperatures would have risen given the massive amounts of asphalt and concrete that cover much of Phoenix. These materials absorb solar radiation during the day and release it slowly at night. On the other hand, perhaps temperatures in town have fallen thanks to an evaporative cooling effect coming from our lawns and gardens, which sport more vegetative mass than the original desert. As these plants transpire, they provide moisture whose evaporation requires energy, presumably reducing the heat load afflicting Greater Phoenix.

To figure out what, if any, changes have taken place in urban climates, a team of climatologists compared the historical record of daytime highs and nighttime lows for the Phoenix area against temperature data from the rural outpost of Sacaton about thirty miles southeast of Phoenix. In the city, daytime maximum highs have consistently been a couple of degrees centigrade lower than in the country, a probable consequence of the effects of evaporative cooling by lawns and trees. But although daytime highs have not increased over the years, nighttime lows have gone up steadily in proportion to increases in population and urbanization over the last one hundred years. As a result of the vast amounts of heat-retaining asphalt and concrete, Phoenix's low temperatures in May are now roughly six degrees centigrade higher (that's ten degrees Fahrenheit) than those recorded in Sacaton (17). Indeed, one of the more depressing features of summer life in Phoenix is to get up early on an August morning and find that it is still over 90 degrees Fahrenheit. The trend toward higher and higher nighttime lows shows no signs of abating, and the overall heat island effect appears to be increasing as well. In another recent study, researchers compared evening temperatures at Sky Harbor Airport, which is located in central Phoenix, with temperature data from a farm on the fringe of the city. These researchers found that Sky Harbor regularly registers ten degrees centigrade higher than the farm site at 8:00 p.m. (38).

It stands to reason that, in an environment that has been liberally moistened with irrigation water and artificially slow-cooked at night, there will be changes in urban populations of animals, especially given the wholesale replacement of native species with exotic ornamentals and the like. Evidence on this point comes largely from studies of birds, which can be readily identified, a great virtue in research of this sort. Phoenix and Tucson, the two major cities in the Sonoran Desert of Arizona, harbor some exotic birds that have taken over many cities around the world. These avian intruders include the pigeon, the house sparrow, and the starling. However, some native species are holding their own in Arizona's cities, such as the mourning dove, the verdin, the house finch, Anna's hummingbird, even Abert's towhee and the curve-billed thrasher. On the other hand, many common desert birds are either very scarce or totally absent in Phoenix and Tucson. The black-tailed gnat-catcher, the rock wren, Costa's hummingbird, and the canyon towhee almost never venture into housing tracts and industrial areas, although they may appear in desert remnants and desert parks surrounded by city neighborhoods. The absence of so many native species swamps the small boost given to bird diversity by the exotic urban contingent led by pigeons and house sparrows, resulting in an overall decrease in species numbers within Phoenix and Tucson (30).

On the other hand, if we add up all the birds living in a hectare of Phoenix and Tucson proper, the total will greatly exceed that recorded in comparable areas of true Arizona desert. So we have two contrasts to explain: a reduction in species diversity but an increase in bird numbers within cities. The two features may be interrelated, as documented by biologists who placed trays containing millet seed both in residential neighborhoods and in some desert locations. When city birds had a chance to take the seed from the trays, they removed all but about 2 percent of the millet during the time the food was available to them. In the same period, birds in desert areas ate so sparingly that 90 percent of the millet was left in their trays at the end of the experiment. The greater abundance of birds in cities apparently generates much stronger competition for food, which favors whatever species are able to win the speed-eating contest. When pigeons and house sparrows gobble up whatever is available, other birds are left with little or nothing, which excludes them from the resource-rich, but intensely competitive, urban environment (30). To add injury to injury, house sparrows and starlings are notorious for their ability to steal good nesting sites from most native species, which lack the exotic species' hyper-aggressiveness.

The situation is very different in the true desert where competition among consumers is kept under control in part by the population-depressing effects of water scarcity. As a result, no one potential super-competitor can build its population up to monopolistic levels. Therefore, some seeds or insects or other foods remain around long enough to support a spectrum of species, none of which ever becomes superabundant.

In addition to water shortages, desert birds have to contend with bird-hunting hawks, especially the formidable Cooper's hawk. The pressure exerted by these predators may further lower the population of smaller birds in the desert, preventing avian densities from building up to the levels found in cities. Conversely, the rarity of hawks in our cities may be the key to why pigeons, sparrows and doves are so common there. The urban environment is largely hawk free, perhaps because Cooper's hawks and the like do not feel comfortable around people, cars, and trucks. As a result, adult seed-eating and insect-eating birds are probably safer and more long lived if they are lucky enough to make their home within city limits rather than in the boondocks.

But what about cats, you may be saying. Cats are indeed a problem for city-slicker birds, something I know from personal experience, having occasionally found the partially gnawed corpses of white-crowned sparrows and Inca doves where they were dropped after having provided entertainment and a snack for one or another of the overfed neighborhood cats. Although cats catch and dismember birds with enthusiasm, they appear to focus on naïve juvenile birds, whereas Cooper's hawks pose a threat to even the most alert and cautious adults. If adult doves and sparrows live relatively long lives in cities, they can reproduce often, overwhelming the capacity of city cats to destroy all their offspring, so the argument goes. As the total number of adult birds grows and grows, there comes a point when they are consuming most of the food available in town. Only then will resource limitation, not predation, keep the bird population from getting even larger (30).

Thus, the general pattern for city birds seems to be "numbers up, species diversity down," a reflection of the fact that cities do offer a great deal of food for those species that are able to take advantage of the urban largesse. This same pattern may extend to some groups of invertebrates as well. Although biologists have generally paid little attention to urban insects and spiders, the bugs of Phoenix have surprisingly been examined in some detail thanks to Phoenix's Long-Term

Ecological Research (LTER) project (83). The team in charge of this research at one time included four spider-studying arachnologists armed with a large quantity of pitfall traps, which consist of two cylindrical plastic cups set so the lips of both the outer and the removable inner cups are level with the soil surface. As spiders march over the ground, some may tumble into a trap from which they can be eventually extracted for identification. Although the familiar web-building spiders do not go on walkabout, the members of several families of spiders, especially wolf spiders, do spend their lives stalking over the ground and so are readily captured in pitfall traps. The LTER spider team focused on these catchable spiders. By distributing their traps equally in different parts of Phoenix, they could determine the number and diversity of spiders inhabiting habitats ranging from remnant desert patches within city limits, to xeriscaped front yards, to urban agricultural fields as well as thoroughly industrial sites.

Why even bother with creatures as insignificant and unappealing as spiders? Perhaps you belong to that large fraction of humanity that actively fears spiders, not altogether without reason since some species are poisonous, as you doubtless know. However, some biologists are impressed, as they should be, by the ability of female spiders to produce silk and to use this quite amazing material in any number of ways, often to capture insect victims. The diversity of silks, body forms, and predatory behaviors exhibited by spiders makes them well worth studying, as does the major ecological role that spiders play as consumers of their fellow invertebrates.

The LTER team therefore did not have to work too hard to justify their interest in arachnids. By the time the team picked up all their traps, they had 5,574 individuals to identify, no mean task. As expected, most were wolf spiders, the generally dark brown or gray, low-slung, long-legged terrestrial types that capture their prey by ambush and stealth. Three-quarters of the team's catch of wolf spiders and others like them came from the two most heavily irrigated habitats: agricultural fields and grassy yards. Desert remnant patches produced a mere 10 percent or so of the total spider numbers coming from alfalfa fields. And yet, in terms of species diversity, the few remaining fragments of true desert left within Phoenix were the richest, far outstripping the area's agricultural fields and traditional yards. In other words, spiders are like birds in their response to man-made environments (83). In places with plenty of water and vegetation, a few species of wolf spiders do wonderfully well, feasting on crickets, other small insects, and even those fellow spiders that also thrive in resource-rich urban environments. The handful of highly successful spider species crowds out all the other kinds. But in the dry, harsh, resource-poor conditions of desert remnants and xeriscaped yards where the hunting is not easy for a wolf spider, the spiders are few in number but rich in variety. When the living is so hard that the numbers of the most common species are pushed down, then there may be room for at least a few individuals of some other species. The result: increased biodiversity in desert environments, a phenomenon that apparently applies to both spiders and birds.

Much the same pattern applies to the bees of central Arizona. Although most of us think that "bee" is synonymous with "honey bee," in reality the honey bee is only one of about fifteen hundred species that make a living in southern Arizona. These bees range from those not much bigger than a fruit fly to others that approximate a hummingbird in size. The various bees cope with desert living in many different ways, but all are dependent on flower nectar and pollen, which nesting females collect and store as brood provisions for their hungry larval offspring. Different native bees often utilize the flowers of quite different native plants, and so it would hardly be surprising to find that the conversion of desert to city habitats has had large effects on the specialist bee species in our city and state.

Documenting this point, however, requires that systematic collections be made in the same way at the same time of the year in different parts of metropolitan Phoenix and surrounding areas. Nancy McIntyre and Mark Hostetler are among the very few who have taken the time to do the necessary work (57). They set out bee traps in four habitats: traditional front yards in residential parts of the city, xeriscaped yards in these same neighborhoods, desert remnants within the city, and desert parks on the outer fringe of Phoenix. Their traps were blue and yellow plastic bowls filled with water to which they had added a couple of drops of soap. Blue and yellow visual stimuli attract some, but not all, bee species. When a bee drops down for a close look at a bowl, it may land on the water surface, only to slip underwater and drown in the slightly soapy water, the fate of slightly more than thirteen hundred unlucky bees during the month of September 1998 when McIntyre and Hostetler were doing their research.

When the bee team examined the species taken from the four habitat types in their study, they found that urban desert and desert fringe traps had yielded about twice as many species as were found in xeriscaped and traditional urban and suburban yards. Moreover, species diversity was significantly higher in gravelly yards with drought-resistant vegetation than in the grassy yards with a preponderance of old-fashioned lawn. Interestingly, in terms of sheer numbers, however, grassy yards in Greater Phoenix had fewer bees overall than desert fringe areas, a numerical pattern counter to that documented for birds and spiders in central Arizona. The distinctive Phoenician pattern of low diversity *and* low numbers of urban bees may arise in part from the fact that those species that specialize on the flowers of a particular native plant simply cannot exist if their desert plant is not in someone's front yard. In contrast, desert areas can support greater diversity by supplying the critical plant species exploited by the relatively rare, specialist pollinators, which are totally absent in the city because they cannot find the plant species that supply food for their brood.

There are, for example, twenty-one species of native bees that collect pollen *only* at creosotebush (22), a plant that has been largely eliminated from cities in the Sonoran Desert, thereby shortening the city bee list by twenty-one species. As a result of this sort of thing, city and desert environments are often markedly different in the faunas they can support, with lower urban biodiversity for birds, spiders, and bees, and probably for other groups of animals as well.

Another aspect of urban biodiversity deserves comment, namely that the diversity of species is *especially* low in the poorer parts of town. In Greater Phoenix, as in cities worldwide, neighborhoods range from the ostentatiously affluent to the unmistakably impoverished. Up in Paradise Valley, where multimillion-dollar mansions are standard housing, some lots are big enough to accommodate not just a pretentious house but a considerable amount of native vegetation, thanks to the appeal the desert has for a certain kind of wealthy homeowner. Down in South

Phoenix, however, the houses and apartments run to the ramshackle and the yards to dust and dirt. Not surprisingly, native birds prefer Paradise Valley to South Phoenix, with the result that avian biodiversity is greater where the rich folks live. Indeed the socioeconomic status of residential areas in Phoenix predicts with reasonable accuracy how many bird species will be found there. Thus, twenty-eight species appear on average in parks located within high-income city regions; only eighteen hang out in parks in low-income areas (44).

If one asks what proportion of a given city's population is living in neighborhoods with below-average biodiversity for that city, the answer can be moderately depressing. Take, for example, Tucson, Arizona, just a two-hour drive south of Phoenix. There, more than 70 percent of the populace lives in places where the avian biodiversity is below Tucson's overall mean value. Equivalent results have been recorded by ornithologists working in Berlin (Germany) and Florence (Italy) (92). What these studies really tell us is that most city dwellers are poorer than average and are therefore forced to live in relatively poor neighborhoods where the combination of abundant concrete, high human population density, and scarce vegetation make life hard for most birds, with the exception of a handful of unloved urban hangabouts, like the pigeon and the house sparrow.

The fact that most city people live, work, and grow up in depleted environments disturbs some conservationists and child-advocacy types who fear that many urban youngsters are missing out on experiences that might promote an eventual interest in natural areas and their protection. Perhaps children who have contact only with degraded urban habitats and computer games are more likely to grow up unaware and uninterested in what strikes the average earth hugger as truly glorious, namely the diverse natural worlds outside of our cities (46). In fact, at least one study indicates that children who have a chance to play in wild areas do exhibit a more positive attitude toward such places later in life (11), while another suggests that if children get into outdoor nature activities before age eleven they are more likely as adults to agree with statements like, "Natural areas untouched by humans should exist." Moreover, these nature-indoctrinated kids are more likely when they grow up to vote for political candidates on the basis of their environmental record (103).

The idea that early experience with Mother Nature is required if a child is to avoid "nature-deficit disorder" may at first seem at odds with an idea advocated by the biologist E. O. Wilson (105). In *Biophilia*, Wilson writes that people have an innate capacity for loving natural landscapes and the biological diversity found in these places. Now, when most of us hear the word "innate" bandied about, we think of automatons programmed by genes to do this or that, automatons immune to learning and the effects of experience. Therefore, you might think that Wilson is saying that we humans have an automatic, robotic love of biodiversity. But the biophilia hypothesis can be interpreted to mean that members of our species have an evolved predisposition to *learn to love* Mother Nature. In other words, our bodies, according to Wilson, contain the kind of genetic information that guides the development of a brain with special learning capacities. One of these could be the ability of the brain to modify itself in response to particular kinds of outdoor experiences. If the biophilia hypothesis is correct, give a kid the chance to play in a forest or fish a stream or wander with buddies across a prairie and that kid should be more likely to develop an affection for these places and the living things they contain than a child who grows up in a treeless cityscape of concrete and asphalt. Wilson suggests that we are genetically predisposed to make use of the effects of our experiences with Nature. Give us half a chance, and we will learn to love the natural environments of our youth, whereas the experience of growing up in the unnatural world of the inner city will not engender the same kind of emotional attachment to Mother Nature.

Neither the nature-deficit disorder hypothesis nor the biophilia hypothesis has been tested with much rigor. True, a handful of marginally relevant studies exist, some showing, for example, that people say they prefer photographs of natural environments over artificial ones (93), a result consistent with the biophilia hypothesis if we assume that most of the respondents had at least some actual experience with natural environments. But perhaps the strongest case that one can make for the biophilia hypothesis is that the argument rests upon the potent logic of evolutionary theory. The evolutionary argument goes like this. In the past, persons capable of learning to respond positively to the natural environments in which they lived as children would have been motivated to settle in similar environments as adults. Given that the places where they had grown up contained sufficient resources to support their survival, other similar places would probably have enabled them to produce a brood of children, who would inherit their genetically based capacity for targeted learning. Learning to like biological diversity and, more to the point, learning to like places that support a broad variety of organisms, makes evolutionary sense given that for tens of thousands of years our hunter-gatherer ancestors usually had to find a variety of plant and animal foods if they were to get themselves (and their children) through the day (64).

Biophilic learning might well underlie my own interest in the outdoors and all things natural. I was lucky enough to grow up in a rural corner of southeastern Pennsylvania rich in plants and animals but relatively free of people and asphalt. Indeed we could see only two other houses from our home. Our nearest neighbors, Mr. and Mrs. Jones, lived in a big red brick farmhouse a quarter of a mile away, surrounded by pastures and woodlots. Mr. Jones, a former cowboy from Virginia by way of Oregon, looked rather like an elderly Marlboro man. He played a fierce game of croquet in his free time, when not doing the farm chores associated with growing hay and running cattle on the land around his house and barn.

Our family and the Joneses occupied a shallow valley bisected by White Clay Creek, a modest stream that kept Mr. Jones's cows well watered. I was free to wander along the creek with my binoculars or my fly rod with no need to ask anyone's permission to enter their private property or fish on their part of the creek. The stream contained many fallfish, a trout-sized minnow that was gratifyingly easy to catch with my amateurish home-tied flies. In the fall, I scanned the trees fringing the creek for "confusing fall warblers," whose illustrations appeared in my *Peterson's Field Guide to the Birds*. I studied this compact guidebook carefully in an effort to sort out the wood warblers in their drab fall plumage as they poured through the valley on their migration south. At times I had dozens of delightful little warblers in view at once, flitting through the creekside maples and sycamores and providing round after round of challenging bird identification problems. These experiences may help explain why to this day I find it exciting to come across a wave of migrant warblers in the mountains an hour or so drive from Phoenix. Even a glimpse of a single hermit warbler darting from creosotebush to creosotebush in the low desert is enough to thrill me.

If it is true that childhood experiences in biodiverse environments do shape our attitudes and interests, then in the future there will almost certainly be fewer and fewer advocates for Nature with a capital *N*. Back East, for example, migrating warblers are now generally scarcer than they once were (88), almost certainly in part because of forest destruction and fragmentation either in the North American breeding grounds or the wintering areas in Central and South America (78, 104). Thus, even those city folk lucky enough to live near an urban woodland park are now less likely to have the pleasure of chasing down one warbler after another in order to secure a glimpse of one of the rarer species traveling with dozens of yellow-rumped warblers or black-throated greens on their way to or from their northern breeding grounds. Tapping an evolved biophilia learning mechanism will be even less likely for that large fraction of urban populations that occupies neighborhoods of low biodiversity. The inferior environments occupied by the urban poor make it tough for them to secure anything other than impoverished natural experiences and all that may imply.

Some conservationists have argued that if we could tap into the human capacity for biophilia, we could ameliorate some of the environmental problems that make reading a daily newspaper or a conservation organization's report an exercise in masochism. Biophilia, however, is not the only human attribute that owes its existence to our evolutionary past. Among our other evolved predispositions are some that may contribute to the very environmental disasters that could be ameliorated by our biophilic tendencies (assuming that we have these tendencies). For example, you do not have to have a PhD in evolutionary biology to realize that humans are far more likely to have evolved the kind of psychological mechanisms that push us toward having and caring for children rather than not having children or not caring for them. Persons in the past who tended to eschew copulation or who consistently ignored their progeny almost certainly did not contribute many of the genes that we find in people today. Instead, those of us alive now carry with us the DNA of ancestors who were able to reproduce more successfully than others in their population. It's no accident therefore that overpopulation and the resource depletion that goes with an overabundance of people are facts of life for all of us today (64).

Indeed, if Wilson is right about the evolutionary basis for biophilia, a love of nature and a fondness for biological diversity are really psychological aids for the production of healthy children with a good chance of eventually reproducing as well. Still, just because we can explain why we love our surroundings in evolutionary terms does not mean we cannot use our feelings to make our environments richer.

In this light, I take encouragement from a project underway in Gilbert, Arizona, a particularly fast-growing suburb of Phoenix right next to older, more established Mesa and Tempe. The alfalfa and cotton fields that once flourished in old Gilbert have now disappeared in favor of housing developments, condominiums, and giant shopping centers, with an overblown drugstore on every corner, or so it seems. But in the midst of all this, at the corner of Guadalupe and Greenfield Road, the city has installed the Riparian Preserve on 110 acres of city land. The primary purpose of the site is ground water recharge, which is achieved by flooding large shallow pools with treated effluent. By letting this water soak into the ground, the town helps recharge the aquifer underlying the area. After the water has percolated down through the soil a sufficient distance, it has been cleansed of any residual unpleasantnesses and so can be removed from the aquifer again and safely consumed, perhaps by the same persons who contributed the wastewater in the first place.

As gratifying as the recycling of treated effluent is to a confirmed tree hugger, my main reason for celebrating the Riparian Preserve does not have to do with its contribution to efficient water use in thirsty Greater Phoenix. Instead, I wish to draw attention to the landscaping at this old agricultural site, which has been converted into a series of ponds surrounded by native vegetation planted there by volunteers who knew how to make the most of desert willows, mesquites, hackberries, cottonwoods, and many other true blue Arizonan plants. The planner of the Riparian Preserve evidently was determined to keep the vegetation honest; as a result, he or she excluded the eucalyptus, the Aleppo pines, the palms, the olive trees, and almost all of the other exotics that so many Arizonans have warmly invited into their front- and backyards.

The contrast between this water project and the one sponsored by my hometown of Tempe could hardly be more painful. The powers that be in Tempe installed an artificial lake at immense expense in a portion of the usually dry Salt River bed where it runs through the northern part of our city. Tempe Town Lake now covers about 220 acres bordered by concrete walls on the northern and southern riverbanks and by large rubber dams at its eastern "inlet" and western "outlet." These specially constructed barriers supposedly can be deflated so as to permit the lake to empty prior to receipt of water rushing downstream should we have a major flood in the future that forces releases of water from the huge dams upstream on the Salt River.

The current lake has not had to be spilled downstream since it was filled in 1999, the same year that saw the opening of the Riparian Preserve. Tempe Town Lake serves primarily as a resource for boaters and a selling point for lakefront development. Sculling crews sometimes practice here, and tourists are occasionally persuaded to take sightseeing cruises run by a commercial operator. Once or twice a year Ironman Arizona stages an over-the-top competition in which contestants run a marathon, bicycle 112 miles, and swim 2.4 miles in Tempe Town Lake. During the big swim, hundreds of competitors churn around the lake. But when the swimmers are not competing, the lake itself does not offer much to see. The shores of the impoundment are barren except for hotels and the like, which are gradually being installed next to the water. Vegetation of any sort, natural or unnatural, is scarce, and so too are birds, which does not especially bother town officials and administrators of the nearby Phoenix Sky Harbor Airport, all of whom were concerned about possible collisions between waterfowl and the aircraft that use the airspace over the Salt River bed as they descend and take off from the airport.

Thus, Tempe Town Lake has been designed in an environmentally unfriendly manner, and I, for one, have avoided the place as a result. In contrast, the Riparian Preserve appeals aesthetically to those of us who

A large group of black-necked stilts resting in a pond at the Gilbert Water Ranch.

(facing page) Avocets feeding socially in treated wastewater at the Gilbert Water Ranch.

stroll about on the large berms that double as trails and pond containers. During spring migration, wood warblers dart from acacia to mesquite as they join the overwintering white-crowned and Lincoln's sparrows on the journey north. The resident songbirds, like song sparrows and Abert's towhees, quickly colonized the reserve and are always there to add life to this reconstituted habitat. The ponds have attracted many waterbirds, which somehow manage to locate this small oasis in the middle of, not just a desert, but a sprawling urban area. In they come, avocets, green-winged teal, pintails, long-billed dowitchers and least sandpipers, snowy egrets, and Wilson's phalaropes. Great blue herons stalk sedately through the shallows in pursuit of mosquitofish or tilapia, while black phoebes sally forth to snap up flies just off the surface of the ponds.

The reserve managers do their best to advertise the spectacle they have created. Bird-watchers need no encouragement to enjoy the "ordinary" species like black-necked stilts, and they go positively bonkers when a rarity like the streak-backed oriole or least bittern shows up. The local bird-watching bloggers regularly alert their fellow birders to sightings of unusual species at the Riparian Preserve, which sends a certain kind of fanatic rushing to the place to add the species to one's state, country, or life list. In addition, some schools have scheduled activities at the spot, and other groups have taken advantage of nature programs offered by volunteers of one stripe or another. Perhaps a few of the younger visitors to the reserve will have their evolved biophilia mechanisms tweaked by the experience, turning them into environmental sympathizers of one sort or another by the time they have become adults.

In any case, Gilbert's decision to turn the clock back in this small part of their city shows what can be done to combat the effects of sprawl and urbanization. Instead of the steady loss of biodiversity that goes with citification, here we have a dramatic reversal of the trend toward the environmental blahs, a world of asphalt, house sparrows, and Bermuda grass. Those of us who have already acquired a dash of biophilia have a place nearby in which to express a fondness for biodiversity without having to travel far outside the ever-expanding borders of our metropolis. For this we should be grateful, and we are.

June *Sonoran Desert Lizards*

Although it is reassuring to know that more or less natural habitats can be reconstructed even from urban lots, it is so much easier to stick with natural desert environments rather than having to start all over again from scratch. The Usery Mountains do not need to be revegetated, restored, reconfigured, or redesigned on a grand scale. They are delightful as is, although they have benefited from official efforts to keep off-road vehicles and weekend gunners under control. I try to do my small part by picking up such litter as I come across these days. Fortunately, I almost never encounter rusted soda pop cans, beer bottles, cardboard boxes, and the like, although once in a long while a deflated balloon drifts in from a birthday party or the celebration associated with opening a new car lot somewhere in Mesa. The string attached to the balloon eventually catches in a paloverde or teddy bear cholla, and then the balloon sags listlessly to one side until I come along to put it out of its misery. What's left of the intruder goes into my back pocket or backpack to be removed from the mountain.

For some reason, however, I failed for many years to remove a broken Diet Rite Cola bottle that someone had stuffed into a rock crevice near the mountaintop after downing its contents, presumably after a hot climb up. This bit of littering must have occurred long ago judging from the primitive look of the bottle's bright red label, which was embossed with "LESS THAN 3 CALORIES PER BOTTLE" in large white capital letters. Royal Crown Cola introduced Diet Rite Cola in 1958, and so I suspect that the bottle left on Usery Peak was verging on fifty years old by the time I finally got around to gingerly picking up the fractured pieces for disposal elsewhere.

After cleaning up the peak, I wondered why I had waited so long to get the job done. The place looked better without the red and blue-green glass shards that I had to step over every time I walked the ridge from paloverde A to paloverde Z. I no longer needed to waste time looking at the broken glass and instead could maximize the attention I gave to the natural landscape with its attractive plants and animals. Of course, some desert animals are more appealing than others. As you know by now, I am partial to insects, but I also enjoy the birds of the Userys, including red-tailed hawks circling overhead, migrant Townsend's warblers slipping from one paloverde branch to another, pairs of white-throated swifts strafing the highest point on the ridge. But I also put the local lizards on a par with the bugs and birds. Several species abound in the Userys. In the spring and summer, in wet years and drought years alike, when I walk slowly along the ridgeline, I am all but guaranteed to see the tiger whiptail *Aspidoscelis tigris*, the side-blotched lizard *Uta stansburiana*, and the ornate tree lizard *Urosaurus ornatus*. These three species are large enough and active enough to be conspicuous, and even a casual nonherpetologist like me can be entertained when the lizards are doing something.

The slinky whiptails always seem a little guilty as they creep along close to the ground nosing into this and that in search of termites and other small insects. But what strikes us as signs of guilt are actually indicators of cautiousness, an adaptive thing for a conspicuous creature that has a good many predators. Even a small movement on my part is enough to cause a whiptail to dash for cover, sending the gravel flying behind it.

In contrast, side-blotched lizards typically sit still on rocks and wait rather than move about restlessly. They run only when I approach very closely or when they have been "defeated" by an opponent of their own species. Male-male confrontations occur now and then when one male advances on another, leading the two lizards to line up side by side and engage in elaborate juddering displays, which involve multiple push-ups and a lateral flattening of the body. In this position, the dark blotches on their sides become visible to one another. After a few moments of ostentatious self-advertisement, one male generally quits the area promptly, sometimes with his triumphant rival in close but brief pursuit.

In the Userys, the most common lizard of all is the tree lizard, another rather sedentary creature that is usually seen from April through September. Female tree lizards are lucky if they live through one summer, during which they lay one or two clutches of five to eight eggs (80). Male tree lizards devote their short and entertaining lives to a competition among themselves that determines how many mates they will secure. Their clashes are all about intimidation. On this very warm June morning on Usery Peak, one aggressive male is perched head down on the vertical face of a large gray boulder at one end of my ridge trail. (Incidentally, although it is true that many tree lizards live in trees, the species is as likely to be found on boulders as on paloverdes and mesquites.) The boulder-defending tree lizard uses the rock face as a platform on which to perform a series of push-ups that involve all four legs, unlike the front leg–only push-ups of side-blotched lizards. After a series of stiff-legged bobs, the lizard adopts a rigid pose, with its entire body held well away from the rock on fully extended legs. This maneuver clearly exposes two baby-blue stripes on its underside, which show up nicely against the lizard's pale underbelly. I am not sure who the male is attempting to dominate with his displays because I cannot see another male tree lizard lurking in the vicinity. But perhaps the lizard would be pleased to learn that I for one am impressed by his maneuvers.

Tree lizards also have one other colorful ornament, a throat patch that in some populations may be blue, orange, or yellow, or some combination thereof. It is odd that individuals vary in throat patch color but

In the Usery Mountains, the ornate tree lizard (*Urosaurus ornatus*) is as often seen on boulders as it is on trees. (right) A male engaged in the distinctive threat display of this species. (above) A closer view of the camouflaged lizard.

not belly patch color, especially since the throat patch also comes into play during aggressive interactions between males. When challenging a rival or being challenged, a male can extend the throat patch into a dewlap, the better to show his opponent the color or colors on this part of his body. Christopher Thompson and Michael Moore wondered if the particular dewlap color of a male offered an indicator of his fighting ability. If so, males could avoid mixing it up with others whose dewlaps signaled that here were lizards that could do serious damage if provoked. To test this idea, Thompson and Moore staged contests in the lab between males that were of similar size but differed in the amount of blue in their dewlaps (the two biologists having decided from their observations of males in the field that a heavily blue dewlap was a signal of high male status). They found that males with relatively more blue in their throat patch were in fact more aggressive individuals. The bluer-throated males put their aggressiveness to work in an experiment in which captive males were given a chance to keep their fellow tree lizards away from a cage lamp, which supplies the lizard with a desirable resource, heat (90).

In addition, Thompson and Moore took a number of males with no blue in their dewlaps and experimentally painted their throats with an orange-blue combination of fabric paints while painting the throats of other lizards plain orange. Males with the experimentally applied orange-blue pattern dominated those with solid orange dewlaps. This result indicates that when males with an inherently low fighting ability see a male with an orange-blue pattern, they are programmed to concede defeat on the basis of this signal alone, presumably because under natural conditions this color combination would indicate that they were up against a superior battler.

In order to test whether natural dewlap colors are honest signals of intrinsic fighting ability, researchers applied orange-blue paint to the dewlaps of some orange-blue dewlapped males and to some whose dewlaps were plain orange. Thus both groups had been handled and painted equally, but the researchers expected the naturally orange-blue males would be more aggressive than the naturally orange ones. Indeed, when a sample of naturally orange-blue males were tested in an experiment of this sort, they performed four to eight times as many four-legged push-ups per thirty minutes as did a matched sample of orange-only males (90).

The males that have considerable blue in their dewlaps have the ability to be aggressive, territorial individuals that can monopolize patches of real estate containing one or more resident females. Males that can successfully control an area with several females are likely to inseminate these females, passing on the genes for their reproductive modus operandi. Incidentally, if one experimentally removes females from a mesquite, the male or males there abandon the tree, demonstrating that male tree lizards use the presence of potential mates as the basis for deciding to defend the tree or a portion thereof (58).

In contrast, males with uniformly orange dewlaps are far less aggressive than their bad-tempered fellow males, whom they attempt to avoid. Instead, these relatively pacific lizards try to sneak onto someone else's territory in order to contact females there surreptitiously. Thus, these "sneaker" or "satellite" males use a dramatically different means to reproduce than territorial male tree lizards. Oddly enough, sneakers grow larger than their territorial cousins, this being one of the very few species in which being large apparently does not confer an advantage in aggressive contests between rival males. Perhaps being large enables the nonterritory-holding male lizards to overpower some unwilling female lizards that they sneak up on while secretively exploring another male's territory.

The evidence collected by Moore and his colleagues strongly indicates that the differences in male color pattern (and behavior) arise early in tree lizard development as a consequence of their different genetic makeups. Indeed, when one takes a population of lizards of varying color indoors and lets them produce the next generation under uniform laboratory conditions, the frequencies of the different color forms in that next generation closely match those of the parental generation. This finding and some other lines of evidence indicate that males inherit their color and behavioral abilities rather than inheriting the capacity to change their appearance and behavior in response to key environmental factors, like population density, stress levels, and experience gained when interacting with rivals.

Now that summer is here, the high temperatures make it possible for males and females of all three lizard species to get started on their soap opera lives early in the morning at times when I am most likely to visit the mountains. As a result, I regularly get to see snippets of lizard melodramas in the late spring and summer. The other day I watched a male tiger whiptail try to snuggle up to a female sliding over the gravel, while two side-blotched lizards engaged in a bout of competitive push-ups on a boulder; nearby a blue-throated tree lizard displayed its status-significant sky-blue throat ornaments to a rival who was hidden from my view. The active lizards offer compensation for the discomforts endured in getting up into the Userys at the time of year when temperatures are getting out of control. These animals make me realize just how central the summer months are to so many desert organisms, a time when the lizards fight and reproduce, a time when a special summer cadre of desert insects rendezvous on the peak to wait for mates, a time when the saguaro cacti prepare a feast for seed dispersers of all sorts, an essential season indeed and one that I do not intend to miss.

June *Saguaro Fruit*

Saguaro spells summer in the Sonoran Desert. True, in every month, the cactus is a keystone species in the sense of dominating the visual landscape and providing it with its special character. But in the early summer, the saguaro becomes more ecologically important than ever by producing a big crop of brilliantly red fruits, which feed a host of animals at a time when they really need the help.

This year, sometime between June 24 and June 27, a three-armed saguaro that grows just beneath paloverde D on the Usery Peak trail produced its first ripe fruit of the year. On the 24th, the cactus had three reddish but unopened fruits among the dozens of unripe green ones perched on its arm tips. On the 27th, seven fruits had split, revealing their spectacularly red interiors. Three of these fruits had already fallen from the saguaro, having lost their grip on the mother plant as they generally do in the final stages of their maturation. The others still clung to their perches on an arm tip.

I had singled out this rather ordinary three-armed saguaro earlier in the year because its buds, flowers, and fruits can be easily observed, since the plant clings to the steep slope just below the ridge on Usery Peak. To check on its reproductive status at close range, I needed only to stand on the hillside just above the cactus. When I visited the plant on May 11, the three arm tips had collectively generated several dozen buds, works in progress in that none was more than an inch in diameter or two inches in length. The buds grew rapidly, however, so that one week later, many had become dramatically enlarged and elongated, the now big-headed buds stretching out three or four inches in an approximation of the trumpet form of mature saguaro flowers. Saguaro buds are aesthetic in and of themselves, with the expanded bulbous heads covered by a sheath of overlapping pale green "scales," each of which is thinly outlined in red. The many scales press tightly down on the interior of the bud, producing a handsomely patterned outer surface.

On May 23, the three arms of the hillside saguaro sported a total of seven superb flowers, probably the first flowers of the year for this particular plant, but because I did not inspect the cactus on the preceding day I cannot rule out a slightly earlier start to its flowering season. Honey bees had located the seven flowers and were actively removing

Saguaros produce fairly large numbers of flower buds, which are attractive in their own right. In due course, the buds open into the large and spectacular flowers for which this cactus is well known.

pollen from them in the company of several species of flies. An unusually large tephritid fly with heavily banded wings applied its proboscis to the creamy white surface of a saguaro petal.

The seven flowers I admired at 7:00 a.m. on May 23 looked radiant at that time, but I knew that within a few more hours they would look considerably less perky. A saguaro flower is an ephemeral thing that usually opens in the evening and withers in less than twenty-four hours. By opening at night, saguaro flowers can enlist the support of bat pollinators, which thrust their heads deep into the nectar-rich, trumpet-shaped blooms, during which time pollen gets smeared all over their faces. The bats then transport pollen from one cactus to another. But bats are not the only pollinators (32), and indeed flowers that are exposed both day and night may be more likely to set fruit than those that are manipulated so as to be available only to nighttime visitors (56). Saguaro flowers attract many diurnal guests, as witness the bees and flies that I saw inspecting the flowers of the hillside saguaro on the early morning of May 23 (and on many subsequent days as well). Hummingbirds, doves, orioles, and other birds are also enthusiastic imbibers of saguaro nectar, the water content of which may be sufficient in and of itself to attract potential pollinators, given the general scarcity of water during the period when saguaros are flowering (107). When temperatures soar into the 100-degree Fahrenheit range, access to saguaro flowers may be the difference between life and death by dehydration for a verdin or black-throated sparrow. But any creature, bird, bat, or bug, that wishes to extract nectar or pollen from a saguaro flower better act quickly.

I visited the hillside saguaro on six days during the last week of May and the first week of June, finding on each occasion between nine and twenty fresh flowers awaiting pollination. However, by June 6 the saguaro had run out of unopened buds and instead was now devoting itself to the production of fruit.

Saguaro fruits develop from pollinated flowers, which undergo a rapid transformation after pollination has occurred. The flower petals quickly close in on themselves, and then the upper two-thirds of the flower begins to blacken and die while the basal third remains green and begins to expand. Within a few days, the blackened distal end bends downward and later the dead topknot often sloughs off, leaving the growing green fruit with a flat blackened tip. By June 8, the three arms of the hillside saguaro supported about 110 fruits, each with the potential at maturity to contain on the order of 2,250 seeds. Given the rather small size of this cactus, its reproductive output in 2006 was about what one would expect, since the "average" mature saguaro supposedly produces about 150 fruits per year (77). Moreover, the three-arm saguaro had managed to generate its dozens of fruits despite the fact that in the preceding eight months rainfall had amounted to less than two inches. That large saguaros so reliably yield a rich bounty of fruits summer after summer is testimony to their ability to quickly harvest and store hundreds or thousands of gallons of water whenever it is available.

The three-armed saguaro required about a month and half for some of its buds to metamorphose into fruits containing seeds capable of becoming baby saguaros in the fullness of time. I suspect that a six-week developmental time is typical for saguaro fruits, but the scheduling of the process varies considerably among individuals. In the spring of 2006, a few highly precocious cacti growing in the flatlands around Usery Mountain produced their first buds in April, but most others waited until the middle of May before buds began to mushroom out of their arm tips and crown.

Early buds yield early flowers, which in turn metamorphose into early fruit. The symmetrical saguaro that grows lower on the same slope as the three-arm saguaro was one of the first in that population to supply flowers and fruit this year. On June 10, two ripe fruits were visible among the ranks of green ones on the arm tips of the plant, as I could see with the aid of binoculars from a point well up on the hillside. For a closer look, I had to work my way down the precipitous slope, which I did very carefully, having learned from unhappy experience that a fall here can have nasty consequences. I placed one foot on a rock poking out of the gravelly hillside and then lurched downward to place my other foot on yet another firm anchor, and in this way proceeded safely on toward the cactus. As I neared my destination, house finches flew up and away from the ripe fruits, which had burst open about two weeks earlier on this cactus than would the fruits on its hilltop neighbor. When the contents of a saguaro fruit are ready to be eaten, the fruit

After they have been pollinated by a bat, bird, or bee, saguaro flowers wither while the fruit beneath expands dramatically in size. When the fruits mature, they split, revealing the crimson inner lining and the highly edible seed-filled pulp.

splits along four or five fracture lines in the outer coat of the fruit; the four or five panels then curl back to expose their bloodred interior surfaces, an advertisement for the mass of red pulp and black seeds in the center of the fruit. In recently opened fruits, this cylinder of food sticks out like a popsicle, inviting consumers to feed upon it.

After watching the finches drop downhill, I sat down on a boulder in the shade to see if they would return to "my" saguaro or go to a neighboring cactus that had five ripe fruits on display. After a few minutes, three reddish house finches came looping back to land on three red fruits. The birds stretched their heads upward and peered around nervously this way and that before turning their attention to the fruits, leaning over to extract either saguaro seeds or the sugary matrix within the fruit or both food items. Shortly thereafter, a white-winged dove in an elegant outfit of white and gray joined the less dapper finches on the top of the symmetrical cactus. The dove turned, presenting the side of its body to show the long white stripe paralleling its wing edge. It then used its surprisingly long beak to extract small quantities of pulp and seed from an open fruit.

White-winged doves and house finches are the most common consumers of saguaro fruits in June. But even during my relatively short stay near the symmetrical saguaro, I also saw a black-throated sparrow, a young flicker (a woodpecker), and a curve-billed thrasher take their places at the banquet table. Saguaros supply food to a whole range of desert consumers during the hottest, driest time of the year when a good meal really counts.

To document the central role of the cactus in getting birds through a difficult period in the annual cycle, Blair Wolf and Carlos Martínez del Rio systematically examined the extent to which saguaro fruits are a source of protein, lipids, sugars, and water to desert birds. The two physiological ecologists have exploited the fact that saguaro fruits have within them distinctive forms (isotopes) of carbon and hydrogen. One can therefore read what a bird has been eating by checking its body tissues or blood for the special isotopes in question. The abundance of certain isotopes relative to alternative forms of carbon or hydrogen in the animal's body can be used to estimate the proportion of its diet that was once saguaro fruit. Wolf and Martinez del Rio have done the requisite analyses and have found that in mid-June white-winged doves and house finches are hugely dependent on saguaro fruits, which provide about two-thirds of their food intake. But even cactus wrens, mourning doves, and curve-billed thrashers rely on saguaro fruit for about half their dietary needs at this time (107).

The symmetrical saguaro offered ripened fruits daily to all comers through June 24, although by this date only a few edible specimens remained, the rest having fallen from the arm tips and trunktop after having been stripped of their contents by doves, finches, and the like. Some saguaro fruits drop to the ground when they still have a considerable amount of edible matter within, and if so, mourning doves and a variety of mammals rejoice. On June 24, I saw a cliff chipmunk, an attractive little character, searching beneath the symmetrical saguaro, clearly looking for a morsel here and there. Later, the chipmunk bounded speedily from boulder to boulder in a gravity-defying performance before scampering up a paloverde and onto a nearby saguaro at a point where the lowest arm of the cactus is connected to the trunk. There the little creature retrieved a fragment of saguaro fruit before leaping back into the paloverde where it could consume its meal without having to perch on saguaro spines. A good idea, it seemed to me.

July *Monsoon Drizzle*

The monsoon began much earlier in 2006 than in the preceding year, and in fact, somewhat earlier than in the "average" year. Although an easterner might imagine that the summer rainy season would not be declared in session until it had actually rained, here in the Southwest our threshold requirements for the monsoon are modest. The dewpoint merely has to exceed 55 degrees Fahrenheit for three days running in order for our meteorologists to declare that the monsoon is under way. It does not matter whether or not the humidity translates into rain. Today is the fourth day of this year's monsoon, and for the first time, rain actually does spatter down on the car as I head for the Userys on the freeway. Actually, "spatters" may be too strong a word, but the shower, or drizzle, is sufficient to require the windshield wipers to operate, which they do despite not having been called upon for months.

Morning drizzles are not terribly unusual during the monsoon, but thunderstorms are required if the rainfall is to have any effect. Today's tranquil little storm drops just enough water to wet the top layer of soil, and no more, a point that I establish soon after getting out of the car

The spines of barrel cacti turn from pale pink (top) to a deep crimson (bottom) when they have been wetted by rain.

The recently fallen fruits of a saguaro cactus on Usery Peak. Any seeds that these fruits contained when they toppled from the crown of the plant have been discovered and consumed by mourning doves and small mammals, which forage on the ground.

at the place where I start my walk up to Usery Peak. But even though the amount of rain seems trivial, it has conspicuous effects, including keeping the temperature down a bit as well as bringing both color and odor back to the desert. As rainwater is absorbed by the dead leaves and stems of brittlebush and bursage, these cold gray plant parts don a warmer coat of yellow tan. The same is true for the spines of the saguaro cacti, while barrel cacti exchange their pale pink spines for brilliant crimson ones. The sun-bleached boulders look much darker after having been rained on, which makes them seem more substantial, and the scorched lichens on these rocks appear to fill out, to get some flesh back on their bones. The wizened mosses also come alive, quickly exchanging their black outfits for new ones of rich dark green. It's almost as if the rain that fell contained a rainbow of pigments that have for the moment rescued the desert from the drabness of June.

Not only have the Usery Mountains been made far more vibrant, they also smell better. As the raindrops evaporate, the air fills not just with water vapor but also with plant biochemicals that give the desert a faintly woody, slightly acrid scent. I revel in the smell of wetted desert vegetation as I walk the trail to the top of the hill.

Near the saddle on the ridge, a group of house finches and white-winged doves flushes from the ground and scatters downhill in a flurry of dull browns and bright white-wing crescents.

Beneath the saguaros, fallen fruits lie together on the damp ground. Some have dried out and are unrelievedly black. Others, recently toppled from their perches, are still bright yellow, green, and red. One fruit of intermediate age has acquired a solid black exterior that contrasts wildly with its still crimson interior; this seedless specimen looks like a disembodied pair of lips twisted in a grimace. Despite the macabre-looking fruit, a sense of optimism fills the air as moisture evaporates from the desert gravel and the dampened brittlebushes.

July *Heat Wave*

The pulse of humidity that produced the glorious drizzle has long since moved out of the state. In its place, a high-pressure ridge has settled in, leading to low humidity and the blinding heat that has afflicted all of Arizona for several days. Today, with a forecast of 115, a mid-July heat advisory is in place. Prolonged work outdoors is discouraged, and everyone is told to head for an air-conditioned workplace or home and to drink plenty of fluids. Actually, it never gets to 115; instead we have to settle for "only" 113. But even this temperature is sufficient to make us wonder why we live here. However, making the best of a bad situation, I decide to see what a heat advisory day in the desert is like—for perhaps an hour or so—and therefore I tell my wife I am off for the Userys in the middle of the afternoon. Sue disapproves, noting my advanced years and the risk of heatstroke. We have both reached the age when we read the newspaper obituaries more often, commenting that this or that notable was our age (or even a little younger) when he or she graduated to the obituary section.

However, one can make a case that persons in their sixties had better seize the moment rather than putting things off. So I tell Sue that if I am not back by six-thirty, she had better send the coroner out to the Userys, since I am off to experience the desert at its most extreme, no matter what.

Less than forty minutes after leaving our home, I turn into my parking place beneath Usery Mountain. Easing myself out of the air-conditioned car, I find myself, as expected, in a highly inhospitable environment. The superheated air can only immediately reach my hands and face because I have on a long-sleeved shirt, trousers, and a hat so that only my hands and face are exposed to the atmosphere. My hands feel more or less normal, but within a few moments I can feel my face heating up as a light breeze imitates the effects of a blow-dryer.

I pace myself, walking uphill even more slowly and sedately than usual. No sense in overdoing it. Although I am here for the novelty of the experience, I have no desire to come to grips with the effects of heatstroke, cardiac arrest, or exhaustion.

On my way upward, I see that the brittlebush leaves, reconstituted by the rain just a week or so earlier, now are bent over on themselves, gray, and burned to a crisp. The same is true for the even less prepossessing bursage. Sweat slides down my back as well as oozing out onto my hands and face, where it quickly evaporates only to be replaced with a new supply. I pause on the hillside and take the first of many pulls on my "canteen," a plastic bottle that once held a quart of Powerade. I have two such canteens in my backpack.

Other than a plane or two overhead, nothing much is stirring. Once I hear a distant cactus wren complaining for a few seconds about something or other. An occasional grasshopper disturbed by my footsteps jumps up and dives away in a flurry of wingbeats. Otherwise, the animal kingdom appears to have taken the advice of the weather service (and my wife) to avoid activity on a day like today.

The long haul up the last grade takes much longer than usual to traverse in the overwhelming heat, which is almost thick enough to wrestle with. When I at last reach the saddle, gratitude is my main emotion. The water jug comes out once again from the backpack. After a deep guzzle and a short rest, I march along the ridgeline track noting what is present—or rather what is not present. No house finches, no flies, no butterflies. I do, however, observe one bird, a turkey vulture, which seems appropriate for the day. The lone vulture soon joins a squadron of five that glides back and forth along the ridge, first sailing eastward, then circling back to the west, passing close overhead several times before finally drifting away. I find it easy to imagine that they are checking me out, eyeing me critically, sizing me up in terms of my potential as carrion.

The barrel cactus that I photographed during the morning of the drizzle has traded its ostentatiously red spines for a set of a bleached pink ones. The transformation is striking. Leaving the now pale barrel cactus, I walk lethargically along the ridgetop, stopping at times for swallows of water. An ash-throated flycatcher hurries from the shade of one paloverde to another. My survey of the local saguaros reveals that the season of saguaro fruit has almost come to a close. Dried, blackened rinds lie on the ground in great numbers by the larger, more productive cacti, which have lost most or all of their red split fruits. True, here and there a rare late-fruiting individual still holds a full complement of fruit on the tips of its limbs. Strangely, all these Johnny-come-latelies carry only green fruits. Will these fruits eventually turn red, split, and offer rewards for a house finch or two? Or are they destined to remain immature until they fall from their perches, discarded by a parent unable or unwilling to complete the investment needed to finish the maturation of those fruits?

Having made it to the peak and having inspected the ridge, I feel that perhaps I should not press my luck. With feverish face but free from any sign of sunstroke, I retrace my steps back down the mountainside. My legs feel heavy but functional. A teddy bear cholla near my starting point has carpeted the ground beneath its body with freshly dropped pale golden joints that contrast with the older blackened remnants cast aside in the distant past. The teddy bear's relative, the chain-fruit cholla, also appears to have sacrificed some body parts recently, perhaps as a water-saving concession to the ongoing drought. Many of this year's fruits and entire chunks of limb lie on the gravel beneath the chain-fruits in the gulleys. The remaining dangling collections of retained fruits are pocked and wrinkled, the tissues having evidently lost some of their water. Just looking at these plants makes me reach thirstily for my water bottle.

July *The Pause*

This morning's return to Usery Peak occurs when conditions are far more equable than those of the previous hike made in the midafternoon inferno two days ago. The temperature is still in the high eighties, a figure that will climb more than twenty degrees as the day proceeds. I will, however, be long gone by the time the afternoon heat has become painful.

Not surprisingly, desert life in its considerable diversity is more evident this morning. At one end of the size spectrum, the harvester ants are out and about, marching rapidly to and from their nests along cleared runways many dozens of feet in length. At this time of day, ground temperatures permit the ants to get their work done; later in the day, the broiling gravel makes it impossible for ants to stay above ground for even a minute.

The largest animal I see today is a diamondback rattler, not a big one, only a foot and a half long, the standard size of rattlers in this part of the desert where snakes sooner or later have a good chance of encountering a snake-hating human eager to put an end to the reptile.

(facing page) A small western diamondback rattler in its defensive posture, as it protests my presence.

Because I had seen only one other snake all year, I had stopped scanning for diamondbacks when making my way to and from the peak. But I have not forgotten what a rattler's tail buzz sounds like, nor have I lost all agility, as I demonstrate by leaping balletically up and away from the snake. I suspect that Rudolf Nureyev would have been impressed at this maneuver.

After my first panicked reaction, it takes me a moment to regain my composure and take a look at the snake, which responds by buzzing more vigorously, its tail tip blurred with the rapidity of its movement. The snake gradually elevates its "neck" and head, assuming an even more intimidating pose. I remain an appropriately safe distance away, admiring the diamondback's camouflaged body pattern, the black-and-white banded tail tip, and its black forked tongue, which slips in and out of its mouth regularly. Unlike most rattlers, this one never drops down to slither under a nearby bursage or brittlebush but bravely holds its ground while keeping its triangular head pointed straight at me. After a few moments, I give way and leave the snake in peace.

I also encounter a modest number of animals of intermediate size, including whiptail lizards, which press their bellies against the desert gravel, and several pairs of canyon towhees, which when surprised by my approach, flutter hurriedly downhill with much the same urgency that I exhibited when confronted by the rattler.

A handful of saguaros still supply a few fruits, enough to attract a couple of white-winged doves and a single house finch, not dozens of consumers like a couple of weeks ago, but more than I saw in the afternoon two days previously.

Despite the presence of some of the standard desert insects, reptiles, and birds this morning, the mood on Usery Mountain is subdued, as if the place is waiting for something significant to happen. We are in an interregnum of sorts. King Saguaro's beneficent reign is over, but Queen Monsoon has yet to provide the Userys with more than a drizzle. Paloverde B is leafless and pallid. The brittlebushes and goldeneyes in its neighborhood are lifeless, mere collections of dried plant parts. All of us are eager for rain.

July *A Pseudostorm*

Yesterday large cumulus clouds began mushrooming in the sky off to the east in the early afternoon. I tried not to get overly hopeful, having over the years seen so many other similar cloud buildups eventually dissipate without ever delivering a drop of rain to Tempe. But the clouds kept bubbling higher and higher as evening approached. The sky then darkened in a most encouraging manner and the wind picked up, shaking the trees I could see from the kitchen window. I thought then that I could afford to indulge in a bit of optimistic forecasting, as it seemed highly likely that the black wall to the east would sweep into town bringing a genuine monsoon thunderstorm with it.

My optimism went unrewarded. We received a fair amount of dust and wind, but not even a spattering of raindrops, and the same was true for the Userys, as I determined when I visited the mountains the following morning. I found no hint of rain from the previous evening: no puddles, no damp soil beneath the surface, not even a suggestion that raindrops had rearranged the fine gravel and sand. At least neither Tempe nor the Userys was hit with the eighty-mile-per-hour winds that came out of that black sky in a few places, flipping planes at a local airport. But I have the feeling that the monsoon is toying with us.

Another day of waiting for a possible thunderstorm lies ahead. For the moment, just a few clouds drift overhead. The high humidity coupled with ninety-degree-plus temperatures makes the hike up Usery Mountain unusually challenging this morning. Nothing much has changed since my last morning visit. The saguaros that had arm tips loaded with unripe fruit then still have plenty of green fruits on display. A white-winged dove stands on one of the rare cacti with a few genuinely ripe fruit. The odd lizard scuttles under a bush on my approach, while a black-throated sparrow slips away as I walk up to the ridge. A couple of mydas flies are still here and there, zooming a foot or two off the ground in their curious bobbing flight. These very large flies with their red-orange abdomens and matte-black wings first appeared in mid-June this year, as they generally do. They will disappear from the scene in late July after having engaged in their form of hilltopping behavior during the heart of summer. Unlike the tarantula hawk wasps, which they superficially resemble, males of *Mydas ventralis* rarely spend more than a couple of hours of one morning on Usery Peak. The few that do come back for a second or third day often shift from one perching area on the peak to another, showing little of the site fidelity exhibited by the tarantula hawks and many other hilltopping territorial insects (1). Male mydas flies do behave aggressively toward one another; those able to chase off rivals presumably are in better position to grab any virgin female that happens to come near the defended jojoba, or brittlebush, or paloverde. These reliable and conspicuous creatures help maintain activity on the mountaintop during the hottest months of the year.

Although I have grown accustomed to seeing white-winged doves and mydas flies over the past several weeks, there are still some entertaining novelties at the top of the mountain. Two white-throated swifts come charging down along the ridgeline hellbent for leather. I cannot recall having seen this species here during the past month or so. In addition, most of the tree lizards and side-blotched lizards that I see are probably newcomers to the ridge, animals that have hatched this year judging from their small size, just an inch or an inch and a half long from the tip of their snout to the start of their tail. With their slim bodies and relatively short tails, they remind me of minnows in the shallows of a rocky creek as they dash for safety across the boulders to slots and cubbyholes into which they slip.

Now that spring is gone and summer well advanced, I realize that some creatures have not shown up this year in their customary abundance. I have seen hardly any of the small "pebble" grasshoppers whose brilliantly ingenious color pattern turns them into what appears to be a collection of small pebbles. With so few annual plants to consume, perhaps these grasshoppers failed to mature or reproduce as they would in a year with a wet spring.

Another no-show in 2006 has been the wasp *Palmodes praestans*. The females of this black-and-orange species specialize in the capture of a very large, very well camouflaged katydid that hides in dense shrubbery. I am guessing that the drought has been hard on the foliage needed by the katydid, whose numbers have fallen sharply as a result. The presumptive current rarity of the katydid would account for a shortage of *Palmodes*, which require this prey to stock their nests with food for their offspring.

A third species that has taken the year off is a huge orange-and-black long-horned wood-boring beetle named *Trachyderes mandibularis*. This beetle is hard to miss as it cruises slowly in to land on a ripe saguaro fruit, a favorite food of females, and thus a favorite place for males to wait for females. Because saguaros produce fruits, drought or no drought, one would think that the beetles should have put in an appearance during the saguaro fruiting season this year, when there was no shortage of saguaro pulp and seeds. But this year I have not seen a single specimen of this most dramatic creature. Their absence meant more food for the house finches and cliff chipmunks of the Userys, but I missed the beetles, one of the largest and most gorgeous of the local insects.

The sun comes out from behind a small cloud where it had been hiding. Heat builds on Usery Peak. Sweat stains my shirt and wets my back, my arms, my face. I scurry down the slope, jump back to the car, and quickly turn on the air conditioner as I drive away from an ever-hotter, ever-drier desert.

July *The Old Burn*

Today, rather than climb up to the top of Usery Mountain, I opt to return to my original study site, the lower ridge that rises to a minor peak well below the top of the mountain. Today offers the chance to have another heat advisory experience, but by getting underway before seven o'clock in the morning, I need only contend with temperatures that are in the low nineties. The humidity has dropped somewhat, as has the chance of a thunderstorm, that most elusive of monsoon events this year. We did have a brief morning shower yesterday in Tempe proper, but nothing in the Userys suggests that rain reached this part of the desert.

Oozing sweat, I walk across the old shooting pit, noting the new tracks of motorbikes and the dirt ramps that macho riders with a desire for serious injury have constructed for their jumps. The ridge angles up sharply at first, then levels off before climbing some more. Eventually, I come to a place where I can survey the old burn, a hillside whose vegetation was incinerated sometime around June 1984. In that month, as I drove along Usery Pass Road, a large triangular blackened patch on a steep hillside off to the left caught my eye. I decided to inspect the site more closely, which I was able to do by leaving the car and climbing the ridge by way of the same ascending homemade trail that I am using today. The trail passed within a few hundred feet of the burned desert. Judging from the acrid odor of smoke and resin hanging in the air on that day, the fire had swept up the hill relatively recently, converting most of the vegetation to charcoal and ash. As I looked out over the devastation, I had no way of knowing whether the fire had been caused by lightning or by a careless smoker or perhaps a malevolent arsonist, but realist that I am, I was inclined toward the hypothesis featuring a careless or malevolent person.

This fire, although a nasty one that burned the grasses, bursages, and many bushes down to the ground, somehow failed to destroy a few shrubby paloverdes and two fairly small, armless saguaros that were growing in a gully in the middle of the burned hillside. A less fortunate larger saguaro growing near the top of the hill was, however, killed, and a few weeks later it fell to the ground. In addition to the handful of surviving paloverdes and the two saguaros, a number of rather small jojobas escaped the disaster. By the next spring, the jojobas stood among low grasses and young annuals competing with one another to see who would get to use the nitrogen and phosphorus deposited in the soil as a result of last year's fire.

///// A word on the jojoba, an intriguing desert shrub despite its rather ordinary appearance. This species achieved a modest amount of fame during the 1970s because of its seeds, which contain a liquid wax that constitutes about 50 percent of their weight (69). Jojoba wax was touted as a potential substitute for sperm whale oil. Interest in a replacement for sperm whale oil grew after 1969, thanks to the Endangered Species Act, which was passed in that year, followed by additional restrictions against importation of sperm whale products. These events encouraged any number of entrepreneurs to develop an enthusiasm for jojoba farming, leading to the purchase of thousands of acres of cotton fields and their conversion into jojoba plantations in the 1970s. However, the jojoba entrepreneurs had not reckoned with reality, which came in the form of killing frosts and insects that were delighted to find entire fields filled with a favorite food. Moreover, many of the surviving jojobas failed to produce much in the way of oily seed. As a result, about two-thirds of the acreage that had been planted with such high hopes has been abandoned by now. Although jojoba plantations persist to this day, the oil produced goes largely into the manufacture of shampoos and other cosmetics, not to the industrial markets that once used sperm whale oil as a high-quality lubricant.

So if you wish to encounter a jojoba, I recommend the wilder places of central Arizona where the plants are still common. Admittedly, the undomesticated jojobas in the Userys have little or no commercial value, although once in the 1970s I did encounter a crew casually harvesting the hard acorn-sized fruits in the hopes of making a little extra money. The fact that the harvesters did not return in following years suggests that the job provided more exercise than cash.

///// On the burned hillside, the remaining jojobas are much too small to generate a large crop of fruits. For these shrubs, survival has been the primary goal, not reproduction. As they have tried to consolidate their grip on life, the exotic grass, red brome, has swarmed over the unoccupied portions of the hillside, all but eliminating barren gravel patches, which are still common on the immediately adjacent unburned hillside.

In October 1988, after a summer in which I visited the Userys regularly without noting anything amiss in the old burn site, I discovered that a repeat fire had recently swept the area clean again. The blaze had been fed by the dried grasses that remained from the past summer, the descendants of grasses that had colonized the hillside after 1984. This time the fire took no saguaro prisoners but instead cooked the lower trunks of the remaining duo sufficiently to kill them both, although some months passed before the cacti collapsed. To my surprise, the remaining paloverdes and jojobas once again withstood this latest trauma reasonably well, judging from pictures of the hillside taken before and after the 1988 wildfire.

In the years since the second fire, there have been no new blazes to the best of my knowledge. The jojobas have not grown a great deal

A north-facing slope in the Usery Mountains that was first burned in the fall of 1984 (top left). Subsequently, the slope was heavily colonized by red brome grass, which reappeared year after year, giving the photograph taken in 1987 (top right) its purplish hue. The heavy cover of the exotic red brome made yet another fire possible in 1988 (lower left), and this time the two armless saguaros that had survived the first fire were severely scorched. They died and fell within a year. Although nearly two decades have passed since the last fire, recovery has barely begun (photograph on bottom right taken in 2006).

since 1988 and neither have the paloverdes, one of which has been blown over and lies slumped on its unfortunate neighbor. When I wander down for a closer look at the scene, I am pleased to find a cluster of three young paloverdes, each nearly two feet high, growing in the gully that marks the border between the burned and unburned desert. In addition, brittlebushes have colonized the twice-charred slope in good numbers. Here these shrubs, with their brilliant yellow flowers in spring and attractive gray leaves, are all much the same height, in the range of eighteen to twenty-four inches, having grown from seed in the eighteen years since 1988. Bursage are common also, perhaps as a result of regrowth from root stock or perhaps as a result of reseeding.

Although brittlebush and bursage have done fairly well in the burn, and indeed appear more common than on the adjacent slope that has never been torched, other plants have failed to return or are represented by a mere handful of juvenile specimens. No cactus is to be seen. Not a saguaro, no barrel cacti, not one teddy bear cholla, even though all occur in reasonable numbers nearby. Particularly conspicuous by their absence are plump barrel cacti, which are sensitive in the extreme to fire; the unburned control patch still has many of these cacti. Of course, it is possible that a few too-small-to-be-seen baby barrels are hiding under a young brittlebush or bursage in the double-burn site. I hope so. But few plants have done well here other than brittlebush and the highly ordinary bursage. I find only one wolfberry seedling and a foot-tall acacia among a sea of the two truly successful colonizers, suggesting that burned areas are suitable only for a fraction of the total desert flora. If true, decades may pass before the local cacti and a good mix of other species reestablish themselves in the burned area, despite the presence of reproducing adults only a few feet away.

But red brome grass isn't going anywhere, and so the danger for yet another native-plants-consuming fire remains high in the burn site. Such a fire would surely destroy any juvenile cactus that had managed to take hold in the interval between wildfires. Even if a fire doesn't come along any time soon, competition from the dense stands of red brome probably reduces the likelihood that cactus seedlings will take root and live long enough to replace some of those killed in 1984 or 1988. Red brome requires very little water to germinate and grow, but it still needs some of this precious fluid if it is to take its place in the desert. Each drop of rainfall absorbed by a stalk of red brome is unavailable for another plant, native or otherwise. In fact, some persons have speculated that the current abundance of this grass now poses a water-resource threat even for established natives, like saguaros, whose shallow root systems are designed to harvest water quickly from the soil whenever it is available. Red brome may take up that water before it ever enters a hair-thin saguaro rootlet, putting the cactus at just that much more risk of succumbing directly or indirectly to the effects of the next severe drought. The thought of red brome grass bullying saguaro cacti is counterintuitive, but there you are.

I leave the old burn and continue my inspection of the Userys. The

The contrast between the old burn site in the Usery Mountains (on the left-hand part of the photograph, which was taken in 2006) and the never-burned desert to the right illustrates the durable damage done to the desert by wildfire.

once magnificent paloverde #10 now looks just a little tattered, presumably as a result of the decade-long drought. What was once a fan of eleven "trunks" radiating from the base has been reduced by attrition to seven, as the tree has discarded a considerable amount of itself. The dead wood lies within and beneath the overarching canopy of the still bigger-than-average foothill paloverde. Today, of course, no male insects of any sort cling to the branch tips looking for females; nor are there any black-tailed gnatcatchers gleaning what they can from the profusion of remaining green limbs and twigs.

Higher on the ridge near my ultimate destination, the local hilltop where paloverde #17 commands the view, things get livelier. I hear what sounds like a baby rattler's buzz, and indeed, the creature responsible for the rather thin, soft rattle I hear is not much more than a foot long, one of the smallest diamondbacks I have ever seen. It performs well, holding its position with head raised defiantly in position for a defensive strike, until I reach the flat area where paloverde #17 grows. Then it drops down and slides beneath a bursage.

On the miniature mesa with its scattered "forest" of sunburned bursages, a single mydas fly competes for my attention with a passing dragonfly outfitted in pale orange. The male mydas fly, the only remaining representative of his species still in the Userys, floats out and around and back to a perch on a little bursage. The heat rises from the stones and gravel, slowly roasting the fly, the dragonfly, and me.

July *A Scorcher*

Yesterday's high—118 degrees Fahrenheit. Today's high—116 degrees Fahrenheit. June 2006 was the hottest June on record for Arizona, and now July is trying to keep pace.

Yesterday did feature a trace of rain on Usery Mountain, judging from the appearance of the open ground on the trail where the top layer of sand and fine gravel had been disturbed slightly by a brief bombardment of raindrops. Each drop left its mark in the form of a tiny crater. Not enough rain fell, however, to stimulate even the most eager of spike mosses, which remain tightly coiled and resolutely brown, tucked in against the edge of small rocks distributed over the hillside.

Still, it feels cooler than 116 as I start up the mountain in the late afternoon, largely because it really is (slightly) cooler, especially in the shadows that have begun to creep down the northeastern side of the peak. Here I find whiptailed lizards and tree lizards out for their evening constitutionals as they take advantage of the chance to scamper over the ground without being fried to a crisp. I also appreciate the shade as I slowly angle up the mountainside. A pair of red-tailed hawks scream

(facing page) A red-tailed hawk, the most commonly seen (and heard) raptor in the Usery Mountains.

in unison far overhead. One hawk slowly circles against the only large white cumulus cloud in the neighborhood. From its position, the redtail can look far up to the north past the hazy Mazatzals and see blue skies with only a couple of rainless clouds in the far distance. The monsoon has completely abandoned us today.

When I reach the saddle just below Usery Peak, it is a little after six in the evening. The descending sun glints off the water to the west, making the canal carrying Salt River water look like a silver ribbon laid out on the ground. Only one saguaro near the peak still has some fruits, and these are just as small and green as they were two weeks ago. None has split open, although one has had its end gnawed off, revealing a hint of its red interior. It's almost as if this cactus simply does not want to feed any foolish house finches that might still be lingering on the mountain.

The southern portion of the ridge bakes in intense sunshine. At first, this part of the mountain seems free of animal life, shut down by the formidable heat of the day. But a dragonfly lifts off from its shaded perch in a paloverde, and then another drifts past on sparkling cellophane wings. So some insects are coping with midsummer conditions in the desert, a point that is reinforced when I see a big gray robber fly perched on an ocotillo stem. The fly orients its slim body so that it keeps itself entirely in the shade cast by its perch. I find a second robber fly, and then a third, in a creosotebush on the secondary peak along the ridge trail. One of the robber flies has captured and killed a honey bee, while the other stabs the body of a winged harvester ant, a male that unwisely flew up to the peak today when few other ants were bold enough to make the journey with him.

Robber flies are regular visitors to Usery Peak during the summer months. In July 1988 one species was unusually abundant, at which time they seemed to be feeding largely on one another, perhaps because other suitable prey were not available. I never saw one robber fly actually capture another member of its own species, but I did see flies in pursuit of other flies. Cannibalistic flies presumably terminate some of these interactions with an outright assault on their fellow robber fly. For one fly to catch, stab, kill, and fly off with a dangerous fellow predator of its own weight is remarkable. (A study of another robber fly species showed that successful cannibals sensibly took individuals of their own kind that were slightly smaller than they [62].) Once back at its perch, a cannibal fly straddles its victim and uses its proboscis to extract the liquefied body contents of the prey. A grisly business, but one can see the advantages of cannibalism for the victors, who secure a large amount of food of a chemical composition likely to be easily digested and incorporated in the consumer's body.

Today the robber flies on Usery Peak do not engage in unseemly acts of cannibalism, even though they do chase one another on occasion. I presume that these individuals have timed their transition to adulthood to coincide with the availability of other edible insects whose flight season begins after the monsoon has begun. Among the group of monsoon-activated insects is the winged harvester ant that the robber fly caught. Until recently, this male lived inside a nest with its mother, the queen ant. There he and many other winged brothers and sisters were cared for by a large force of sterile worker ants, which are the wingless sisters of those they help. Usually it takes a good rain before the workers usher what may be the next generation of queens and kings out of the nest. These winged ants fly away in search of a sexual partner from another nest with whom they will mate. Once inseminated, the future queens move on to find a place to start digging a nest. Males focus completely on their mating activities, spending hours hovering over or roosting near the paloverde or creosotebush that they have selected as their landmark rendezvous place. Eventually they die. At times, windrows of deceased ants pile up in and around paloverde B.

I am guessing that the mini-rain on the preceding day provided just enough humidity to stimulate workers in a nest or two to release a very few winged reproductives. But when these few males reached the hill-tops, they found no receptive female ants, only hungry dragonflies and robber flies. These predators and others make male harvester ants and other hilltopping insects pay a heavy price for using Usery Peak as a rendezvous site. For the moment, however, most ants are still waiting for the right conditions before leaving the nest in search of a mate on this hilltop. The harvester ants need a real rain, and they need it now.

July *The Season of the Ants*

Yesterday morning the weather prognosticators were all atwitter with the possibility that the monsoon would finally deliver later that day. A pulse of moisture was said to be on its way from old Mexico, a forecast that I wanted to believe. But by the late afternoon and early evening, I could see no sign of a thunderstorm in the making—no majestic cumulus clouds rising up like slow-motion nuclear explosions, no black skies, no tremulous gusts of wind sending fallen leaves tumbling down the street—just a dull gray sky and the all-engulfing heat. I resigned myself to disappointment.

Well after dark, however, lightning began to flicker and burst in the distance, followed by a pause, then the deep drumroll of thunder. I perked up. As the lightning continued, I turned on the patio light and looked out, afraid to let optimism take over completely but eager to see what would happen next. Not long after that the first fat raindrops hit the patio bricks in the circle of light, enabling me to rejoice, albeit cautiously because I knew that we might just get the trailing edge of a storm, enough to wet the bricks but not enough to trigger a genuine celebration.

To my delight, however, the rain pounded down in a most emphatic manner, at least for fifteen minutes or so before drifting into a light patter. In response I felt my spirits lift and my heat-induced depression ease a little.

Considerably later, after I had retired for the evening, a loud thunderclap woke me up. A new storm was on the way, and this time, hallelujah, the heavens did not back off quickly. Instead, the rain pelted the roof for a good forty-five minutes. I knew then that we had had the real McCoy, a genuine monsoon moment, a turning point in the year. Excited by this bonus, it took me some time before I went back to sleep.

The next afternoon, I was off to the Userys thinking that I would almost certainly find the peak humming with ants and ant consumers. By the gate that blocks access to the upper part of the road to the AT&T towers, I met a friendly looking character who was standing by his truck. Bart proved to be a local landowner who had just been doing a good deed by sending five teenagers on their dirt bikes back the way they came rather than letting them proceed up the wash to tear up still more desert. Bart wanted to know what I was doing. After he heard my short course on bugs and hilltops, he knew.

Soon I was climbing toward whatever insects were actually on the peak. On my way, I saw that all the largely quiet harvester ant nests of a few days ago were now heaving with activity. Workers raced out from and back to the nest. Here and there a winged individual or two came out of the nest entrance only to turn right around again and slip back into the ground in the company of worker nestmates. One such worker from a nest along the trail managed to make her way up my calf undetected until she had inserted her stinger in my flesh. A harvester ant sting at first feels like a minor irritation, but the unpleasantness of the sensation grows into a deep aching pain. Upon sensing the start of this progression, I agitatedly shook my pant leg and tried to feel about for an ant. In short order, a satisfied worker crawled out around my trouser cuff. I flicked her onto the ground and tucked my pant legs into my socks, closing the barn door after the horse had left, so to speak.

At this time of year, worker harvester ants are all in attack mode, the better to defend those of their winged sisters and brothers that are about to embark on life outside the natal nest. As mentioned already, these "reproductives" use their wings to fly to a rendezvous point, like Usery Peak, where they can meet members of the opposite sex from other colonies. At the top of the mountain today, I was gratified to find that thousands upon thousands of ants had indeed preceded me to this place. After the rain, many colonies had obviously urged their reproductives to leave, and many of these had congregated by paloverde B and other landmarks high in the Userys. Even now, dozens of individuals were flying upwind to land in the paloverde. Many of these latecomers dropped onto the ground near the tree where thousands of their kind had already assembled.

The main sexual drama played out on the broad apron of gravel that surrounds paloverde B. The whole eastern and northern sectors of this area were dotted with balls of ants, some composed of three or four males and a female, others with as many as a couple of dozen males surrounding the object of their desire. Mating generally takes place within these bundles of ants when one male succeeds in grasping the posterior tip of the female's body with his abdominal claspers, which is followed by the insertion of the ant equivalent of a penis. The lucky or competent male then transfers his sperm to his partner. But even after a pair has coupled, other males continue pulling and tugging at their rival in an attempt to shorten his sexual union. Females encourage this sort of thing by remaining sexually receptive during and after the first mating and several subsequent copulations, insuring that they receive sperm from a variety of partners. Eventually, the queen-to-be breaks free from her horde of admirers and flies or walks away from the mating site in search of a spot where she can dig a burrow into the ground. There she will live long enough, perhaps, to produce some daughters who will act as her assistants in the expansion of the nest and the formation of a colony. If the queen-in-waiting is exceptionally fortunate, the day will come when some of her eggs, fertilized by the sperm she received long ago on her nuptial flight to Usery Peak, have developed into future queens and kings.

This afternoon, however, all of the young queen's attention is focused on getting a supply of sperm on board from more than one partner. This task is not without risk, given that she must run a gauntlet populated by dragonflies and flycatchers to reach her mates. Moreover, even after having found sufficient males, she may ironically enough die at the hands or jaws of her suitors, who have been known to pull a potential mate to pieces as they try to gain control of her in the heat of their sexual frenzy.

///// My visit to the peak took place in the late afternoon, around six, which falls within a period of several hours when harvester ants (*Pogonomyrmex rugosus*) are known to engage in their extraordinary mating activities. Therefore, when I returned to the hilltop the next morning, I did not expect to see many members of this species mating, but I hoped to find other ant species hilltopping during the early morning time slot. There are any number of species of harvester ants, and the various species apparently partition the day into blocks of time when each one holds more or less exclusive rights to a given rendezvous destination (40).

On my way to the top, I spot the first giant red velvet mites of the season, further evidence of the stimulating effect of the recent good rain. Although small in the absolute sense, they are immense as far as mites go, a good third of an inch long, and brilliantly vermilion, so that they cannot be overlooked. Their plump ticklike bodies are wrinkled and uneven, as if they have been partially dehydrated, and perhaps they have been given that they spend almost all of each year in a dormant state, underground, unable to feed, living off their reserves. Only when there has been a sufficient monsoon shower or storm do they leave their sheltering burrows and come out to hunt for prey over a day or two, which may be all the time they have to secure the food they will need to sustain themselves in the months ahead (89).

When I reached paloverde B, I saw two red velvet mites moving very deliberately over the gravel as if they had all the time in the world, when in reality they had only hours left in the day to do what they had to do aboveground. One species of harvester ant on the peak was even

After the first respectable monsoon storms, males of two species of harvester ants (*Pogonomyrmex pima* on the left, and *P. rugosus* on the upper right) fly to Usery Peak to compete for virgin queens of their species, which also arrive at the peak in search of mates. The ants then attract a host of predators, among them the robber fly shown in the lower-right photograph, which has captured and killed a *P. rugosus*.

more lethargic than the mites. Large numbers of male *Pogonomyrmex rugosus* clung quietly to rocks, the main stems of a brittlebush, and the trunk of paloverde B. They were taking it easy until later in the day when fresh queens would begin arriving and another round of their mating game would get under way.

Far more active was another harvester ant, *Pogonomyrmex pima*, a very small black, not red-brown, species easily distinguished from its much larger relative by its size and color. Thousands of tiny *pima* males were on the move, many flying to the top of paloverde B to festoon themselves on the outer twigs of the tree. There they raced frantically up and down the twigs in search of females, who were almost immediately grasped upon their arrival and quickly mated.

In addition to the treetop landing sites used by *pima*, other swarms of ants formed in the open air near paloverdes and creosotebushes on the hilltops and ridgeline. In these chaotic aerial swarms, males swirled rapidly about one another as they attempted to be the first to intercept females coming to the mating aggregation. Some of these groups were composed of *pima*, but more than one species of ant had chosen this morning as its mating day, as I was told when I brought specimens of a tiny leaf-cutter ant to a colleague.

The higher places along the ridge were, as is typical for hilltopping insects, the very locations favored by the ant species out and about on this monsoon morning. The highest points were enveloped in a cloud of ants. When I stood by the creosotebush on the second peak along the ridge, I became the focus of masses of *pima* harvesters. They quickly shifted from the creosote to swarm above my hat before dropping onto me. I had reason to be relieved that male ants do not sting, as dozens also settled on my shirt, ears, hands, arms, and back. When I removed my hat and examined it, I found it positively crawling with ants, some of which were mating quite happily (I presume). I had become an acceptable mating landmark for *pima* simply by standing next to and being taller than creosote #4.

One wonders why *pima* uses hilltops in the early morning, while *rugosus* becomes active only in the afternoon at these same locations. This division of the day hardly seems likely to have evolved to reduce the risk of cross-species matings, given that the two harvester ant relatives are so very different in size. But by separating themselves temporally from each other, they eliminate the mutual interference that might occur should members of the two species attempt to land upon the same landmarks at the same time.

After serving briefly as an ant-mating rendezvous site, I abandon my post near creosote #4 and head down the mountainside, leaving the *pima* harvester ants behind. But I intend to return later this same day to see if *rugosus* really does resume its mating activities in the afternoon.

///// So it is that around 5:00 p.m. I am back in the Userys trudging uphill with Juergen Gadau, an ant specialist who wishes to collect some male *rugosus* for his research on the population genetics of this species. Juergen also hopes to secure some recently mated queens, but driving into the parking place in the Userys, we note that the sky is gray, indeed dark gray, over the mountain. Is it about to rain? If so, will this shut the *rugosus* mating aggregation down for the day?

We do not know what is in store for us as we begin our climb. The local red-tailed hawk circles silently against the ominous clouds over a neighboring ridge. A very few raindrops begin to fall, making me wonder if we are going to have to scamper back down the mountain with lightning bolts nipping at our heels.

Juergen and I discuss the consequences of being halfway uphill during a lightning storm, but then Juergen draws my attention to a handful of winged termites that have materialized out of nowhere. They flutter up into the air just overhead. My companion sees where the termites have come from, a gravelly slope immediately adjacent to the trail. We quickly move to this area, and soon Juergen is able to show me one source of some termites, which are becoming more and more numerous by the second. One gray-winged termite after another surges out of a tiny crack in the hard soil barely large enough to accommodate the bodies of the departing insects. But despite the narrowness of the exit, a torrent of winged bodies flows out of the ground and into the air. These adults are less than an inch long from head to wingtip; their black-and-tan-banded abdomens announce that they belong to a subterranean species, *Gnathamitermes perplexus*, one of the commonest of the seventeen termite species found in Arizona.

The exit crack is completely ringed by several layers of tiny white, wingless workers, who are prepared, I assume, to give up their lives in defense of their departing nestmates should they be attacked by spiders or ants. These sterile termites behave protectively in much the same way as sterile harvester ant workers when they form a defensive circle around their brothers and sisters before their siblings take off on a nuptial flight.

The sky above the hillside quickly fills with fluttering wings, and then the emergence subsides and diminishes to a trickle. But in the space of a few minutes thousands of termites have taken wing from just this small part of the mountain slope to join tens of thousands more that have flown up elsewhere. Every raindrop that fell to earth today appears to have been transformed into a termite.

The winged termites are males and females in search of mates, which they achieve by landing after flights of varying distances. Once on the ground again, both sexes click off their disposable wings, which enables the unencumbered males to pursue females as these search for the start of a burrow in the damp ground. A male that has found a female follows her extremely closely; the pair look like a miniature two-part toy motoring over the ground. Only a ridiculously small fraction of these pairs will ever succeed in finding a burrow in which to set up housekeep-

The pale-bodied corpses of a great many termite reproductives lie on the ground by the entrance to a nest of the harvester ant, *Pogonomyrmex rugosus*, where they have been dropped by dark red ant workers. Note the gray termite wings scattered on the carpet of corpses.

ing, and only a tiny proportion of the pairs with a home will manage to produce a new colony with thousands of workers in the employ of their king and queen parents. The released termites obviously do not know the odds against them, which is probably a good thing.

As Juergen and I proceed toward the hilltop, we see evidence everywhere of the horrors that confront termites as they leave their natal colony, select a mate, find shelter, and found a new colony. One of the enemies they must overcome is a chunky tarantula that has come out of its nest for the occasion, the first one I have seen this year. Much smaller spiders are also searching for termites on the ground. But the termites' main enemies are their fellow social insects, especially *rugosus* harvester ants. Worker ants are on the move everywhere, racing in and out of their nests, marching smartly up and down the trails that they make to facilitate their movement into foraging areas. They are tracking down termites, grabbing them, stinging them, carting the corpses back to the nest entrance, dropping them off there, and then dashing back to slaughter some more. The pale, banded abdomens of termites form a tableaux of death next to the nest entrance of every colony we pass.

Once at the top of the hill, Juergen and I find, as expected, the *rugosus* mating aggregation in full operation. While their sterile sisters are efficiently hunting termites downslope, the reproductively competent males and females are putting their energy into supplying or receiving sperm. The open gravelly border around paloverde B is once again dotted with bundles of ants, males struggling with males, females trying to avoid being pulled apart, with still more ants arriving by the minute.

///// Three days have passed since the afternoon of the termite massacre. Today in late July the sky is largely clear and sunshine abundant. Not a single termite flutters through the air or scampers urgently over the ground. Not a single termite corpse remains by a harvester ant nest entrance, their remains having been gathered up and taken inside the nest for processing and distribution to the ant grubs growing within.

I walk slowly in the extreme humidity toward the peak. As I approach paloverde B, a young gray fox strolls confidently out from under the tree but then freezes as it spots me. Ears erect, the fox's eyes, set in a sharp little face, stare intently at me before the animal decides that I pose a probable danger. Suddenly it leaps out from under the fringe of the paloverde and bounds fluidly across the gravel apron and over the edge, out of sight.

Underneath the tree, thousands upon thousands of male harvester ants have assembled, waiting for an opportune time to compete again for mates. I suspect that the fox was feasting on these stingless ants; gray foxes are well-known gourmands with a taste for insects. Around the outer edge of the tree on the ground a few small groups of male ants battle over control of a female somewhere in their midst. Five, ten, or two dozen males try to force their way down to the female, wings flickering, bodies pushing. But although the individual battles are intense, the overall number of combatants is vastly fewer than on those previous days when the entire apron was dotted with writhing bundles of ants.

The now fading harvester ant aggregation is not the only residual sign of the recent rains. Everywhere, once leafless or nearly leafless plants are preparing to photosynthesize in earnest. Every ocotillo on Usery Mountain is completely leafed out, their thin gray limbs covered with rows of full-sized teardrop leaves. Backlit by the sun, the ocotillos look positively radiant in their new outfits. The brittlebushes never lost all their leaves during the long dry spell that began in mid-March. But what were once shrunken and twisted leaves have now somehow been brought to life again. Admittedly, they do not look especially fresh and vibrant, but at least they are harvesting sunlight for their owners after a prolonged period of dormancy.

Several other desert plants have moved more slowly than the ocotillos and brittlebushes but are also getting up to speed again. The brown twigs of the goldeneyes have sprouted bright green circlets half the size of a dime. These half-leaves will become bigger quickly.

Tiny leaf buds are also lined up on the twigs of the paloverdes, which have been leafless ever since the spring when the trees disposed of their leaves to make room for their flowers. Soon the paloverdes will look more like normal trees instead of seeming to be haphazard collections of green twigs, stems, limbs, and branches.

The rains have also provided the starting signal for a new generation of paloverdes to give life a go. Here and there paloverde seeds have recently germinated, and the infant plants have forced their way through the softened soil, popping their cotyledons out of the ground. In less than a week, some of these recruits have added the first feathery leaves to a thin stem growing above the fleshy cotyledons. Their odds of survival are terribly low, but for the moment they look healthy and confident.

Two recently emerged seedlings of the foothill paloverde, which disappeared not long after the monsoon ended.

The rain-wet soil has sprouted more than paloverdes. Scattered here, there, and everywhere are half-moons composed of recently excavated pellets of earth, the work of queen harvester ants that have built their shallow little starter nests, no doubt soon after mating with males at the hilltop rendezvous site. The dark semicircular tumuli contrast sharply with the paler sun-dried gravel. Underneath the surface, out of sight for the moment, the new generation of inseminated queens prepares for the struggle ahead. Their chance of founding a colony of reasonable size, one that gives rise to yet another generation of winged queens and kings, is infinitesimally small. Some will fail to collect enough food to support the production of a few worker-daughter assistants, who are absolutely necessary if the colony is to go forward. Most other queens and their retinues will be attacked and destroyed by workers from other colonies. But for now each new mound represents a chance to win the lottery and change the dynamic of life on Usery Mountain ever so slightly.

Overhead, rows of cumulus clouds are lined up between the Userys and Four Peaks far to the north. The monsoon is not over, but no rain will come from these tame cumuli. If the baby paloverdes and the fledgling ant colonies are to have a chance, another thunderstorm or two will have to build out to the east or north and come crashing down on the Userys in August or early September. It seems greedy to ask for more, but I do so anyway on behalf of the seedling paloverdes.

August *The Beginning of the End (of Summer)*

The monsoon has withdrawn from Arizona for the moment, as it often does periodically during the late summer. Perhaps it will return in a few days. In the meantime, the morning climb to the top of Usery Peak can be accomplished with marginally less heat- and humidity-induced stress, for which I am grateful. The sun skirts the edge of a blanket of cloud, while black-throated sparrows sing vigorously for the first time in a while.

The horned lizard on the mountain slope is the first one I have seen in more than a month. I presume that the lizard's current walkabout stems from the abundance of harvester ants earlier following the monsoon rains that briefly soaked the Userys. Horned lizards feed almost exclusively on the formidable stinging workers of various desert ants. Today, harvester workers mill about the entrances to almost all the colonies of *Pogonomyrmex* in the Userys, although with none of the hyperactivity that they exhibited in the period immediately following the rains, especially on the orgiastic afternoon of the termite feast. But they are still up and about, available for a horned lizard willing to tackle them, not hidden within their underground redoubts.

Unlike the worker ants, the winged male and female harvester ants have almost entirely disappeared from the mountaintop. One or two late-arriving representatives of the little *pima* cruise slowly into paloverde B as I scan the largely empty crown of the tree. Here and there on the ground an old male of the much larger *rugosus* staggers around amid a carpet composed of the corpses of his fellow males. Their race is run. Thousands of moribund males lie on top of one another in the shade by the trunk of the paloverde; the dead ants generate a sour-sweet odor of decay, which hangs in the air around the tree today. Some of the females they mated are surely waiting within their underground burrows nearby.

On the gravelly apron around the paloverde, I find just three of the four paloverde seedlings that were growing here three days ago. The missing seedling has presumably disappeared down the gullet of a woodrat or some other smaller rodent. I wonder how long the three survivors will last. (All had disappeared by late August.)

But although examples of death and dying are commonplace on the mountain today, so too is new life. The leaves of the brittlebushes have expanded, and the local wolfberries are revived, although their leaves are small and pale. One wolfberry has put out hundreds (perhaps thousands) of white flower buds as the plant gives reproduction another try, perhaps in part because the spring effort generated remarkably few fruits and, thus, seeds.

In addition, the smallest cactus in the neighborhood, the pincushion cactus (*Mammillaria grahamii*) has responded to the monsoon rain in much the same way as the wolfberry and the harvester ant colonies—by attempting to reproduce. The species possesses the ability to put its flower buds on hold until a rain comes, at which time the buds are released to complete their development in less than a week. One cluster of three little pincushions has lived up to its reputation and sports eight gorgeous flowers with strawberry red centers rimmed with a paler pink. Several of the flowers have attracted minute bees that are pushing their way through the bright yellow stamens to the nectar below.

Brittlebush shrubs are quick to respond to drought by permitting their leaves to shrivel and die; but they also rapidly regenerate fresh, vibrant blue-green leaves as soon as the summer drought is broken.

(facing page) The flowers of the very small pincushion cactus appear after rain at almost any time of the year.

Competing with the pincushion cacti today for the honor of being most colorful are the wandering dragonflies, with a few handsome white-belted ringtails (*Erpetogomphus compositus*) sprinkled in among many flame skimmers (*Libellula saturata*), whose males are an attractive orange-red and whose females are only slightly duller. The skimmers cruise the ridge, down the slopes, and over the rises, where they regularly pause to perch on the exposed branch tips of paloverdes and creosotebushes. Some perched individuals launch short flights out and back from their resting sites. They appear to be ambushing midges or other very small hilltopping insects, which have become far more numerous after the rains.

The dragonflies are gathering strength for their reproductive efforts, which take place well away from the mountains in backwaters along the edges of the Salt and Verde rivers, among other places. The females have to bulk up to get the raw materials for their eggs; the males need energy reserves if they are to be successful in the competition to control territories that enclose the aquatic sites that egg-laden females like to visit. Territory holders sometimes get to mate with those females, which then will use their sperm to fertilize the eggs they toss into the slow waters patrolled by their partners.

But first things first. Because feeding must precede sex for flame skimmers, I have the company of a great many of these good-looking, hungry dragonflies today in a place where all the water is out of sight, hidden in the soil, in the fresh leaves of the ocotillos and the flowers of the pincushion cacti, in the bodies of ants and termites and the dragonflies themselves.

August *Hilltopping Wasps*

Another afternoon in which the forecast of a 40 percent chance of rain is wildly at odds with reality, reality being sunny skies with just a few scattered clouds in the vicinity of Usery Peak. The nearest thunderheads are so far away I can barely make them out. I march doggedly up the mountainside in stifling heat. I am in a bit of a funk thanks to the monsoon's failure to match the forecast and because I forgot to bring my camera. I console myself with the thought that nothing new is likely to be on the top when I get there, and so my camera will not be missed.

I am partly right in that most of what I see is familiar: whiptails slithering over the gravel from shrub to shrub, flame skimmers drifting along the ridge or perching on branch tips of paloverdes, and harvester ant workers milling about their nest entrances. However, the harvester ant mating aggregation has all but disappeared. Indeed, the only male harvester ant on the hilltop resides in the jaws of a flame skimmer, which presumably intercepted the ant on its way to paloverde B. The dragonfly perches with its prey on the dead branch of a deceased paloverde near the old aggregation site. The skimmer slowly rotates

The cadre of insects that uses Usery Peak as a mate rendezvous site changes from spring to summer, with the large fly *Mydas ventralis* (above left) active during the early summer, while males of the skipper butterfly, *Erynnis funeralis* (above center), sporadically appear on the peak throughout the monsoon months. Males of the sphecid wasp, *Tachytes ermineus* (above right), defend their perch territories on the ridge during the late summer (August and September), a period of extremely hot and humid weather.

the half-eaten body of the ant, methodically munching its way through its victim.

On the botanical front, things are also pretty much the same as they were two days ago. Most of the recently germinated paloverdes are still in place. Other plants exhibit at best modest changes compared to the recent past. What were leaf buds on the paloverdes a few days ago are now small pinnate leaves with stems about a half-inch long. The collective effect of the burgeoning output of leaves makes the paloverdes look considerably darker and more substantial than they were a week ago.

But there are some surprises as well. Two males of the funereal duskywing, a skipper butterfly (*Erynnis funeralis*), have set up shop at different spots along the ridge. The males' choices illustrate yet another variation on the theme of the hilltopping mating system; in this species, males fly to peaks, but instead of waiting for females at the very highest points they perch in dips in the ridge on the dead branches of small shrubs. The funereal duskywing was present quite regularly during midday in the late spring; to find it now in midsummer after a long absence gives me something to add to a page in my notebook.

In addition, I discover a hilltopping insect that I have never seen before (because I have more or less sensibly spent so little time in the mountains on sweltering August afternoons). The "new" species is a small but attractive digger wasp (a member of the wasp family Sphecidae), whose males occupy paloverde B (of course) as well as plants growing on two of the other highest points along the ridge. The bulging yellow-green eyes of the wasps announce that they are males whose modus operandi is to wait on an elevated tree or shrub from which they can spot and chase after passing females. Although female digger wasps also use vision to spot their prey, their eyes are usually smaller than those of males.

I am pleased by my modest entomological discovery, a discovery that admittedly needs to be fleshed out with many more details. All I need is time, my camera, an insect net, and some paint markers, as well as a suitable number of cooperative male wasps.

///// The very next afternoon, I make my way uphill with some anticipation. My camera is nestled in its bag, my insect net is clutched in my sweaty hand, my notebook is at the ready. True, I have forgotten my paint marker pens for the second day in a row, another mental lapse that disturbs me. But still I hope to make some progress—provided that the wasps are on their perches once again. Hiking along the ridgeline, I find, as I had hoped, one to three males in each of the three plants where they had been on the previous day. My net comes in handy when I wish to remove one of the three males from paloverde B to serve as a voucher specimen to be sent to an entomological colleague who can give me its scientific name. Without a name, I will not be able to publish a scientific paper on the wasp, should I secure new information on the insect's behavior. I choose as my sacrificial lamb a male from paloverde B because there are up to three males present in this tree and because they confine themselves to the crown of this tree, where they are hard to observe closely. At the other sites, I usually find only a single male at the lookout, and these males can be watched more easily since they occupy relatively small shrubs. With a vigorous swoop of the net, I catch the unfortunate wasp, quickly dispatch the male, and pop the corpse in a vial for transport home. Later the specimen will be mounted on an insect pin with the appropriate information on an associated label prior to being shipped to someone willing to give me the species' name, a precious commodity as far as I am concerned.

Later I walk over to two other perching sites: a small jojoba bush on a high point along the ridge and the creosotebush on the second-highest peak on the ridge. Camera in hand, I intend to photograph rather than kill the males at these spots. Getting a decent photograph, however, proves more challenging than I had anticipated. The wind is blowing quite strongly today, enough to shake the branches of the creosotebush chosen by the male wasp. In addition, my subject rarely stays put more than fifteen seconds or so before shifting perches, usually just as I have maneuvered my Nikon into position and am on the verge of getting the wasp in focus. Moreover, the males in the jojoba and creosote have the irritating habit of disappearing completely for several minutes or more before materializing again. Perhaps they travel around a short circuit of shrubs in which they perch, shifting from one to another and then back again. In keeping with this hypothesis, I follow one male in flight as he lands on three different jojobas a short distance apart on the ridge. He stays briefly in each of the other two bushes before returning for a spell in the jojoba where I found him originally.

So I do make very modest progress in documenting the natural history of the wasp, but I really must get some males marked with identifying dots of paint if I am to get anywhere. Only when I can recognize individual males will I be able to determine if a wasp that comes and goes from a given creosotebush is one and the same male, or if several males share the same site.

In the meantime, anonymous wasps dart in to land on the hilltop plants they have selected, and then, after shifting from one perch to another and another, they dash off for a while. This pattern differs somewhat from that of the male tarantula hawk wasps that occupied these very same plants for hours each day in the spring of the year. Today, gray hairstreak butterflies keep the new wasps company on their chosen landmarks, although they prefer perches on the very outermost edges of these shrubs and trees rather than inner twigs and branches.

As the sun descends slowly in the west, a bevy of dragonflies hungrily patrols the ridge on flickering wings. I head downhill to the east past mats of spike mosses that have given up hope for a sustaining rain and have now returned to their dormant state, brown and crumpled, on hold until the next shower or storm. In contrast, the brittlebush are greener than they have been for months, having committed themselves to a new canopy layer of full-sized green leaves. The plants have acquired some substance, a rounded semihemispherical shape that I suspect maximizes their light-capturing capacity given the constraints they have imposed on themselves by growing only a single outer layer of leaves. These days at least the brittlebushes have plenty of sunlight with which to work.

///// Another afternoon, another round of wasp watching. This time I make a major show of competence by bringing my net *and* my paint pens. Shortly after reaching the top, I also have my first male wasp in hand after a crisp swing of the net. After the wasp has been extracted, it receives two dots of green paint, and I release it from my grip. The wasp shoots off like a bat out of hell. Unlike the tarantula hawk wasps that I have spent so much time marking and watching, the little sphecid fails to return during the time I spend monitoring its perch shrub thereafter. And although I see male wasps at the other two sites, my clumsy attempts to capture them only scare my quarry away. Are the wasps supersensitive to attempts to capture them? Or have I come to observe them at a time when they were about to leave the ridge anyway? I just don't know.

///// In the middle of the afternoon the next day, as I drive the freeway toward my study site, I see that clouds are billowing up all round the Usery Mountains. Here and there the cumuli spew out gray streamers of rain. I do not know what to wish for: that the showers move right over the Userys, providing a welcome monsoon drenching for the area, or that they stay away so that I can climb to the peak to check on my hilltopping wasps without risk of getting wet or, worse, getting electrocuted by a lightning strike.

When I reach my parking place, a small storm cell with sporadic

A huge monsoon thunderhead billows over the valley behind paloverde B on Usery Peak.

thunder and lightning has formed close by. The storm seems very local, however, and so I nervously decide to go for it, hoping not to make the evening news posthumously. In an effort not to seem to thumb my nose at the lightning gods, I leave my aluminum-handled net in the car and carry the one with a wooden handle up to the ridge, hoping that it is less likely to serve as a lightning rod.

Happily (from the perspective of my personal safety), the nearby shower thins out and slides off to the east of the Userys during my climb, so that when I reach the top I am safe and sound, although the sun is mostly hidden behind a layer of low clouds. I wonder if the wasps will tolerate the partial overcast, a question that is answered as soon as I reach the jojoba site where I had marked green-two-dots the day before. There he is, perching alertly on a jojoba leaf. Then he darts to another leaf, pausing there briefly before shifting again to a bare twig. After staying in place for perhaps a half minute or so, he is off, looping about the shrub for a few seconds before disappearing. For the life of me, I cannot see where he went. A check of nearby shrubs reveals nothing.

I head on my way to creosotebush #4, where to my pleasure an unmarked male is flipping from perch to perch. I wait until he selects a place where I might attempt to capture him before launching my attack. With a swoop of the net, the wasp is mine. He receives a dot of pink paint prior to his release.

I march back along the ridge to the opposite peak where paloverde B is outlined against a gray sky, and here too I am quickly rewarded with the capture of an unmarked male. This wasp is soon on his way, carrying a single dot of green paint on his thorax.

The rest of the afternoon is spent checking and rechecking the three landmarks. Green-two-dots shows up several times on his perch plant; likewise, pink dot comes back to creosotebush #4 after a short interval. But although I see up to two males in paloverde B, they appear only occasionally and briefly. To my exasperation, the darn things never perch in spots where I can exercise my net effectively. Perhaps green-one-dot was one of the males in this tree, but I am not able to confirm that possibility today.

When the sun disappears completely behind a thick mat of clouds, I end my session on the peak. The pattern of male behavior is becoming increasingly clear. Individuals do have at least one favorite perch but are not consistently on station from the midafternoon onward.

///// Yet another day, with its masochistic opportunity to overcome the challenges of an extreme climate. My rewards for this afternoon's work are modest. I fail for another day to catch a single male in paloverde B even though at times two wasps occupy this tree simultaneously, darting erratically from perch to perch before leaving. I do find green-two-dots at his perch again, but for the most part he appears to have abandoned this shrub, which he occupies only twice on the many occasions when I check the plant. Pink-one-dot does return to creosotebush #4 but only after I capture and mark a new male here, a male that disappears after the trauma of being netted.

The monsoon continues to tease with cloud buildups that generate showers far in the distance. But the rain dissipates long before it reaches the Userys or Las Sendas, let alone Tempe. The seedling paloverdes with their shriveled cotyledons and pale leaflets look stressed to the limit. How many more days can they hang in without rain? They may well be doomed. As I ponder the paloverdes' fate on my way back down the mountainside, I spot a loggerhead shrike carrying a reddish object in its beak. When it lands, I can examine the bird and prey with my binoculars, which reveal that the shrike has caught a flame skimmer. The bird stuffs the dragonfly in a fork of a branch and proceeds to tear it apart, one hunter consuming another in the shadows cast by the Usery Mountains.

///// Today as part of my continuing series of afternoon visits to Usery Peak, I decide to arrive earlier than usual. Originally I had assumed that the male wasps set aside the late afternoon as their special period for getting together with females, but recently I have begun to notice the wasps temporarily disappear more frequently as evening approaches. I wonder therefore if the peak period of activity might be earlier in the afternoon, rather than later. When I arrive at 2:00 p.m. rather than 3:30 p.m., I find that all the perch sites are occupied by male wasps, which stay put rather than darting off to who knows where for a time. Evidently I am going to have to come out earlier still to find out when males actually begin their daily round of perching and waiting.

To the north of the Userys, the thunderheads climb up in the sky like an immense eruption of snowy ash. Long ribbons of rain descend to a presumably grateful desert to the accompaniment of the occasional lightning flash and thunder roll. The cell stays north and heads east away from the Userys. On my way back to Tempe, the radio speaks of a flash flood warning for the desert well to the east of my hometown.

///// In order to document just when my new hilltopping subjects begin their work, I am out to the base of the Usery Mountains by 10:00 a.m. in anticipation of a productive day with the wasps. My enthusiasm stems in part from the fact that we had our second major rain of the monsoon last night, which followed a night when storms skirted past our part of Greater Phoenix. This rain came just when I had pretty much given up hope that Tempe would get another good drenching this season. As evening approached, nothing in the clouds offered a hint of what was to come after dark, namely thunder, lightning, then a feeble shower followed by periods of outright rain with fat raindrops banging into the roof and off the leaves of the citrus trees outside our window.

As always, however, I was worried that the Userys missed the fun, given the highly local nature of so many of our monsoon storms. My fears were unwarranted. The soil is soaked out in the Userys as well as in my front yard, and the humidity in the mountains leaves me soaked, too, as I make the uphill climb yet again.

The effects of the rain here are immediately apparent in the revived spike mosses, which have in the space of a few hours gone from crinkly brown to plush green. Likewise, the mosses on some boulders have become far plumper and much greener than they were before last night's rain. When I finally reach paloverde B, I find that the crown of the tree is alive again with winged males of *pima*. They swarm up to the tips of the branches to grasp a twig, only to drop off and repeat their approach to the tree. The colonies of this ant must have retained large numbers of their winged males and females after the first big rain but have now decided to release a new wave of adults to mate at hilltops, after which the queens can burrow into the rain-softened ground.

In addition to the hordes of little black ants, the mountaintop features any number of other hilltoppers today, apparently also stimulated by the storm. Among these insects is a pair of pipevine swallowtails mating in a ridgetop paloverde, always a rare event. This pair is remarkably tolerant of me and my camera; on the few occasions in the past when I have found a pair of these big black butterflies on the peak, the female has always skittishly lifted her partner from the perch and flown away long before I could get close enough for a decent photograph.

As for the sphecid wasps, they too are out in force, although not at first in paloverde B where the hundreds of black ants may make it difficult initially for male wasps to set up shop. But at the other plants where I have found the wasp in the past, no *pima* are present to interfere with males that have taken up their perches before 11:00 a.m. These small wasps obviously are willing to put in a long day at the office. I bet that some show up well before 11:00 and I know that some stay past 6:00 p.m. I will have to get out to the Userys even earlier than today in order to establish the males' true arrival times. (I eventually learn that some appear at the mountaintop as early as 8:30.)

Today I go from spot to spot surveying the males on their perches, recording the number of flights they make out and back in a two-minute sample period, and trying to catch and mark those individuals that lack paint dots. At paloverde Q, I succeed in capturing a rather large male, and as I apply a dot of green paint and a dot of white paint to his thorax, I notice that the base of his abdomen is bright orange-red. Suddenly it occurs to me that most of the wasps I have been capturing along the ridge have had uniformly dark blackish abdomens. Whoa, I say to myself. I then begin to systematically check the color of the abdomen of each of the wasps on the study site, a process that reveals there are indeed several specimens of each type here. Some trees, like paloverde B, harbor both a "red" specimen and a "black" one. I ask myself, "Are there two species of wasps, not just one, hilltopping in my study site?"

I confess that I was worried about the implications of this question. I had not imagined that there could be two members of the same genus of wasp occupying the same trees at the same time and behaving in much the same manner. Most of the hilltopping insects at the peak do not have close relatives present while they wait for their partners to appear. Thus, the tarantula hawk wasp *Hemipepsis ustulata* is the only

member of its family, the Pompilidae, that engages in hilltopping behavior in the Userys (and elsewhere as far as I know). Likewise, the gray
hairstreak *Strymon melinus* is the only member of its genus to employ
the hilltopping mating system in the Userys.

The data that I have collected to date have not been tagged with respect to the abdomen color of the male sphecids I have been observing.
So I am going to have to start over to some extent. I will also have to enlist the assistance of an expert in wasp naming to help me out here. Fortunately, there are such experts still, despite the fact that the training of
insect taxonomists has fallen on hard times in this era when molecular
genetics rules supreme in academic circles and taxonomy is considered
"old-fashioned." The colleague I will impose on, Dr. Wojciech Pulawski,
works at the California Academy of Sciences and is an expert in the
classification of wasps in the family Sphecidae. I will offer to supply
Pulawski with specimens of the two types in the hope that he may be
willing and able to tell me whether they are two species or simply two
color forms of the same species, a not uncommon phenomenon in the
animal kingdom.

Later, while I am watching pink 123, a male with an all-black abdomen, at creosotebush #4, a small insect flies into the bush in a flurry
of pale wingbeats. What is this thing? A termite? A miniature ant lion
adult? No, it is a pale gray moth with a wingspan of less than an inch.
The wonderful thing about the moth is the way in which it perches on a
creosote limb. The insect has spread its narrow wings apart and almost
wrapped them around the branch on which it has settled, while projecting its abdomen straight up into the air at right angles to its wings. The
function of this weird pose is pretty obvious. The moth has made itself
look nothing like an edible insect by concealing its wings while making its abdomen look exactly like a creosote twig stub. Although I peer
at the moth at close range, it holds fast, immobile. Had I not seen the
moth fly into the shrub I wouldn't have spotted it in a million years, and
I assume that the creature's camouflage also poses a challenge for the
little flycatchers, black-tailed gnatcatchers, and Townsend's warblers
that sometimes forage for insects in creosotebushes and other desert
plants.

Finding such beautifully camouflaged animals always enlivens a

(top) A dull and tiny moth whose behavioral tactics seem designed to camouflage the insect and protect it against bird predators. Note the position of the abdomen and the wings, which are curled around a limb of the creosotebush.

(bottom) Chemically protected insects, like these milkweed bugs, typically forgo cryptic coloration in favor of ostentatious warning colors that advertise their unpalatability.

visit to Usery Peak. Invariably these creatures use behavioral tactics to enhance their cryptic coloration. Horned lizards press their bodies close to the granitic gravel and are reluctant to move unless they are about to be stepped upon. Likewise, just the other day, my heavy footsteps disturbed a praying mantis, whose unwillingness to move was nearly its undoing. Long and skinny, with pale gray colors, the insect was nicely color coordinated with the long thin stems of the desert shrub in which it was perched. Moreover, the creature held its predatory front legs straight out in front of its head, in keeping with the goal of looking more like a twig than an edible insect.

My wasps are not camouflaged, nor do they appear to try to keep out of view. Instead they sit out in the open on leaves and twigs, from which sites they launch their conspicuous exploratory flights. The males' cavalier attitude toward predators probably stems from the fact that male wasps look like stinging female wasps, which educate predators to leave them alone. The males are also probably taking advantage of the fact that educated predators learn to associate striking color patterns with venomous stings, toxic sprays, or bad-tasting flesh. This fact has led many protected species to go out of their way to make themselves conspicuous and easy to remember. For example, the milkweed bugs feeding on the pale green pods of the foul-smelling climbing milkweed, *Sarcostemma cynanchoides*, are almost certainly repellent to birds, thanks to their ability to recycle defensive chemical compounds present in their food. The bugs, which are brilliantly crimson, often assemble in groups, which magnifies the conspicuousness of all to predators, warning them to avoid repeating an earlier mistake in which they tried and failed to consume one of these memorably disgusting animals.

///// I can report progress on the wasp-naming front, thanks to Dr. Pulawski, who not only promptly agreed to examine my specimens but equally promptly identified them. He tells me that I have sent him not one, not two, but three species, all members of the genus *Tachytes*. The black-bodied males are *Tachytes ermineus*, but the partly red-bodied males include representatives from two species that Pulawski tells me are so similar in appearance that they can be distinguished only by examining their genitalia under the microscope. This finding definitely encourages me to pay close attention to the color pattern of the wasps I am marking and to see if there are some consistent behavioral differences that might enable me to distinguish between the wasps with red abdomens.

In the following days, I come to realize that there indeed appear to be two kinds of males with red abdomens. Males of one type perch high up in paloverdes and creosotebushes, where they regularly interact with the largely black *ermineus*, which also likes to sit in the center of trees and shrubs just below their crowns. Males of the putative third species perch on the ground or near the ground on the outermost twigs and leaves of jojoba shrubs. The low-perching males are also noticeably smaller than their cousins in the tops of trees. I collect an additional set of specimens of the two types and ship them off to Pulawski, feeling confident that he will give different names to the males taken from these two very different locations.

He does not.

Instead, according to Pulawski, all eight wasps in the second batch that I sent him are members of what we can call species A, a surprising conclusion as far as I was concerned since I had managed to convince myself that there were two species, a larger one that perched high in paloverdes and a smaller one that perched low in shrubs or even on the ground. In the face of Pulawski's report, I wonder if the slightly smaller, lower-perching males actually belong to a previously unrecognized species nearly identical in external form to the paloverde perchers. A more likely alternative possibility is that the larger males of species A monopolize all the prime territorial spots high in desert trees and shrubs, leaving the smaller males of this species to do the best they can at inferior sites close to the ground where they at least will not be assaulted or chased off by larger, more powerful opponents.

///// Because of my uncertainty about what's going on here, I collect a new batch of wasps for shipment to Dr. Pulawski, and he continues to patiently work his way through the specimens. As he does, he himself becomes confused (he later tells me), so much so that he puts to one side the formal identification key to *Tachytes* that he has been using and goes back to the original published description of one of the species that he thinks I have sent him. When he does, he realizes that the key he has been using has been leading him astray and making life much more complicated for him (and for me) than it has to be. The upshot of it all is that eventually Pulawski is able to tell me that there *are* two species of *Tachytes* with red abdomens after all, and my notes tell me that these two species do correspond to the two behavioral types, one that perches on or very close to the ground, and one that perches from three to ten feet high, typically in the center of paloverde trees.

What a relief.

Knowing what I now know, thanks to Dr. Pulawski's diligence, I am able to concentrate on the species whose males appear to be defending perches within paloverdes, as these are more abundant than males of the smaller, ground-perching species. If males of what I now know are correctly called *Tachytes spatulatus* are indeed territorial, in that they defend their landmarks against rivals who would usurp these perch sites, then I predict that males occupying these perches should be larger than those that they keep away (since being bigger is almost universally associated with a greater capacity for territorial defense in the insect world—and among animals generally). I think I know how to check this prediction out.

On my next afternoon visit to the Userys, I come supplied with a little cooler filled with two blue ice packs and a large number of small plastic vials. The cooler does not weigh much, but even so, I blame it for adding to my woes as I struggle to the top of the ridge. It's a great relief to reach the saddle and pull off my heavier-than-usual pack, placing the two water bottles in the shade of a paloverde, after first emptying a liter's worth down my gullet. I then extract the cooler from the pack and set off for paloverde A with my Mini-Mate, notebook, net, and binoculars. Shortly after arriving at my destination, I capture the resident red-abdomened male with an unusually deft swing of my insect net, if I do say so. He's an unmarked male that has apparently taken the site from green 12. I slip him into a vial and pop him into the cooler, where he will become inactive in the cold.

Over the next hour, I monitor that tree and succeed in capturing four "replacement" males that come in to take command of the tree in the absence of any resident male. One of the four is the previous resident, green 12. Was he returning to reclaim the site from the unmarked usurper? Or had that unmarked male thoroughly defeated him in an earlier clash, with the old resident merely stopping by to check on whether the usurper was still in charge? I do not know. But in any event, green 12 and the other three unmarked males are also placed in vials and chilled.

The experiment at paloverde A is repeated at paloverde B with similar results, with three replacement males arriving in the hour after the removal of the male defending the site in the midafternoon. Clearly there are more males around Usery Peak than there are attractive landmark paloverdes for males to claim and defend.

Having done all I can do on this broiling afternoon, I then cart the chilled captured males down the mountainside and take them back to my home in Tempe, where I have a wonderfully sensitive, compact little scale that I purchased long ago for research of this sort. My scale reveals that four of the seven replacements are indeed smaller than the current "resident" male. Moreover, two of the three larger males are former residents that had apparently lost their perch trees to slightly smaller rivals, in violation of the general rule that bigger males win; only one of the three relatively large replacements is an unmarked male with no known previous connection to the tree where he was captured as a replacement. These results are hardly conclusive, but they give me reason to continue my simple experiment in the future. (And when these experiments were done later, the results fully supported my original prediction: statistical analysis tells me that residents are indeed significantly larger on average than replacement males.)

///// Having made modest progress in describing male behavior in two species of *Tachytes*, I want to determine whether my observations are novel. I am willing to wager a large sum of money that no one has ever studied the behavior of *ermineus* or *spatulatus* or the third species, *sculleni*. In the first place, such studies would require an observer to find and watch these southwestern wasps during the hottest part of the summer. Although entomologists regularly subject themselves to discomfort, there are limits for most of us. After all, I had lived in central Arizona for more than thirty years before venturing out this year to the Usery Mountains in August when "my" wasps were active. However, most insects have been ignored by the scientific community simply because there are so many species and so few entomologists. Pick an insect species at random, and odds are that little or nothing has been written about its behavior in scientific journals.

But to make sure that this rule really applied to my wasps, I searched the scientific literature for any mention of *Tachytes*. In so doing, I assembled a modest list of four papers that made mention of male behavior. The entomological researchers who had written these papers described, generally very briefly, how males of *Tachytes amazonus*, *Tachytes distinctus*, *Tachytes intermedius*, and *Tachytes tricinctus* appear to locate mates. (To my surprise, I learned that I myself was an author of one of these papers, having penned a few notes on *amazonus*, a species that I had watched for several days near Buenos Aires, Argentina. In defense of what is left of my memory, my venture into the world of *Tachytes* took place long ago, in 1974 to be exact.) Because there are 394 species of *Tachytes* in all (according to www.calacademy.org/research/entomology/Entomology_Resources/Hymenoptera/sphecidae/Number_of_Species.html), 390 remained fair game in 2006 for those of us who wanted to discover something entirely new about male behavior in this genus. The unstudied total included, of course, *Tachytes ermineus*, *Tachytes spatulatus*, and *Tachytes sculleni*, the three members of the genus found in the Usery Mountains. I was happy that I had these three species all to myself.

The four *Tachytes* for which at least something was already known about male behavior are species in which males assemble near places where many females nested the previous nesting season. In these places at the appropriate time, many females will eventually make the transition from pupa to adult, after which they will burrow up to the surface and fly away. These fresh females are almost certainly receptive to males that catch them soon after their emergence. Accordingly, males of these species perch either on the ground or close to it, leaving their perches to chase potential mates flying nearby, although males of one species are also said to defend active nests of presumably already mated females. (I wonder about this claim, but if it is true, I suspect that these males are guarding their previous mates to prevent them from acquiring additional sperm from a rival male.) The fact that I did not see a single nest of any *Tachytes* in the Userys, let alone aggregations of nesting females, coupled with the male preference (in two species) for perches high in the center of trees and shrubs, suggests strongly that in the wasps I studied, males are employing the standard hilltopping regime as described earlier for various other insects. Indeed, the two species of *Tachytes* wasps that perch high in paloverde trees use exactly the same set of plants favored by other hilltopping insects, including the tarantula hawk wasp that comes to Usery Peak in the springtime. The *Tachytes* males are probably waiting for virgin females to rendezvous with them at these conspicuous landmarks.

Admittedly, I have no direct evidence on the attraction of females to the perch sites selected by males. I did get stung once when reaching into my net to grab what I thought was an unusually large unmarked *ermineus* that I had just captured at paloverde M. Perhaps this female mated at that very paloverde not long before it stung me, but of course I do not know for sure. Given that females of many hilltopping insects copulate only once in their lifetime, and get the job done quickly, it is not surprising that hilltopping male insects are rarely seen achieving their life's goal, namely, mating with females. Indeed, I have recorded only thirty matings by the much larger and more conspicuous tarantula hawk wasps in ten full seasons of observing this species.

Even though I do not have all the parts of the natural history puzzle in place for my three *Tachytes* wasps, I am pleased at the payoff for climbing Usery Peak during this monsoon, painful though it has been at times during the uphill haul. Although it is not at all surprising to encounter insect species whose life stories are unknown, there is joy in getting to know even rather ordinary insects as individuals, a pleasure in the discovery of something new, of overcoming obstacles both physical and mental in order to make these discoveries, of getting to know the inhabitants of a particular place. Thanks, *Tachytes*!

August *The Big Wash and the Vanished Seep*

When I look out to the northwest of Usery Peak from a vantage point near the paloverdes occupied by male *Tachytes* wasps, I can see a major wash far below that drains this sector of the mountain. Where the land flattens out, the wash is broad and wide initially, but as it moves roughly westward the watercourse splits and splits again, forming a delta of ever smaller, but still significant, elements. At its start, the big wash with its smooth tan surface looks extremely inviting as it wanders through the corridor of paloverdes and ironwoods growing on its borders. Years ago, I occasionally made forays from a ridge far lower on the mountain to this wash. My usual destination was a shaded corner where I sometimes found a little pool of water oozing out of the mountainside next to a big acacia. Recently, I have begun to idly contemplate descending to this seep from the very top of the mountain, a plan that I might actually put into action were it not for the daunting prospect of having to climb back up and over the Userys to return to my car.

So instead on this Saturday morning in early August, I decide to approach the upper reaches of the wash from the west by walking in from the Bush Highway. To do so means stepping over a barbless wire fence that the Forest Service, bless their hearts, erected some years ago to keep ATV owners and truck drivers out of the desert. Previously these self-absorbed maniacs churned up and down any and every wash able to accommodate them and their machines. They paused only to deposit bullets in saguaros and gaily scatter garbage here and there. The effects of their previous activities are still evident today even though motorized vehicles have been blocked from entering this corner of the Tonto National Forest for several years. No tire tracks remain, but there is still a smattering of aluminum cans and plastic bottles, mostly riddled with bullets, to which we can add several ancient piles of palm fronds and one noisome mound of decaying asphalt shingles. The folks who took the trouble to dump the palm and shingle debris in the desert really went out of their way to make a mess. One wonders why they didn't just drop the trash off in a suburban alley somewhere closer to home.

The heat and humidity seem unusually intense today, but this has to be something of an illusion since the morning is young and the monsoon has been waning, not waxing, of late. Still I find myself pausing at frequent intervals, even though the incline up the wash is gradual and the walking is easy. As I dawdle along, I find several prominent plant species that I do not encounter on my walks up the side of the mountain itself. Desert hackberries are one such plant, and they, like the paloverdes, fairy dusters, wolfberries, and more, have fresh coats of green leaves, which make them look very much alive and well. The whole landscape has been revived since the last big rain. The leafed-out ironwoods and the paloverdes by the border of the wash have a really substantial air about them.

Speaking of ironwoods: soon after beginning my walk I come across several full-grown specimens standing just upstream of large groups of one- to three-inch-tall seedlings that have popped out of the gravel of the wash proper. I have never seen clusters of this sort before but assume that the baby plants must be ironwood seedlings that germinated following the rain. Earlier this summer, the local ironwoods produced masses of seedpods, and I suppose that pocket mice immediately ate some proportion of the seeds within those pods before burying the ex-

The two vibrant seedling ironwoods (left) were among the many that died (right) quite soon after the end of the monsoon.

cess in the wash for later consumption. The rodents' failure to return for every last seed has been a boon to the ironwoods.

But are they really ironwood seedlings? The question arises because I subsequently find numbers of green seedlings growing in the gravel next to acacias far from the nearest ironwood. Acacias also produce big fat seeds enclosed in a pod, and rodents no doubt also collect and bury these seeds as well. So are the small leafy seedlings I have been finding infant ironwoods or baby acacias? I lean toward the ironwood option because the thin delicate spines on the plantlets are more similar to those on adult ironwoods than to the short, stocky spines found on acacias. I will have to impose on one of my botanical colleagues to get a definitive answer. (And when I do, Les Landrum weighs in gratifyingly on the side of ironwoods because of the "stipular" spines of the seedlings.)

I continue "upstream" following the river of gravel and sand past many a healthy ironwood, both adult and presumptive seedling. A handful of Gambel's quails burst from the brushy border of the wash and whirr off into the desert.

The main motivation for this hike is to relocate the seep pool that I found long ago in the upper portion of the wash. Because of the recent rains, I imagine that there is some chance of finding some water where it used to be. But when I reach that part of the streambed where the semipermanent puddle used to be, not a hint of moisture remains. The big acacia whose branches shaded the seep in the past has been partly uprooted by a flash flood that ripped down the wash following a storm that took place some time ago. The flood deposited a truckload of gravel on the spot where javelinas and honey bees once came to drink, more evidence that desert washes are constantly being reorganized in a never-ending process.

My walk reaches its anticlimax just about the point when the wash has run its course. So I turn around and begin the descent back to the highway. On the way I concentrate on picking up aluminum cans, fourteen total, all but three of which once contained beer. Although Coors, Millers, Pabst Blue Ribbon, Keystone, Old Milwaukee, and Budweiser are all represented in my sample, the favorite of the local litterbugs is Budweiser, which makes up four-elevenths of the total. Even though I shake out the cans before popping them in my daypack, I later find that the pack is in need of a cleaning.

As I stroll along plucking beer cans from their hiding places, I pass a telephone-pole saguaro. Near the top of its unbranched trunk, one lone flower looks up to the blue sky. The flower represents a probably futile attempt by the cactus to reproduce at this late date, perhaps in response to the recent rain, perhaps not. There is no question, however, that the rain has triggered flowering in some of the wolfberries growing along the wash. Hundreds of very modest pale yellow flowers festoon the tangled branches of a particularly large and leafy specimen. The flowers have attracted nearly a dozen lyside sulphurs, a pale butterfly with whitish wings tinged with yellow. The sulphurs hang from the outer twigs of the wolfberry like Christmas ornaments while professionally probing the little flowers with their long gray proboscises.

The sun bathes the desert, while I try to ignore the sounds of the traffic rumbling along the highway to which I must now return. Retracing my steps, I relocate several of the "flocks" of baby ironwoods that I had encountered earlier in my hike. The tiny trees look cheerful and healthy for the moment. But since each cluster occupies only enough space for no more than one adult tree, I realize that from the dozens currently dotting the gravel of the wash, at most a single survivor will be selected. The future will almost certainly not be kind to these small ironwoods.

The *Tachytes* wasps are not the only insect species that I had not seen before this summer's desert explorations. Another addition to my Usery insect list is a dobsonfly perched in a paloverde on the ridgeline. Until today (August 14), I have never seen a dobsonfly anywhere in Arizona, let alone on the top of Usery Mountain. These insects are pretty hard to miss, since adults are four or five inches long. During their larval stages, dobsonflies live in the water, and one would think that adults would hang out by water as well because females typically lay their eggs, after mating, on vegetation above a stream or river so that the hatchlings can drop into an aquatic environment (23). There they will develop, if all goes well, into hellgrammites, very large carnivorous grubs with dangerous-looking jaws. Admittedly the Salt River is visible from Usery Peak, as it is only a few miles away, but this adventurous, or confused, adult dobsonfly has flown a long way from the river in order to explore a desert mountain. Why?

I have no answer to this question, but I am not about to miss the opportunity to photograph the wandering dobsonfly, which clings to the outer branches of the paloverde. Almost certainly it will wait for nightfall to move on. For the time being, it more or less patiently allows me to examine its large, superbly camouflaged wings and its inch-long pointed jaws. The jaws provide a clue that I am looking at a male, because female dobsonflies typically have short, powerful cutting jaws, not these strange almost tubular mandibles.

Whenever the sexes differ in the size and shape of potential weapons, be these jaws, horns, or antlers, odds are the male's armament is larger and more elaborate than that of the female. In addition, we can bet that the males use their special body parts either to impress or control females or to intimidate or harm their fellow males, which are competitors for potential mates. Either way, the special structures can help males leave more descendants by enabling them to overcome female resistance to mating *or* to prevent rivals from monopolizing the pool of potential mates.

The only dobsonfly seen on Usery Peak in 2006. The male's jaws are impressive but surprisingly delicate.

The male dobsonfly's jaws may help him hold or stimulate a female, should he find one, or they may come into play in combat if he encounters a rival that must be intimidated or driven away from a willing female. In the case of a Mexican species of dobsonfly, males use their projecting jaws to stroke the wings of females, a counterintuitive use for what seem at first glance to be weapons (23). But males of other dobsonflies are also known for their ability to make love, not war. For example, males of the Japanese species *Protohermes grandis* may donate 20 percent of their body mass to their mates in the form of a gelatinous secretion that females consume after their partners have attached the edible material to the female's genitalia (39). This donation presumably encourages the female not to mate again but instead to use the sperm of the male that supplied her with a large postnuptial meal.

Perhaps the big male dobsonfly resting in paloverde K uses its mandibles to pet potential mates before copulating with them, or perhaps he uses his jaws to maul rivals. I doubt whether anyone knows which hypothesis is right, because studies of dobsonflies are few and far between, probably because dobsonflies themselves are relatively rare. The scarcity of adult dobsonflies is the product in turn of the rarity of hellgrammites, the larval form, which must find, capture, and consume large amounts of prey, a difficult task that can take three or more years, if the big grubs are fortunate enough to live this long. The general rule, whether one is dealing with dobsonflies or lions, is that it takes about ten pounds of food to produce and sustain one pound of consumer. Because large predators must consume great quantities of prey, the numbers (and total weight) of meat eaters found in any given area will generally be far less than the numbers (and total weight) of the prey from which come the unlucky ones that unwillingly supply the calories and nutrients required by big carnivores.

If the 10 to 1 rule is truly general, then there should be some other large carnivorous insects, besides dobsonflies, that are relatively rare and so seldom appear on Usery Peak, and there are. Among the many species of robber flies are some fairly big ones that snatch other, generally smaller insects from their perches or out of the air before stabbing them with their stiletto mouthparts. These hunters are vastly outnumbered by the smaller ants, flies, and other insects that regularly show up on the hilltop in season. So, for example, I saw only a few specimens of the sleek gray robber fly that showed up in July around the time of the harvester ant flights. The same rule of rarity applies to another heftier, hairier species of robber fly that I spotted one morning in August. This species happens to be the same size as a bumblebee, and indeed it looks remarkably like a bumblebee, particularly in flight, thanks to the beelike alternating bands of black and yellow hairs on its abdomen. Presumably the fly is relying on deception to keep birds like ash-throated flycatchers at bay, since the birds may be reluctant to test the proposition that a creature that looks so much like a painfully stinging bee is actually harmless to them, perhaps even tasty. Freedom from attack by birds gives the robber fly the chance to dash after its prey without risk of being attacked by a deadly enemy of its own. The fly in paloverde B on August 8 had put this ability to good use because it was feasting upon a winged harvester ant, a real Johnny-come-lately to the hilltop. But this was the first and only bumblebee-mimicking robber fly that I encountered in the Userys in the summer of 2006.

We humans have a real eye for rare things. The rarer the antique, the coin, the bird, the robber fly, the you-name-it, the more likely we are to place a high value on the item. I have no doubt that there are a host of reasons for this peculiarity of human nature, sometimes involving the competitive elements of our behavior. I know that being able to announce to other bird-watchers that you have seen, and identified, a rare vagrant species is likely to enhance your status within the community of birders.

Alas, no such comparable community of insect watchers exists, nor is it likely that I can derive any other advantage from making it known that I have seen an out-of-place dobsonfly or relatively uncommon robber fly. Perhaps my personal interest in rare bugs arises as a nonadaptive side effect of some element of brain operation that encouraged our distant ancestors to take an interest in natural history, the better to catalog the available resources in their surroundings. For our Pleistocene ancestors, knowing what kinds of animals and plants were available in their environments could have had real practical value, at least with respect to those animals and plants that people find palatable. Surely there is some reason for my ability to feel a small frisson of excitement at the appearance of a dobsonfly or an unusual robber fly. Whatever it is, I am happy that I can derive enjoyment from the rarer local insects as well as the common ones.

September *Monsoon Plants*

Five weeks have passed since I discovered large numbers of ironwood seedlings growing in the washes to the west of the Userys. Because we have had several good rains during these five weeks, I expect to find the infant ironwoods in good shape on my next visit to the washes—if the plants haven't been eaten by jackrabbits, cottontails, woodrats, and the like. As I approach a parking spot by the edge of the Bush Highway not far from the baby ironwoods, a few fat drops of rain splat against the windshield; to the north a large monsoon shower obscures all of Four Peaks. This may well be the last of the monsoon, but even so the desert here has little to complain about this year in terms of quantity and timing of rainfall. The incipient shower moves over the highway and off to the west where it appears to be developing a little more punch.

It takes me only a few minutes to climb over the wire fence and march up to a big ironwood by a little wash, where I had found the first of several colonies of seedling ironwoods on my last walk here. Today I am gratified to find a good many seedlings still standing in the wash. True, a substantial proportion, perhaps half the original group, has died.

Some of those that have gone to their reward remain in place, pale tan upright stems with whitish leaflets still attached. Despite the rains, it appears that these plants have simply dried up and died. None of the young ironwoods is much taller than it was five weeks ago, and even the ones that are alive do not look particularly vigorous. Many show signs of insect damage in the form of nibbled or perforated leaves. The living seedlings appear to be holding on by the skin of their teeth.

The same applies to the little foothill paloverdes that sprouted so eagerly after the first heavy rains of the monsoon. Most of what were once fresh, deep green seedlings have either disappeared, probably into the bellies of small mammalian herbivores, or are now mostly pale, tattered specimens about the same size they were weeks ago. Here and there a youngster seems to be doing well, growing out of a patch of dried plant matter or next to a sheltering rock. But these specimens are definitely exceptions to the rule.

Indeed, the entire crop of plants that appeared after the monsoon's inception is pathetically small compared to that produced in springs when winter rains have been adequate. True, in this postmonsoon season, I can find scattered groups of a skinny little plant that has clearly grown from recently germinated seeds. My botanist friends have told me that it is *Ditaxis neomexicana*, a common late summer annual with rather narrow green leaves and some of the smallest, least flashy flowers imaginable; to see them properly requires a hand lens. I also find a couple of nice-looking vines named *Phaseolus filiformis*, a fairly close relative of the garden pea. And some weeks earlier the effects of the monsoon were evident in the flowering wolfberries, pincushion cacti, and a few others, adding a dash of color to the desert. This cohort also included a perennial vine, *Janusia gracilis*, which first put out a number of small yellow flowers that in the fullness of time became reddish winged fruits similar in form to the winged fruits of maple trees. But as one surveys the Userys in mid-September, the ground between the paloverdes and jojobas is mostly bare. The small number of plants colonizing these patches and the small size of their flowers make the desert look brown instead of green, orange, and blue, the predominant colors of wet springs.

(facing page) A view to the north from Usery Peak during the monsoon; a shower dumps rain far from the mountain.

Some possible causes of the difference between the spring and fall flowering seasons are not hard to imagine. First and foremost, July, August, and September are far hotter than February, March, and April, which insures that much of the summer moisture evaporates before it can be collected by monsoon-dependent plants. Moreover, most of the water that is taken up during the summer is promptly transpired as the plants moderate their internal temperature. Therefore, even when rainfall amounts are more or less equal in the winter and the summer, the water available for plant growth will usually be much less in the summer. This factor may explain why the number of arms on saguaro cacti, which varies from region to region, is positively correlated with winter rainfall amounts but not summer precipitation (27). Saguaros apparently grow during the winter, adding mass to their arms, which are then used as platforms for the less expensive flowers and fruits when they are produced in summer.

Some other factors magnify the differences between the winter and summer rainy seasons. For example, when it rains in the winter, the storms are almost always gentle and the water has ample time to soak into the soil. In contrast, during a summer thunderstorm, much of the water pounding the hillsides sluices off to race away down gullies and washes, shortchanging most of the local vegetation. Finally, winter rains are reasonably predictable in the five-month period from November through March. Summer rains are less predictable. Since they rarely begin much before mid-July and are almost always over by mid-September, the summer growing season lasts only about two months. So both the amount of water and time available for plant growth are reduced in the monsoon versus the winter, which may help account for the feeble late summer flower show relative to the often exuberant display in the spring.

I don't mind. I would not want the two seasons to be identical anyway.

September *The End of the Monsoon*

With the arrival of mid-September, the monsoon has faded away in keeping with tradition. Not one cloud floats anywhere in the perfectly blue sky that runs from horizon to horizon. The temperature this afternoon is only about 90 degrees Fahrenheit, a huge improvement for a walker over the standard temperatures of a month or so earlier. The humidity is a mere 12 percent, according to the weather report on the car radio. I cannot say that I enjoyed the climb to the mountaintop today, but when I arrive at the saddle I do not feel that my existence is in jeopardy, nor do I have to desperately gulp down the better part of a bottle of water before proceeding.

On the other hand, I miss the little *Tachytes* wasps that flourished under the superheated, superhumid conditions of monsoonal August. No wasp currently maintains a lookout in any of the paloverdes or creosotebushes growing on the ridgeline. Their numbers had been in sharp decline even before this day's check, which confirms the downward trend. Nor are the wasps the only no-shows. The flame skimmers that once cruised the ridgeline and hillsides by the dozens have been reduced to a handful of tattered individuals that perch on the tips of ocotillo limbs, from which vantage points they sally forth sedately after the few remaining midges. The California patch butterflies, which were practically swarming over the mountainside just a couple of weeks ago, are almost entirely gone—except for a handful of small black spiny caterpillars that I find on a goldeneye shrub next to my access trail. Could there be another generation in the making of these attractive little butterflies? Or are these larvae doomed to die before pupating? I suspect the latter is true (and later inspection of the peak will tell me that I was right in this case to be pessimistic). For the moment, the only hilltopping insects of note are some pipevine and black swallowtails and a couple of great purple and gray hairstreaks, all of which restrict themselves primarily to a few large paloverdes growing along the ridgeline trail.

The paloverdes themselves have lost many of their once multitudinous leaflets to the small moth larvae that took advantage of the trees' leafy response to the first major rains of the monsoon. Not long ago, whenever I attempted to catch a male *Tachytes* wasp in a paloverde, I was as likely to sweep up an inchworm or two. Sometimes, I replaced these gray-brown caterpillars, putting them back into the tree from which they came. Once I watched one of these rescued larvae, a fairly large individual, inch its way along a green limb at remarkably high speed, given its restrictive mode of locomotion, before turning up onto a dead twig. After climbing several inches, the pale caterpillar stopped abruptly and pressed its body tightly against the shaded underside of the pale brown twig. The effect of this maneuver was to cause the inchworm to all but disappear. Had it selected a green twig of similar dimensions, it would not have been able to pull off its disappearing act. No wonder I almost never see these creatures except when I knock them from their perches with wild swings of my insect net. Given the caterpillars' fine camouflage and astute choice of hiding places, I have nothing but admiration for the insectivorous birds that search for these insects. Now, however, most of the warblers that search for caterpillars have left the Userys and are somewhere far to the south, leaving a depleted stock of late-maturing caterpillars for the resident black-tailed gnatcatchers. Meanwhile, the paloverdes stand partly unclothed, no longer looking nearly as green and bushy as they did for a short time in midsummer.

The paloverdes are not the only plants that seem a bit subdued in this dry pre-autumn. The spike mosses gave up the pretense of being green and alive long ago in favor of crumpling back into their dormant, deathlike stance. Likewise, the brittlebush leaves have folded inward; many bear the signs of insect damage. The ocotillos have begun to let their leaves turn from green to yellow. It won't be long before the yellowed leaves give up the ghost and flutter to the earth.

It is still hotter than blazes, but things are changing. Fall will come someday.

September *The Hackberry Hike*

The Peralta Trailhead provides access to one of the most utilized hiking trails in the Superstition Mountains, which border Greater Phoenix to the east. Cars regularly fill the parking area near the trailhead, and latecomers are sometimes reduced to leaving their vehicles in a rough clearing some distance back down the road. Close to the overflow site, an automated fee machine once took four dollars in bills or coins (or a credit card) in return for the privilege of walking in the Superstitions. On my most recent visit to the trailhead, I discovered that the machine had been removed, which enables me and my fellow weekend walkers to avoid having to feed quarters into the machine. Freed from this onerous responsibility, those of us who have bounced down the occasionally rough dirt road from the highway are able to start hiking slightly sooner than otherwise. Most will choose to take the Peralta Trail to Fremont Saddle. Once at the saddle, walkers get to admire a massive stone spire, Weaver's Needle, which offers a powerful visual reward. Hikers tend to hang around the saddle for a while, admiring the Needle, snacking on trail mix, or sucking an orange before turning around for the two-mile walk back. A few of the less environmentally aware types drop their orange peels on the return trip.

An alternative and considerably longer option is to march across the huge flat basin just over the first ridge to the east of the main parking lot. I prefer this hike for several reasons, chief among which is the reduced number of fellow hikers in this part of the Superstitions. As a result of my preference for solitude, I have on many occasions trudged along the rarely used Coffee Flats Trail to Randolph Canyon and then on to Red Tanks Canyon. I have experienced this rugged country under a variety of conditions in different seasons and different years, sometimes in the middle of long droughts and other times just after vigorous rainstorms. When I visited the Superstitions in September 1991, for example, it had not rained for some time, and no water of any sort flowed over the red rock ledge at the entrance to Red Tanks Canyon. Whatever water had been in the stream earlier during the monsoon had evaporated or had slipped into the sand and fine gravel that cover long stretches of the wash. What was left was an empty watercourse, a dry creek, an anti-stream. Evidence that the stream could flow was obvious, however, in the form of the sand and fine gravel that had been deposited during past floods. In places, great quantities of this material had been dumped on the streambed by storm flows that had run out of oomph.

By examining my photographs from a walk in February 1995, I see that almost all of the sand, gravel, and other debris evident a few years earlier in Red Tanks Canyon had been swept away, revealing the once-hidden big rocks, boulders, and smooth red sheets of rhyolite. The old gravel deposits had evidently been picked up and carried farther downstream by one or more flash floods that follow thunderstorms in the Superstitions. Here, as in other parts of the Southwest, these impressive demonstrations of water power regularly rearrange the landscape, stripping a portion of streambed here, dumping the stuff downstream, and occasionally jamming flotsam and jetsam around the trunks of big cottonwoods in the canyon bottom. These mementos of flood action remain stranded above the streambed, where they offer a hint to hikers to avoid the wash when rain is falling heavily on the watershed.

In February 1995, the tranquil stream sliding over the red rock pavement at the junction of Red Tanks and Randolph canyons was just a few inches deep and a few feet wide, not an angry frothing wall of mud and water intent on really tearing things up. A few weeks earlier in the winter, a gentle rain had settled in over the Superstitions, wetting the soil and sending trickles of rainwater slipping down canyon walls and into rivulets throughout the mountains. Gravity pulled the water along, letting it puddle up in the basins carved out of solid rock in stream bottoms. The slow release of water after the storm gradually restored stream flows and brought out the color in the red, pink, and blue-gray rocks that have been scoured and tumbled thousands of times during their long residence in the Superstition's streams. By February the creek was already contracting in anticipation of its gradual but inevitable return to a largely water-free state. By May or even April, water is almost always gone from Red Tanks Canyon except in the deepest rock-lined basins, where stagnant wading pools shaded by boulders and cattails may persist for months, sustaining the thin chartreuse strands of algae, diving beetles, introduced sunfish, Sonoran mud turtles, and dragonfly larvae.

In September 2006, almost exactly fifteen years after my first photographic foray into Red Tanks Canyon, I am back at it again on a quiet Sunday. I know that it will take me three hours of steady walking to reach the canyon, and with temperatures due to reach ninety in the afternoon, I must get an early start. To this end, I am up at five in the morning in order to arrive at the trailhead before six thirty. After hopping out of the car, I decide to leave one of my three full bottles of water behind as a weight-saving maneuver. It is hard in the relative cool of the morning to remember what it will be like in the heat of the afternoon when one's mouth feels as if it has been stuffed with cotton. But it will be hours before I have my refresher course in the punishments of being thirsty and out of water. For the moment, I am happy to have a lighter backpack as I march off into the early morning dusk.

Once I have crested the first ridge to the east of the parking area, which contains only three SUVs, I can see the sun lying just above the eastern horizon. Great shadows stretch across the portions of the caldera that are west of some physical obstruction, large or small, a rock outcrop, a hill, or bare stone spire. The local vegetation looks positively

exuberant, a function of the heavy monsoon rains that blessed this part of the desert and have been translated into lush growth of the acacias, jojobas, and other shrubs. So thick is this new growth that I will lose the trail briefly on several occasions once I leave the relatively well traveled Dutchman's Trail to venture onto the less-traveled Coffee Flats Trail.

As I pick my way carefully along this second trail, which is not only somewhat overgrown and hard to follow but also endowed with many loose rocks, I find that I am in grasshopper heaven. As I push through some of the shrubbier sections, every step sends grasshoppers leaping up and flailing off their perches in clumsy attempts to reach safety in another plant. One of the commonest species is also one of the largest, about three inches long, a heavy-bodied yellow-green hopper that crash-lands into jojobas, hackberries, cacti, you name it, at the end of its escape flights. A thoroughly nervous animal, few allow a close inspection, but a handful of unusually tame or unusually tired individuals permit me to look at them carefully. They have handsome dark blue eyes set off by the bright green of their heads. Another bush-dwelling species is even better looking, with its deep yellow and black patches and its reddish lower hindlegs.

A third grasshopper species that rewards my attention lives on the ground rather than in bushes. This hopper, with its appropriately earthy red-brown color pattern, is reluctant to move when approached, but it can be induced to fly a short distance if prodded. During these flights, it exposes its hindwings, revealing them to be a magnificent deep blue outlined in black. As soon as the grasshopper lands, it draws its hindwings under its camouflaged forewings, abruptly canceling the blue look. One presumes that the grasshoppers' predators might continue to look for a prey with large blue patches, after watching one fly low over the ground, and if so, they would probably overlook the hopper after it had plopped down. Certainly there are times when I cannot find individuals that have made the dramatic transformation from a conspicuous blue-winged animal to one that looks like the dark reddish earth on which it sits. I assume that this is why members of this species that have flown once or twice often then refuse to budge from their sitting position even as I approach closely in order to photograph them.

Insects other than grasshoppers have also responded to the vegetative largesse of the season with population explosions of their own. In areas where hackberries are numerous, empress butterflies by the dozens flit this way and that before settling on perches in the little trees. There they usually remain even when I come within inches to have a look. Evidently these are among the tamest of butterflies, the antithesis of the exceedingly nervous big green hoppers. Their current abundance must reflect the fact that the hackberries have taken advantage of the extra rain to produce thick canopies of healthy-looking leaves, the food on which empress butterfly larvae feast. After eating their fill, the caterpillars then pupate within the plant. When the adult females emerge from their pupal cases, they find males eager to court them. All about the hackberries, I see males pursuing unreceptive, presumably already mated females. Here any sexually responsive female hackberry butterfly would not have long to wait before being contacted by an eager male.

The orange-brown butterflies appear to have adopted a subdued version of the color of the hackberry fruits, which brilliantly ornament every hackberry bush along the trail. This is a bumper crop to end them all. The butterflies do not eat the berries, of course, but I enjoy them in moderation. The currant-sized fruits are dominated by a large central seed, but the outer ring of flesh is pleasantly tasty, with a hint of apricot, or so I imagine. I am not the only mammal to find the fruits appealing, judging from the orange-colored seedy feces deposited on the trail here and there by some midsized animals, perhaps ring-tailed cats or gray foxes. Tens of thousands of hackberry fruits still wait to be harvested.

The leaves and edible fruits of the desert hackberry (*Celtis pallida*).

The many distractions along the way mean that three hours pass before I reach Randolph Canyon, which will be my route into Red Tanks. As I expected, the canyon contains stretches of flowing water, barely flowing but a pleasant sight nonetheless. The monsoon storms must have dumped runoff that carried sand and gravel downstream, rearranging the stream bottom once more. In some places, where in recent years bare rocks and water once filled the streambed, a blanket of pale gravel now rules.

I hurry along, increasingly aware of the rising temperature and the declining level of water in my first bottle. But there are many distractions to keep me from getting to Red Tanks as quickly as I would like.

A late-summer Gila monster (top) on the move near the stream in Randolph Canyon, a stream that harbored thousands of red-spotted toads (bottom) in September 2006.

For one thing, the damp patches in the streambed are literally hopping—with red-spotted toads, most not much bigger than a fat grape. These toads delight me with their plump babyish bodies, big eyes, and ornamental orange-red pimples on their backs. Then there is the Gila monster that marches across my path in the middle of the morning, encouraging me to pause and extract my camera once again. The beautiful lizard seems aware of my presence, for it puts some streamside vegetation between us, lying still behind a shrub before deciding to make a break for the dense cover farther from the stream.

Eventually, despite the opportunities to pause and poke around, I reach Red Tanks Canyon, with its dramatic entryway, a sheet of handsome red rock complete with stream flowing down the center. As I walk into the shallow canyon, I record the current incarnation of the streambed, which is neither buried beneath tons of sandy gravel nor emptied of all sand and stripped of streamside vegetation as well. Instead, modest amounts of sand and gravel have been deposited in pockets between the big sheets of rock that lie across the streambed, but nothing like the avalanche of debris that smothered the canyon bottom fifteen years ago. And some new vegetation has come in after the last big floods, notably some young cottonwoods on the right-hand bank and large clumps of grass, some even in the very center of the streambed. Unfortunately, some of the newcomers are Bermuda grass and fountain grass, two outsiders that do not belong here. But I can still wander up the canyon appreciating both the novelty and familiarity of the place.

The big saguaros on the stream borders and hillsides provide a sense of continuity, as do the handful of distinctive tanks, the deeper pools nestled in basins of solid rock, which are distributed at intervals along the stream.

All along the way to the Red Tanks, I had congratulated myself not only on the pleasures provided by toads, Gila monsters, and trickles of water, but also on the absence of people and cows in Randolph Canyon. No footprints, no hoof marks, no cowpies. But as I make my way up Red Tanks Canyon, I discover a line of deep hoofprints that violate an otherwise clean sheet of gravel in the streambed—a cow obviously has been here before me, perhaps just one, maybe two individuals, judging from the small number of prints. Are these strays that were not rounded up the last time cows were moved out of the canyon? Or are these forerunners of a mob recently released into the Superstitions? Whatever the answers, the hoofprints in the streambed and the muddy borders around a pool of water are reminders that cattle have been and continue to be part of this environment.

Although the nearly permanent water sources provided by the rock pools in the canyon help make Red Tanks Canyon a particularly attractive and biologically rich site, they also make it possible for the rancher who owns the grazing permit for this part of the Superstitions to run his cows in Randolph Canyon and Red Tanks Canyon, even in summer, if he so chooses (provided that the U.S. Forest Service agrees, which it often does). Cows, like people, are fond of water, especially if they are lactating, as many of them are on the lands administered by the Forest Service. The grazing permit holders in the Superstitions run cow-calf operations designed to produce calves to be sold when they reach a certain size and are sent to eat corn in a feedlot prior to a visit to a slaughterhouse. Because the cows in cow-calf operations are either pregnant or providing milk for their youngsters, we can assume that they are generally thirsty creatures.

///// Dairy cattle operators have figured out to the tenth of a pound how much water a cow needs each day. Their calculations revolve around an equation that says for every pound of milk produced per

day, a cow needs 0.9 pounds of water, and for each pound of dry fodder consumed, a cow needs another 1.6 pounds of water. In addition, cows sweat. Dairymen must therefore take temperature into account when calculating the water required by their charges. This they can do via an elaborate formula for figuring out how much extra water is needed for each degree increase in the "weekly mean minimum temperature," a measurement that requires its own arcane calculation. Suffice it to say that plant-gobbling, heavily perspiring cows must drink a great deal if they are to remain healthy, milk-producing animals. Indeed a fifteen-hundred-pound dairy cow requires between twenty and thirty gallons of water a day to keep going, depending on the air temperature.

Now, the cows out in the Superstitions are not dairy cows capable of manufacturing eighty pounds of milk a day, nor do they weigh fifteen hundred pounds. Still, even a nonlactating rangeland heifer needs a gallon plus for each hundred pounds of body weight. A decent-sized animal will therefore consume on the order of ten gallons of water during an early summer day in central Arizona. Even a small herd of cows therefore must go through a great deal of water in a short period during a Superstition summer. I suspect that they can substantially deplete the water in the red rock tanks scattered along Red Tanks Canyon, as well as alter the vegetation in the areas they can reach.

Removal of cattle, especially from riparian zones, can allow the area to recover. Once the little dogies were hauled away from the San Pedro River in 1988, grasses and other small nonwoody plants returned in numbers in this southern Arizonan site. Indeed, the density of herbaceous plants increased by four- to sixfold between 1986 and 1992 (45).

The San Pedro would not be called a river in almost any other state. A watercourse that you can jump over in some places or splash across in three or four steps would be called a stream, brook, or creek. Here in southern Arizona, however, permanent flowing waterways are so rare that the San Pedro has been elevated to river status, while its modest flows have kept it safe from dams. Thus, water slides along a narrow channel moving from south to north, soaking into the ground where it supports many a majestic cottonwood, albeit only in a narrow band on either side of the "river." Keep this riparian zone in operation and the cottonwoods and other special streamside plants (and the animals that

(facing page) The entrance to Red Tanks Canyon in September 2006.

depend on them) can flourish (71). Graze riparian habitats to the bone and a region's biodiversity declines.

The San Pedro illustrates this point. In the spring, the cottonwoods leaf out, creating a gorgeous green ribbon that guides a host of migratory birds north from Mexico. On some days, it's almost as if every Wilson's warbler in the west has been funneled into the San Pedro corridor. Everywhere you look, a bright yellow warbler with a black skull cap is on the move, slipping into or out of stands of willow on the riverbanks or flitting from one dense patch of tall weeds to another. This species, and many others, such as the trim gray Lucy's warbler, keeps largely or entirely within the riparian zone while avoiding the nearby chaparral with its beat-up little mesquites and spindly acacias.

Because of the San Pedro's importance as a major migratory pathway in the West as well as a hotspot for breeding birds, like summer tanagers and hooded orioles, ornithologists were especially interested in what would happen to the bird community after cattle had been sent packing. Researchers therefore monitored portions of the forty-mile-long San Pedro Riparian National Conservation Area both before and after cows were declared non grata there. Of the approximately sixty species of breeding birds studied, only a few became less abundant after the cows were eliminated, while nearly half increased in numbers in the space of just a few years. For example, in the period from 1986 to 1990 the rate at which yellow warblers were seen or heard increased from about five observations per mile of transect to nearly thirty observations per mile (45).

Just a few years of freedom from cows were required to generate significant quantitative changes in both the vegetation and the breeding birds present in the San Pedro corridor, probably because the persistent availability of water made it easier for plants to recover from cattle damage. When the plants came back, so did the birds, especially those that nest low to the ground in open cup nests.

But even out on the open range, where the land has become desertified thanks to year after year of cattle grazing, ecological restoration is not necessarily out of the question despite the fact that livestock not only remove vegetation but promote more rapid drying of the soil and warming of the air (19). Hope for recovery of cattle-damaged real estate comes from a study by T. J. Valone and a team of researchers who studied two protected sites within the intensely grazed San Simon Valley of southeastern Arizona. Both places, which were only four miles apart, had been fenced to keep the cows out, but one exclosure had been in operation for twenty years while the other had been cattle-free for nearly twice as long. The twenty-year site showed little improvement compared to the surrounding rangeland, which had been eaten to the bone by cattle year after year. Within the exclosure perennial grasses remained scarce, and in their stead, grazing-resistant woody shrubs dominated the scene, as was true in the surrounding range. At the other exclosure, however, which had had thirty-nine years to recover, perennial grasses were significantly more abundant inside the cattle fence than outside. Moreover, small rodents appeared to have benefited from this change, as they were more common inside as well (94).

The ecologists who did this study suggest that in arid, desertified regions, twenty years might be too few to permit a recovery of an ecosystem subjected to overgrazing, whereas forty years just might do the trick. Forty years seems like a long time to wait for ecological restoration, but we'll take it.

It's not just classic overgrazing that can make life hard for grasses and the animals that depend on these plants. Even relatively benign grazing regimes have serious effects on wildlife, despite the claims of a band of ranchers led by Alan Savory who argue that "holistic resource management" offers the means to feed one's cows and help maintain wildlife populations at the same time. This happy outcome is said to be achieved by quickly rotating large numbers of cattle through a series of pastures. At each stop, the cattle are permitted to graze for only a relatively short period before they are rounded up and moved briskly to the next field (75). Yet, when Carl and Jane Bock examined the grass cover and birds found in areas subject to rotational grazing in southern Arizona, they found the same pattern noted above. Grazing, even if it occurs for a modest number of days, has long-term negative effects on the abundance of grasses and on the abundance of those birds, some nineteen species in the Bocks' study, that live among these plants and feed on their seeds. In cattle exclosures, the nineteen species in question were nearly three times as abundant as they were within the holistically grazed pastures (12).

///// By the year 2004, our planet was populated by livestock to the tune of about 1.5 billion animal units (in which one cow = one animal unit = five sheep). Thus, for every four humans on the planet, the equivalent of one cow roamed the land, with the 1.5 billion such equivalents grazing more than a quarter of the entire surface of the available land area (3), generally those parts of the globe least able to support wheat, rice, and corn because of aridity, poor soils, and harsh conditions.

I do not think of these things as I leave Red Tanks and head toward the distant parking lot on my late September hike in 2006. I ignore the occasional signs of cattle grazing in the past, the gray, dried cowpats, the abandoned water trough, the shot-up windmill. Instead, I look fondly at the hackberries, the grasshoppers, and the red-spotted toads, which are as conspicuous and abundant on the walk back as on the way in. I cannot, however, claim that the last part of my hackberry hike is deliriously enjoyable. With the temperature now above 90 degrees Fahrenheit, the relative coolness of the early morning seems like a faint dream. I am reduced to taking one small swig of water every fifteen minutes or so in order to husband my reduced supply, which now consists of a pint or so. I have two hours to go. Yes, I have read that when thirsty, one should just go ahead and drink up rather than trying to conserve a few last sips of water, but it is somehow reassuring to know that the water is not all gone when one's destination lies a long way down the trail.

By the time I finally get back to the Honda, I eagerly reach for that third bottle of water that I so casually left behind in the cool of the morning. The water, now superheated by the radioactive interior temperatures of the car, tastes absolutely delicious. Somewhere out in the Red Tanks, a thirsty cow no doubt stands by the stream and contemplates the tepid algae-filled, urine-tainted fluid contained in a basin carved out of solid rock. I feel sorry for the cow but have even more sympathy for the canyon.

September *Boulders and Treefrogs*

After September 21, we are supposed to have achieved autumn, so they tell me, and yet the weatherman forecasts another day of hundred-degree-plus temperatures for downtown Phoenix. Cruel but usual punishment for this time of year in our part of the world, where the climate invariably procrastinates when it comes to putting summer out of its misery. But even if fall won't come when it should, we can pretend that it's hiking weather, which my fellow walker Max Werner and I do, by heading out to another part of the Superstition Mountains where we think we will find a streambed with water. Thanks to getting a fairly early start, we have the pleasure of being bathed in relatively cool temperatures when we hop out of the car at seven-thirty in the morning. The illusion of fall grows substantially in the first gully on the shaded western side of the hill. There, cool, dare I say chilly, air has pooled up in the depression; as we drop down into this glorious pocket of coolness, we luxuriate in the sensations it provides.

We have to take advantage of the cool air while we can because the sun soon gets the upper hand, insuring that we will walk along in ever-increasing heat after reaching the top of the first ridge on the Boulder Creek Trail. After that initial climb, the route stays more or less level before dropping down a long slope to the dry creek bed. There we find an abundance of gray rocks to test our rock-hopping skills as we head up to the LaBarge Narrows, our destination today. Cows would be unhappy in this rugged terrain, and I have never seen any in this part of the Superstitions.

When we reach the Narrows, we enter a closed-in canyon with such high rock walls that we have the benefit of shade even as the morning winds down. A thin sheet of water slides from one rock pool to the next in the floor of the canyon. A black phoebe leaves its perch in a stunted tree growing in a small pocket of soil by one of the larger pools. The flycatcher snatches an insect just above a swirl of green algae floating on the water and then loops back to its perch.

Given our leisurely approach to the Narrows and the time we spend appreciating the shade and water there, it is nearly noon when we decide to retrace our steps back to the trailhead. Moving cautiously downstream, we come to a jumble of immense boulders that we had avoided on our way up to the Narrows. This time we decide to slip down among these chunks of cliff that have tumbled from the hills above the streambed. As Max lets himself down cautiously through a slot between two boulders, he exclaims with surprise that he has found a frog sitting next to his handhold. A frog hanging out on bare rock in the middle of a day like today? When I get my chance, I maneuver into position cautiously, hoping not to disturb what I know must be a canyon treefrog, a species that likes rocky perches rather than tree trunks. My cautious approach is unnecessary. For all intents and purposes, the three-inch-long frog might as well be glued onto the vertical rock face it has chosen as its resting place. It does not flinch as I raise my camera into position and take the first of many photographs.

My subject's speckled skin matches the color of the granite boulder quite beautifully, providing a plausible reason why the animal is willing to sit tight even as I shift position in order to take a whole series of photographs. Canyon treefrogs evidently bet the farm on their camouflage, and so stay put rather than leaping away to safety when confronted by a potential enemy in the manner of your typical frog.

As my camera and I are putting the treefrog to a test of nerves, Max keeps finding more and more specimens on the other boulders in this Stonehenge in the Superstitions. The frogs are camouflaged, but even so they are not all that hard to find. Sitting out in the open not only seems an invitation to predators to come and get it but also would appear to increase the frog's risk of desiccation. And yet the frogs sit within a few feet of damp crevices, pools, and puddles in the bottom of the drying creek bed, eschewing all these logical daytime resting spots in favor of far more exposed ones. Given that Max and I are sweating profusely, even though we too are largely in the shade of the big boulders, one would imagine that the treefrogs must also be losing water at a great rate.

But in reality our canyon treefrogs are not about to dry up and blow away, thanks to skin that is far more resistant to water loss than the skin of typical aquatic frogs, which are highly vulnerable to desiccation. Moreover, canyon treefrogs can also safely maintain a higher body temperature than most other frogs. These attributes are obviously useful for a frog that spends so much of its time out of water during the hotter months in the desert Southwest.

If the canyon treefrog's skin truly has the function of reducing evaporative water loss, other frogs that live in out-of-water habitats should have skin with similar properties. Although this prediction has rarely been checked, one study by a team of Australian biologists revealed that, as expected, treefrogs have skin with relatively high water retention values compared to the skin of frogs that live in water. (The Australian treefrogs sampled in this study have to cope with the lengthy dry season in northern Australia, which has favored individuals whose skin slows the rate of water loss.)

The skin of a canyon treefrog is not its only line of defense against desiccation, as my photographic subject tells me with its body language. Plastered tightly against its boulder perch, the frog will lose very little water through the delicate skin on its belly. Moreover, the treefrog minimizes its exposed upper surface area by folding its limbs and tucking them in close to its body. Just by staying put in this position, the frog saves water that would be lost by evaporation if the animal were to extend its legs and expose its belly in order to walk or jump forward.

Four canyon treefrogs packed tightly into an open geode in a streambed boulder. The tactic may reduce water loss from their bodies.

As I continue my photographic onslaught, Max makes another discovery that surely is relevant to water conservation by these "boulder-frogs." While rummaging about, finding one treefrog after another, he announces with satisfaction that he has located a cluster of four individuals. I hurry over to take a look. The little frogs have wedged themselves into a half geode embedded in one of the larger boulders in the jumble and are stacked up one on top of another. From within their stony container, four black eyes peer out at me, each eye surrounded by a membranous circle of gold overlain with black filigree. I suspect that by piling on, the frogs conserve even more water than they would otherwise, since as moisture evaporates from one individual, the other frogs can take advantage of their neighbor's contribution to the humidity in their immediate surroundings.

It makes sense that a desert treefrog would have evolved a variety of stratagems to reduce the risk of drying out in an environment where high heat and low humidity rule the day. Indeed, the importance of remaining hydrated on a hot day along Boulder Creek takes on personal significance as we slowly work our way downstream back to the trail up the mountainside. At the start of the hike, I had two bottles of water in my backpack, one of which is still available as I begin the long steep climb upward. Under the fierce midday sun, I soon realize that I have once again greatly overestimated the amount of water contained in my two bottles. As I puff slowly up the trail, Max gets farther and farther ahead. I stop from time to time to take another swig and to transfer a small additional amount of water from my rapidly emptying bottle to the palm of my hand and then onto my face, which feels unpleasantly hot and dry unless artificially moistened. Oh, to be as waterproof as a canyon treefrog, at least until I can get back to the jug of water I left in the car.

Although I manage to negotiate the remaining distance to the trailhead without experiencing a lethal amount of evaporative water loss through my skin, I have nonetheless acquired a deeper appreciation of the skin and special skills possessed by canyon treefrogs, which enable them to cling comfortably to boulders on a hot September day in the desert.

October *Summer Resurgence*

The overheated weather that dominated much of September simply will not quit even though we are now well into October. With temperatures hovering with depressing persistence around the century mark while humidities register in the teens and low twenties, the desert has become thoroughly parched. The Userys have the same exhausted, brittle look they had in June before the monsoon came to rescue the mountains. The leaves of the bursage have become wispy and dry. The ferns have curled themselves up into brown balls, and the spike mosses look as if resurrection is out of the question. For these species and most others, photosynthesis is on hold while everything waits for the next rain, and who knows when that will be.

The baby paloverdes that once numbered in the dozens along the trail to the peak have mostly disappeared. I know of just a couple survivors, and they are looking more than a little stressed at the moment. The round leaflets that these seedlings once boldly exposed to the sun's rays are now folded up against one another, held out of action for a better time, or else just plain missing, having been eaten by insects or dropped by the plant in a game attempt to conserve water. The hard times experienced by the young paloverdes in my small sample are par for the course. In a study of 1,008 tagged seedlings at a site in Tucson, Janice Bowers and her colleagues found that barely one percent survived for a single year, a figure that fell to one-tenth of one percent in the second year. By the fourth year, not one of the original cohort of foothill paloverdes was still standing, the combined result of drought, jackrabbits, and other herbivores (14).

Speaking of herbivores: on my most recent visit to the Userys, I got to see a big mule deer trotting out of the saguaro forest growing on the side of the ridge. A handsome animal with big antlers, the buck paused on the top of a side ridge to look back at me through a wispy paloverde before calmly dropping down the other side and out of view. The deer seemed to be in much better shape than the nearly leafless paloverdes littered with old caterpillar silk. On one set of twigs belonging to paloverde B, a small spider has constructed a complex trap with a retreat fashioned in part from the dried fragments of past victims. Next to this shelter, which is just big enough to accommodate the spider's oversized abdomen, the web contains two white egg sacs composed of heavy duty silk. What is the spider catching and consuming these days given that the paloverde apparently no longer attracts the male midges and other small insects that once flocked to this mating rendezvous landmark?

Paloverde B and several other conspicuous trees on the ridge are, however, still focal points for male pipevine swallowtails and black swallowtails, which circle and swoop about the spindly trees as if they fully expected to find a female of their species waiting there. From time to time, one of the males alights on the outer twigs of a paloverde and pauses there in the shade only to be flushed out by the arrival of another male. Two black swallowtails fly up above Usery Peak facing one another as they ascend ever higher in the blue sky. They come so close that they must be hitting each other with their wings. Then the males separate, and one sails off slowly, dropping into the open space downslope while his rival circles around to reapproach paloverde B in another fruitless inspection of the tree.

Once the swallowtails move on and a juvenile Harris's hawk flaps past, all is quiet on the peak. I start back down the mountainside, slid-ing on the loose gravel in the steeper places. The spiky limbs of the ocotillos growing by the trail, which just a few weeks ago were blan-keted with deep green leaves, are now either utterly barren or else sport a tattered collection of fading yellowish leaves about to flutter to the ground.

The same is true of the ocotillos in the Sonoran Desert National Mon-ument, which I visit a few days after inspecting the Userys. The gray limbs of the ocotillos here are also becoming more and more exposed as the plants shed their leaves. The fact that almost all of the ocotillos still have at least some greenish leaves suggests that a good rain fell on this part of the desert perhaps a month ago, stimulating the local oco-tillos to invest in a new set of leaves. When I was here last in late July, the ocotillos were universally leafless, as were the paloverdes and the Mexican jumping beans, a large bush or a small tree that goes by the scientific name of *Sebastiania bilocularis*. Now most of the paloverdes have a decent crop of little leaves, while the jumping bean trees along the washes have grown a dense coat of much larger, broader, and darker leaves. The washes themselves have obviously been swept by sheets of runoff, which has cleaned out most of the tracks left by illegal off-road vehicle drivers during the preceding months. The water flowing down the usually dry bed was probably only a few yards wide and a couple of inches deep, but the surge pushed a wide range of debris downstream before depositing the flotsam and jetsam high and dry when the stream reverted to form. The bleached sticks, twigs, and grass stems left be-hind on the white gravel look like a random collection of fragile bird bones.

In the desert flats, grasshoppers flush up at my approach. After fly-ing a short distance, the hoppers settle back down on the ground where they usually disappear from view thanks to their drab brown and gray outfits. Although this one species of *Trimerotropis* is abundant, I do not see a single representative of the larger bush-dwelling grasshop-pers so common in the Superstition Mountains some sixty miles to the northeast. Even though the monsoon clearly came to the Sonoran Des-ert National Monument this year, far more rain fell in the Superstitions than on the Maricopa Mountains, as is the standard pattern for these two areas. The Superstitions therefore support a much denser, shrubbier vegetation than the more ascetic Maricopas, with the result that the two areas differ in the abundance of and diversity of their plant-eating insects.

Given the near total absence of small October annuals in the Maricopas, I am not at all sure what the one common grasshopper can be eating here. Because this species rests on the ground, I guess that it grazes there too, but other than a few inch-high seedlings of a late summer annual, I can find nothing small and green on the desert floor. Perhaps the grasshoppers eat the leaves of perennial shrubs rather than the leaves of young seedlings. The same food may have kept some cattle alive after they were released into the Maricopas following a monsoon storm or two. Although I do not spot any cows today, the washes are dotted with occasional cowpies, not freshly deposited but not old and crumbled either.

Any cow wandering through here will not find anything comparable to the lap of luxury available in Red Tanks Canyon, where water in permanent or near-permanent pools is at hand and the shrubs are dense and leafy in good seasons. No, whoever owns the Maricopa Wilderness steers must not feel much sympathy for them prior to pushing them off the truck into the wilderness. I suspect that one of these abused steers, a really hungry one, was responsible for the mutilated paloverde before me, which has had the tips of its green branches severely clipped. When this plant made its sacrifices on behalf of a local rancher and his charges, the high temperatures were surely above 100 degrees Fahrenheit. Even today, we are on our way to 90 degrees, and the forecast speaks of more of the same for at least one more week. Summer does not give up without a struggle in the Sonoran Desert.

October *Autumn Is Really Here*

One week can make all the difference at this time of year. I am back on the edge of the Maricopa Mountains just seven days after my last visit, but today no one could complain about the heat. The temperatures are actually bearable, thanks to a front that has drifted in from the Pacific Northwest and is taking summer away with it as it slides eastward through our state.

My hiking partner, Doug Newton, has guided me to an isolated mountain island that rises sharply from creosote flats in the eastern part of the Sonoran Desert National Monument. I have not been here before, and Doug wants to introduce me to the modest collection of petroglyphs that the Hohokam pecked into some boulders near the northern end of the little range. We turn off from the corrugated dirt road that follows the gas pipeline onto a smaller track and in short order find a parking place near a hillside composed of a great mound of desert-varnished boulders.

Others have been here before us. A half-filled carton of fermented orange juice lies in the middle of the barren dirt parking area. A plastic mannequin leg hides within a creosotebush nearby. Twenty or so red plastic cups, large ones suitable for beer and other beverages, are scattered hither and thither out in the open, under bushes, by rocks on the hillside, along with a great many other items ranging from Styrofoam coolers and white plastic plates to the beer cans that were drained by the litterbugs. I have brought two large plastic trash bags, expecting that they might be needed, and we quickly fill them; the bulging bags occupy all the space in the back of my Honda CR-V. Many other bits and pieces remain for another pickup. But the area does look better than it did before, although collecting other people's fresh garbage is not our favorite pastime.

Afterward, Doug and I wander around the nose of the mountain, and Doug locates the scattered petroglyphs, which can be easy to overlook. I admire his finds: a lizard figure here, a stick human there, a tight and elegant spiral (or is it a snake?) pecked into the dark rock. Gunners have blasted away at some of the vertical rock faces available to them, leaving behind small whitish circles in the ancient rocks. Fortunately they do not seem to have noticed most of the petroglyphs, or if they have, they are, thank goodness, bad shots.

From even a short ways up the hillside we have a magnificent view of the vast creosote flats that lie between us and the nearest adjacent mountain ranges several miles away to the west and south. A broad band of blue paloverdes, mesquites, and wolfberry shrubs snakes along the western edge of the mountain island on which we stand. The narrow belt of thick vegetation closely tracks the sinuous wash that must sometimes be filled with plant-sustaining water.

A monarch butterfly drifts south, following the wash by the edge of the mountain. Soon it has left the petroglyph boulders and the remaining uncollected trash far behind on a migratory trip that may bring it to a destination where the human imprint is somewhat less overwhelming. I hope so.

October *More Evidence of Autumn*

Time has already swallowed the better part of October. Perhaps that is why the high temperature today is forecast to be a downright delicious 81 degrees Fahrenheit, a major improvement over what we had to endure earlier in the month. No clouds disturb the blue of the sky as I set out from my home in Tempe and head to the Userys to check on the males of a small syrphid (hover) fly, *Palpada mexicana,* a species that is apparently actively hilltopping again after a long summer hiatus that followed its springtime mating competition. At a time of year when most hilltopping species have disappeared, this fly is filling the research void as best it can.

Climbing the mountain seems remarkably easy when sweat is not oozing from every pore and one's core temperature is stable. In my exuberance, I almost trot up the mountainside. But when I get to the saddle, I find a stiff north wind pummeling the trees and shrubs along the ridgeline. What with the wind chill factor, it almost feels cool at ten o'clock this morning.

Certainly the brisk wind appears to be too much for the little hover flies, whose creosotebush perches swing wildly back and forth. I do not see a single individual, marked or unmarked, during my hour on top of the mountain. But not every animal is intimidated by the wind. Soon after my arrival on top, a Cooper's hawk glides past, buoyed by the updraft produced by a north wind striking the northeast-facing slope of Usery Peak. A little later, a sharp-shinned hawk duplicates the flight path of its predecessor, sliding off eastward before curling south. This is the time of year when migrant raptors take advantage of the favorable flight conditions.

Seeing the two hawks heading south without a wingbeat reminded me of fall days when my father and I would go bird-watching at Hawk Mountain in central Pennsylvania. On these outings, we would join many other birders hiking up to a lookout where we would collectively pray for wind out of the northwest. At Hawk Mountain, as in the Userys, October has always been an excellent month to see Cooper's hawks and sharpshins, which ride the updrafts as they sail along the north-south running Appalachians. Indeed, on October 19, 2006, the same day I spotted the two hawks passing the Userys, the many birders at Hawk Mountain racked up a total of 224 sharp-shinned hawks and 30 Cooper's hawks flying by the lookouts that day, according to information posted on the home page of the Hawk Mountain Web site.

It is sobering to realize that the bird-eating accipter hawks, including the two species mentioned above, were not protected in Pennsylvania until 1969 (10). Before then, shooting sharpshins and Cooper's hawks was much more popular in the Appalachians than watching them migrate, with many hunters eager to destroy these "chickenhawks." I learned about this firsthand when in the summer after my eighth or ninth grade, I was chosen to go to a conservation camp in central Pennsylvania. There we learned many useful things about protecting stream banks from erosion and how to fill gullies on farmland. But we also heard from an official of the Pennsylvania Game Commission on the desirability of killing hawks of all kinds. I knew this could not be right, and so I wrote about my experience to Maurice Broun at Hawk Mountain. He then contacted the Pennsylvania Game Commission to protest the kind of instruction we youngsters were receiving at the camp, because even at that time, hawks (with the exception of the accipters) were supposed to be off-limits to hunters.

I am glad that hawks of all stripes now enjoy the full protection of the law in every part of the United States. Even so, here in Arizona, raptors are hardly a dime a dozen, not because they are still shot, but because predators near the top of their food chain are limited in numbers by the energetic "rule" that it takes about ten units of prey to support one unit of predator. Thus, although I regularly see one pair of red-tailed hawks circling in the sky above the Userys, all the other species found in Arizona are rare enough here to provide a little thrill on those unusual occasions when they make an appearance.

Today provides another small excitement when I come across a predator much smaller than a Cooper's hawk or a redtail: namely, a young regal horned lizard no bigger than a fifty-cent piece. I would never have seen the lizard had it not scampered a few inches forward just as I was about to step on it. The disturbed reptile moves as fast as it can in search of shelter beneath a creosotebush. This brown and gray lizard is by far the smallest I have ever seen in my study area; its color pattern lacks the complexities exhibited by older and larger specimens. In particular, the diminutive lizard does not have the two conspicuous pale elliptical patches that run down either side of the back of its bigger relatives. I suspect that these gravel-colored elements may draw the eye of an observer away from the outline of the lizard's body, the better to keep a predator from recognizing a possible meal. This antipredator tactic goes by the label of *disruptive coloration*, an option not available to the little horned lizard, which must instead rely primarily on matching its color pattern with that of an appropriate background. Mixed gray and pinkish gravel patches are common on Usery Peak, and so the small lizard should have no difficulty finding a safe place in which to blend into the earth.

In addition to the two hawks and one horned lizard, I have yet another noteworthy encounter before leaving the peak. This meeting involves an unusually large grasshopper that flushes upon my arrival at the saddle and flies up conspicuously in a flurry of wingbeats for a short distance before dropping precipitously onto the ground by a

The relatively large regal horned lizard (top) has two conspicuous gray stripes running down the animal's back, which may serve to attract the attention of predators and distract them from seeing the outline of the lizard's body. The much smaller immature regal horned lizard (bottom) appears to rely strictly on a camouflaged color pattern that matches the pink and gray gravel on which the lizard is standing.

Four cryptically colored grasshoppers found in the Usery Mountains. (upper left) This large gray species features several conspicuous dark bands and patches that may draw the attention of predators away from the overall outline of the body. (upper right) An immature hopper whose body color very closely matches the color of the rocks on which it was found. (lower panels) Two members of the same species of grasshopper that exhibit potentially disruptive coloration (the dark bands that cut across the body) and background matching (pink on pink and gray on gray).

jojoba shrub. I see precisely where the hopper has landed, and yet when I go over for a closer look, the darn thing has apparently vanished. After a minute of peering befuddlely at the spot, I suddenly pick the three-inch-long insect out from the background of assorted small twigs and grass stems on which it has come to rest.

Closer inspection of the grasshopper reveals the secrets of its disappearing act. First, at rest its wings are folded together, creating a thin, flat, straight-edged dorsal strip, which is colored pale gray in contrast to the much darker surrounding wing material. As a result, the upper edge of the wing looks like a gray twig or stem. With my mind's eye drawn to the pseudotwig, I failed to see the grasshopper. In addition, the light tan antennae were colored very differently from the rest of the body, the better to make it difficult to associate it with a gray, white, and charcoal-colored grasshopper. Instead, the antennae look to me like bits of dried grass stem, which also naturally appear here and there on the desert floor. Without this trick, the grasshopper's antennae could provide cues for an alert predator to use in detecting its prey. When I was helping a fellow biologist collect beautifully camouflaged leaf-mimicking katydids in Australian acacias, we both found it easier to look for their distinctive antennae rather than trying to pick a green katydid body out from a background of exactly the same color.

I have not yet finished cataloging all the elements of my grasshopper's color pattern that may make it harder for predators to recognize that they are looking at a large, edible insect. For example, small but conspicuous patches of cream, white, and pale gray-white are distributed on the top of the head, the side of the head and thorax, and on the top of the femur, respectively. The pale patches are all bordered by black or brown lines or dark blobs, which accounts for their conspicuousness. These elements of its color pattern are just the right size to mimic the gravel that litters Usery Mountain and many other parts of the Sonoran Desert.

This big handsome grasshopper is only one of many grasshoppers that engage in visual deception. Some species in the Userys rely strictly on the match between their color pattern and the dominant color of the rocks or gravel on which they sit for much of the day. But others make good use of disruptive coloration. Some species have dark bands that cross their hindlegs as well as underline the break between thorax and wings. These marks seem to disassemble the body of the insects into gravel-sized bits and pieces.

When prey items possess disruptive coloration, they may gain an advantage when their color patterns activate edge detectors in the eyes of predatory vertebrates. Messages from the visual neurons in question are produced when the hunter's eyes are stimulated by regions of high contrast, resulting in signals being sent to regions of the brain devoted to visual analysis. As a general rule, predators benefit from having visual systems of this sort because edge detectors usually help them see the outline of their prey's body, which contrasts with the animal's background. However, grasshoppers like the big one that I eventually saw, seduce their enemies' visual systems into treating the small conspicuous patches on its body as separate and distinct objects and not as part and parcel of a larger object, like a grasshopper's leg or head or body. When a bird or small mammal focuses on the distracting patches, it may not see the bigger picture, namely, the outline of all or part of a grasshopper, which does the insect a world of good in places populated with curve-billed thrashers and scrub jays. The same applies to the larger regal horned lizards, whose pale gray dorsal ellipses may keep a coyote from seeing the animal's head, and thereby recognizing it for what it is—a potential meal.

No one has tested these conjectures with respect to the large gray grasshopper in the Userys, but some excellent studies have been done elsewhere in which artificial prey were pinned to trees where they could be found by wild insectivorous birds. Some of the "prey" (which were moth-shaped pieces of paper with tasty mealworms concealed beneath) had disruptive elements, that is, small high contrast patches that broke up the edge of the "wing." Other kinds of prey were also the same size, shape, and color, but the conspicuous patches were located *within* the wing, away from the edge. The prey with a disrupted outline "survived" better than the other "moths," which were more often recognized and "attacked" by birds that had learned to associate these "moth wings" with an attached mealworm (76, 87).

The beautiful thing about disruptive coloration is that it can work independently of the background, whereas pure crypsis (camouflage) works well only if there is a close match between the prey's coloration and the background on which it rests. If a nondisruptively colored baby horned lizard happens to wander onto soil that is not the same color as its skin, its odds of survival are presumably reduced. If true, the lizard must restrict itself to a limited subset of available habitats, a choice that carries costs of its own. In contrast, a creature like the disruptively colored grasshopper on Usery Peak can in theory access a wider range of habitat types more safely because its "camouflage" involves patches that are actually designed to be seen, to stand out against the background but in ways that lead the observer astray. In practice, however, some animals can have their cake and eat it too, as in the case of those disruptively colored grasshoppers and horned lizards that select backgrounds that match a good portion of their bodies, a tactic that actually enhances the conspicuousness of their nonmatching patches, lines, and bars.

I applaud the theory of disruptive coloration, the experiments that the theory has stimulated, and the big grasshopper on Usery Peak with its disruptively colored body. The adults of this magnificent grasshopper can be seen and admired only in the late summer and early fall, which provides one more reason, along with the migrating hawks and the last horned lizard of the year, to celebrate the different seasons of the Sonoran Desert.

October *October's End*

Even now on a sunny midafternoon, the temperature barely tops seventy degrees. I did not break a sweat on my way to the peak today. The blast furnace conditions of a couple of months ago have more or less faded from memory.

I have come to the Userys today to check on the little hover flies that earlier in the month provided an addition to my list of fall hilltopping insects. As expected, they are nowhere to be found, even though only light breezes ruffle the sun-drenched creosotes on the ridgeline. But I do find a single member of a hover fly species, almost certainly *Eristalis tenax*. This species looks rather like a honey bee with its golden brown abdomen marked with black bands. The resemblance to a male honey bee is so great that the fly has received a common name, the drone fly.

Drone flies have attracted the attention of many biologists, several of whom have asked, is this species attempting to mimic honey bees, the better to deceive predators into mistaking them for stinging female bees (not a harmless drone)? The answer seems to be yes. Toads that have been stung by honey bees presented to them in a laboratory by heartless researchers show much greater reluctance to attack drone flies dangled before them than do fellow toads that have not been stung (18). In addition, schoolchildren and young adult humans are more likely to claim that drone flies can sting (which they cannot) compared to other flies. If human visual perception matches that of the actual predators of drone flies, then these results also support the bee mimicry hypothesis (33). A third line of support for the mimicry hypothesis comes from films of the flight patterns of flower-visiting *Eristalis tenax*, honey bees, and other flies. Analysis of these films shows that the percentages of time spent in hovering flight were more similar for the honey bee–drone fly duo than for pairs composed of honey bees and other flies (33).

Today's drone fly is not flying at all, but sitting on a rock near one of the saguaros that crashed during the latter part of the summer. I wonder if it is a female attracted by the residual odor of decay. Drone flies are known to lay their eggs in polluted or rotting fluids, but not much moisture is left in the collapsed saguaro.

The female drone fly, if it is a female, soon travels on without pausing to hover. The fly leaves behind a mountaintop where only a handful of other insects are out and about this afternoon. A single tattered pipevine swallowtail flies up to paloverde B, circles back, and drops down toward paloverde A, only to reverse course and return again to the higher tree. It then repeats itself, and does it again, and again, like a captive panther repetitively retracing a route about its cage. During the pipevine's maneuvers, a small skipper butterfly wings in to land on the ground near the hilltop paloverde. Although some skippers are well-known hilltoppers, including the funereal duskywing skipper, which makes occasional appearances in the Userys, I have never seen this particular species here before.

Another novel insect perches in paloverde B, the dragonfly *Sympetrum corruptum*, a solitary specimen that uses the tree as a platform from which to launch short flights after small insects, when any make the mistake of approaching the tree. No other dragonflies perch or patrol anywhere along the mountaintop, a great contrast to the dragonfly fest that took place here a couple of months ago. The dragonfly and the new skipper demonstrate that I have not yet exhausted the insect biodiversity present on this one hilltop in central Arizona.

Two great purple hairstreaks, very familiar hilltoppers on the mountaintop, also put in an appearance. One black and blue male perches in paloverde N, while another has stationed himself in paloverde T. Although the species is a regular in the Userys from March to October, the extravagant gorgeousness of the butterfly makes it special no matter how often I see it.

In addition to the handful of hilltopping insects, a couple of lizards add a little zip to an otherwise quiet afternoon. First, a side-blotched lizard spreads itself out on the near vertical face of a pale rock by the trail. Flattened against the granite, it exposes as much of its dark back to the sun as possible. The lizard, however, is on guard, and when I take one step too many in its general direction, it slides like a snake over the top of its sunrock and slips into the protective shade offered on the other side. Later I see a single ornate tree lizard dart for shelter, but that's the lot today.

The current scarcity of insects and lizards may stem in part from the cooler temperatures of late October but also perhaps from the dryness of the area, which has received no more than a third of an inch of rain this month, less than half the average amount. Moreover, this October's total has been assembled in several dribs and drabs that have moistened only the uppermost layer of soil, which quickly dried out again. Without a deep soaking, many plants in the Userys have temporarily forsaken photosynthesis again. The leaves of brittlebush and bursage are mere ghosts of what they were at the height of the monsoon, while the leaves of goldeneye have fallen to the ground, leaving the shrub naked and dormant. The spike mosses greened up when a tenth of an inch of rain fell earlier in the month; they then turned brown again in about a day. There is little chance that they will revert to a coat of green any time soon since no rain is forecast for the next two weeks. Life in the desert is a roller coaster of brief highs followed by longer periods of decline and dormancy, a pattern produced by occasional days of rain sandwiched between seemingly endless spells of unadulterated sunshine. Thanks to the bright days of October, however, those of us who live in the Sonoran Desert need not fear seasonal affective disorder, the depressed state induced by exposure to a long series of gray fall and winter days. In order to get a full dose of sunshine in southern Arizona, all we require is to get off our backsides and climb a desert hill on a day like today.

October *Eagletail Wilderness*

Following my own advice about taking the weight off my backside, I decide to spend some time walking in the Eagletail Wilderness, a decision that sends me west on the freeway toward California. I get off at Tonopah, Arizona, about sixty miles west of Phoenix, while it is still early in the morning. Clouds blanket the sky. Where's the sun today? Perhaps it is planning to burn its way through those clouds later.

Tonopah supposedly has a population in excess of one thousand, but if so, the good folks here are well dispersed. The only prominent features of the place are a café, a gas station, and a nursery that specializes in Australian plants, which would be a brave commercial choice even in Greater Phoenix with its millions of potential consumers. Out here in the unpopulated boondocks, the nursery looks like a money-loser, although I appreciate its neatly drawn signs that trumpet the water-conserving attributes of Australian trees and shrubs.

I am out of the commercial district of Tonopah so quickly that it barely registers. A few miles south, the road splits, and I take the western turn, which in due course becomes a smooth dirt road. To the south of this road, a herd of cattle forage on what appears to be an old farm field; to the north, creosote flats dotted by the occasional paloverde and ironwood stretch off forever, or so it seems. However, the northern section is for sale by realtors associated with Century 21 and other well-known concerns. One new sign in unforgivable chartreuse advertises the availability of a sixty-acre plot. The Internet later tells me that one other sixty-acre property in the area can be had for slightly more than one million dollars, which comes to somewhat less than $17,000 per acre. "Great property for investment in a very pristine area with views of the Eagletail Mountains." I can only hope that the recent deflation in the real estate market will at least slow the inevitable transformation of this area from "pristine" to something else.

Today I do indeed have a clear and unobstructed view of the Eagletails, which I admire as I hurry past the real estate signs on my way to the start of Pipeline Road. Here I will park the car, rather than continue northwest on Pipeline Road to a trailhead by Courthouse Rock. At the moment, the Rock is a dark spire jutting up far away into the gray sky. Rock climbers speak glowingly of the pleasures experienced by climbing up this huge chunk of granite, but since I do not have an overactive death wish, I have avoided climbing it in favor of walking along a well-marked trail into the clusters of hills and ranges to the west. Four miles down the trail is one of the most attractive petroglyph sites in Arizona, a whole series of blackened cliffs at the junction of two large washes. Major portions of the cliffs are covered in ancient artwork of various sorts. Some items look like an outline of a net or a floor plan, while others are composed of zigzag lines or circles. My favorites are the simple but lively images of deer and bighorn sheep, which were frequent subjects of petroglyph makers here and elsewhere in the Sonoran Desert.

Having already visited this site twice in 2006, today's walk will instead take me to a new destination along a route due west from a point three or four miles to the southeast of Courthouse Rock. No trail here, but with the big rock standing like a beacon to the northwest and much open plain due west, the chances I will get lost are vanishingly small. I leave the car by an ironwood and start out on the lower flanks of an east-west running line of hills and ridges. The sun has begun to open up the cloud cover overhead.

Many Sonoran Desert sites contain petroglyphs of game animals hunted by aboriginal desert dwellers. Mule deer can be seen in the upper photograph of a petroglyph panel by the Gila River near Sentinel, Arizona. The lower rock walls, both in the Eagletail Mountains Wilderness near Tonopah, Arizona, feature desert bighorn sheep.

The walking is easy, so much so that I have plenty of opportunities to examine the views and vegetation along the way. The Eagletails usually receive less rain than the Userys, but it is apparent that the place has benefited from a combination of a good monsoon and (probably) a decent late rain in October. Here and there the floor of the desert has acquired a smattering of a ground-hugging little composite with the unattractive name of foetid marigold. Despite its label, the small but bright yellow flowers of the admittedly strong-smelling marigold lift one's spirits. The creosotebushes are not in flower, but they look good too with their green leaves shiny with resin; the specimens growing along the dry washes and the even drier little sandy rivulets are especially deeply colored and fully leafed out, the signs of past rain. Surprisingly, a handful of brittlebushes are also in flower. The number of yellow flowers per shrub is not great, but to see any brittlebush blooms at this time of year is unusual. In the Userys, all the brittlebushes are holding back, waiting for the customary time, March or April, in which to flower—with the proviso that the winter rains materialize.

I make my way slowly up one after another of the small hills that stand in my way. Looking across the desert from the tops of these hills is a fine way to appreciate the fondness of the paloverdes and ironwoods for the minor washes that cut across the sparsely vegetated plain. The little puffs of green form lines that outline the barren patches between the washes and gullies. Far in the distance, Courthouse Rock stands tall, helping me keep directly on line to the mountains ahead. Sometimes the spire is in the shadows, while the hills behind are briefly illuminated by the sun. Other times the situation reverses itself, when the Rock turns pale red under a band of sunshine while the hills in the background become nearly black.

About an hour into my hike, it occurs to me that I cannot remember turning off the headlights of my car. I tell myself that I must have done so. I know that the Honda bleats out a warning if one opens the front door while the lights remain on. I could not possibly have ignored that signal even if I had forgotten until that moment to turn off the lights. I know this is true. But something perverse in me keeps coming back to this possibility, which leads me to contemplate my subsequent moves if I return to a car with a dead battery. I am not enthusiastic about the

(facing page) Courthouse Rock in the Eagletail Mountains.

prospect of adding some six or seven miles to what will be a fairly ambitious hike as well as having to deal with the uncertainties of finding someone to help me out of a predicament of my own making. I tell myself that the odds of leaving the lights on is one in a thousand, but then I ask myself, "Do you want to deal with the consequences of that one in a thousand event?"

Although the answer to my rhetorical question is all too obvious to me, I do not wish to retrace my steps, especially since the mountain ridges ahead are appealing. I therefore force myself to ignore my inner worrywart and plunge ahead, up ridge and down slope, across plain, down washes and up the other sides, keeping my eyes and to some extent my mind focused on a narrow canyon opening in the main mountains ahead. If I can negotiate that opening, I am pretty sure that I will have an entrée into a hidden and little explored world.

As I approach the opening, the mountains in front rear up higher and higher. A big chunk of rock has recently, in geologic time, split from a spire slightly to my right. As the chunk (or chunks) tumbled down the slope, they fractured, leaving behind a trail of smaller pieces marking the line of descent. The very biggest pieces occupy the lowest point in this trail of destruction.

I make my way to the canyon opening and see that a shallow wash jumbled with boulders provides me with a manageable route round the bend and into the mountains proper. Very cautiously I descend into the wash and then pick my way up the watercourse, which is, needless to say, totally dry. However, the combination of a good rain in the not-too-distant past and the shelter against the sun provided by the canyon walls provides an unusually congenial environment for some common desert plants, like brittlebush, goldeneye, oreganilla, janusia, and more, all of which have produced at least some flowers.

Although I expected to find the way up the narrow passage blocked by tangles of acacia and paloverde, I have no difficulty, at least for a while. In fact, a narrow homemade trail of sorts created by the footsteps of the occasional hunter, or deer, or bighorn sheep snakes along the southern edge of the wash. When I finally do come to what looks like challenging obstacles in the path, I have a clear view both up into the mountain ahead and down the canyon behind me. The sun has long since chased the clouds away, and everything not shaded by a rock wall or immense boulder basks in full sunshine. The near vertical slope on the north side of the canyon has repeatedly been swept clean by occasional deluges over the course of thousands of years. During a storm, the water must come bounding down the hillside from one rounded ledge to the next, taking what it can with it, and spilling it all into a V-shaped gully that joins the wash. From there, the water splashes, slips, and slides into the wash, sustaining all manner of plants and creating an oasis in the Eagletails, a temporary one with respect to surface water but much longer lasting with respect to canyon vegetation, which can thrive long after all the water has eased itself underground.

Having arrived at a natural turning-around point, I turn around. My decision allows me to avoid a struggle through the plant blockade and also reduces the chance that I will slip, twist an ankle, or break a leg or bang my head. Although my wife, Sue, has a general idea of my location, she does not know in any detail about my path through the Eagletails for the simple reason that I did not know exactly where I was headed when I set off earlier in the day. Were I to become injured in this remote and secluded canyon, I have the feeling that could be it, light's out, the end of the game. My tendency toward anxiety expresses itself again, forcing me to once more seek out a distraction, such as making absolutely certain that I am putting my feet on firm surfaces.

Going down the canyon is easier than going up. Once out of the canyon, my route at first follows the wash, which runs downhill to the east. The floor of the wash is made up of sand and gravel so that I do not have to hop from one boulder to the next or balance myself on something that could give way with a crash. After moving far enough downstream on the veritable highway provided by an ever-widening wash, I make my way to the flat plain nearby and head directly toward the place where I have left my Honda CR-V, ideally with the headlights off. I cannot see my destination, of course, but the end of the east-west mountain range near my parking spot is visible, as is a white water tank that I saw soon after heading out this morning. The faraway tank supplies a beacon even better than Courthouse Rock for my current purpose.

The trek has some ups and downs, but for the most part I need only put one foot in front of the other on level ground. An occasional group of black-throated sparrows and some pods of Gambel's quail provide modest entertainment on the way back. A rock wren teeters on a boulder set into the bank of the wash. The smooth dirt runways constructed by Merriam's kangaroo rats radiate out from the base of a creosotebush growing from the pebble-strewn plain. I half expect to see a toy car racing down these tracks. To see a kangaroo rat in action, I would have to wait patiently for the rodent to appear in the early evening on a day when it was collecting seeds. Kangaroo rats often store what they have found in an underground cache, and their runways may lead to favorite collecting areas, just as harvester ants clear paths to their favorite seed-producing patches.

Although I am pleased by the sparrows and the sign of kangaroo rats, I derive more pleasure from what I do *not* see: no off-road vehicles (although old tire tracks are irritatingly common on the flatter ground), no other walkers, and almost no litter (only two small discards to carry out). The sun beams overhead. Courthouse Rock gets smaller and smaller on the horizon behind me. And when I finally do open the car door, with just a residual hint of anxiety, I see that the lights were indeed turned off before I hiked off into the desert. My happiness is complete.

November *November Heat Wave*

Although the calendar indicates that November is already well under way, temperatures will hit the mid-80s today, with the prospect of 90 degrees Fahrenheit tomorrow or the next day. Nearly a month has passed since the last feeble shower of October wet the ground in the Userys. The subsequent heat and rock-bottom humidities since then have produced an intense drying trend, which has left the desert gasping. When I stop to check on the ironwood seedlings in the wash below the Usery Mountains, I find that since my last visit three weeks ago death by desiccation has carried off all but two of the once abundant ironwood-lets. The only survivors have lost most or all of their leaves. Their green stems reveal that they are still hanging on to life, but only barely.

On my way up the wash to see the last of the ironwood seedlings, I pass several mounds of fresh horse dung. For reasons that I cannot fathom, the Forest Service appears to tolerate a small herd of horses wandering within the fenced-off desert on the eastern side of the Bush Highway. I was once told that these animals were released here by the local Indian community, which I am guessing prefers to have the horses forage for themselves rather than ante up for the hay and oats necessary for their survival. If my guess is correct, the horses' owners are doing no favors either for their hungry livestock or for the desert, which has precious little vegetation to sacrifice at this time of year. I wouldn't be surprised if the horses have contributed to the depletion of the seedling ironwood patch, although I have no direct evidence of that. I am confident, however, that the horses are up to no good here, although the fault lies with their owners and perhaps the Forest Service.

When I contact a ranger with USFS in the Mesa office, he tells me that although the feds are aware of the horses' presence, they lack the funding, the mandate, and the staff to tackle the problem. He agrees that the horses are an environmental disaster but cannot offer me any hope that something will be done about them at a governmental level. I am disappointed.

Having confirmed the dire state of the ironwood seedling population and seen the mounds of horse droppings in the wash, my mood has shifted downward. Nevertheless I carry on to my parking place in the Userys and stoically climb the ridge one more time. The day is warm, but the pre-winter sun has slipped so far off to the south that the northern slope of the Userys is in the shade even though it is just three in the afternoon. The cooler shadows make the climb less challenging than it would be otherwise. The local red-tailed hawk protests once far overhead, perhaps in response to yet another intrusion into its home range.

Once on top, I take a swig from my water bottle and then use my binoculars to peer down at the Las Sendas development at the bottom of the Userys to the south. Work continues on the trophy homes nearest the mountains. With their turrets and towers and tiles, these houses seem to have been designed for minor members of the European royalty instead of local real estate magnates and lawyers. The construction crews have been working on these homes for a long time.

The sounds made by roofers and carpenters float faintly up to the mountaintop from time to time. The warmth of the afternoon has encouraged a few ornate tree lizards to come out to bask on exposed boulders. The hilltopping season continues as well, with a couple of thoroughly faded pipevine swallowtail butterflies on the prowl around paloverde B and other prominent ridgeline paloverdes. The old

(facing page) By 2006, the development at Las Sendas was nearing completion, having spread from the south up to the border of the Tonto National Forest just below Usery Peak.

swallowtails have lost the bright bluish iridescence that once adorned their wings. The trees visited by swallowtail oldsters have also attracted much fresher looking great purple hairstreaks, which perch in the crowns of the paloverdes. From time to time, a hairstreak will launch into a flight that takes it around its perch-tree before it settles down again to wait on the tree. Paloverde B not only has a resident hairstreak but also a single adult praying mantis, which hangs upside down with its forelegs in the classic prayerful position. I wonder if the large green mantis is waiting for the hairstreak to make a mistake in its selection of perches. Or maybe the mantis is hoping for a *Leschenaultia adusta* to land within striking distance, given that a male of this black tachinid fly is here today. Tachinids practiced the art of hilltopping avidly in the early spring, but I had not realized that they would be here in November as well.

I pick my way downhill a short distance to a saguaro that I expect to find toppled any day now. In the 1980s and '90s, this taller-than-average specimen sported two prominent limbs that projected out at more or less right angles to the main trunk, as shown in my photographs of this individual taken from 1987 to 1999. One limb pointed east, the other west. But some time after 1999, both limbs drooped sharply downward, with the west-pointing appendage suffering the added indignity of an amputation of its outer half. Whatever charm the cactus once had was lost as a result of these alterations. Recently I noticed that a big chunk of cuticle was missing well up the main trunk, revealing a blackened, oozing wound. Streaks of decay ran down another small arm that also had slumped over, perhaps in response to freezing temperatures some years ago.

Death comes for saguaros in more than one way. Those that collapse during a storm are effectively dead in an instant, although once I came across a wind-thrown specimen that managed to flower even though uprooted and flat on its back. The toppled saguaro used its stored energy reserves to keep an arm tip or two alive long enough for one last hurrah of blossoms. But in addition to more or less instantaneous death by fractured trunk, saguaros sometimes succumb in a manner less violent and more prolonged but no less final than the clean, abrupt end provided by a monsoon storm. A black spot of decayed skin, like the one on the saguaro in front of me, is usually the first sign that something has gone terribly wrong. Soon the damaged patch begins to ooze a dribble of brown fluid, which slides down the trunk. Over time the liquid forms a dark lacquer coat that reaches down to the ground, discoloring the soil at the base of the cactus.

The organisms causing the saguaro to decay from within are microscopic bacteria that somehow manage to get past the barrier of a saguaro's tough exterior. In a study of Tumamoc Hill saguaros, researchers found that, at any one moment, about 1 percent of these plants had oozing wounds caused by the bacterium that specializes in attacking saguaros (65). Some of the unlucky cacti in question had become damaged through abrasive contact with a branch of a neighboring paloverde or ironwood, which provided an entryway for microorganisms capable of converting a cactus into a compost heap. (Although some researchers have claimed that the bacteria invade only already moribund cacti that have been essentially killed by a hard freeze (86), I have seen saguaros succumb at times when lethal frosts were very unlikely to have preceded the cactus's decline.)

Once saguaro-eating bacteria have a foothold inside the plant, ugly things happen from a saguaro's perspective. Installed in the relatively moist interior, the bacteria often overcome the plant's chemical defenses and go to work using saguaro chemical compounds to produce generation after generation of bacterial offspring. As the bacteria multiply, they are joined by infective fungi and other microbes as well; the combined work of these organisms creates an agreeable environment for the larvae of a variety of flies. Together, these saguaro consumers devastate the cactus in relatively short order, creating a standing carcass that differs from that of the typical wind-thrown saguaro, at least initially. The skin of the cactus begins to crack and pull apart, revealing the blackened flesh within. Fruit flies assemble by the thousands to lay their eggs in the decay, which nourishes the minute larvae even as the saguaro loses its life by degrees. The jig is up long before whole sections of the main trunk slide down to the ground to join decayed and decaying chunks of saguaro already there.

In a matter of a few months, all that is left of a once healthy cactus may be an upright partial skeleton with an assortment of brown sleevelike remnants covering the broken trunk. The upper portions of the skeletal rods that once were contained within the trunk splay outward in an unkempt manner. The whole process removes all the grace of a living saguaro. In just a few months, a brown and blackened partial skeleton stands as its own gravestone, surrounded by what is left of the rest of the plant.

Thus even a small rot blotch in the main trunk of a saguaro is never a good sign, almost always preceding the rapid deterioration and eventual collapse of the cactus so afflicted. Indeed, the saguaro beneath paloverde B does not look good, the upper part of the main trunk curled slightly to one side, the specimen much thinner than its companions, its trunk discolored and indented. Upon close inspection, I see that a dozen or so specimens of the chunky syrphid fly *Volucella isabellina* have gathered on its trunk like vultures at an elephant carcass. The flies hover slowly up or down along the main trunk, sometimes perching for a while, other times hanging in the air by the open wound. Females of this fly typically lay their eggs on the spines of the cactus. When the eggs hatch and the larvae exit, they make their way into places where the saguaro is decaying. Within moist or even liquid pools of rotting saguaro, they grow by consuming the resources found there (59). The numbers of the adult syrphids on the cactus indicate a substantial amount of decaying material, a treat for the fly's offspring but bad news for the cactus. And yet it is still standing, with twisted and mutilated arms, rotten skin, and an undetermined amount of internal damage. I wish the saguaro luck, but it won't do any good.

November *Determined Hilltoppers*

We are now more than halfway through November and yet the temperatures continue to be absurdly high; a maximum of 88 degrees Fahrenheit is forecast for Phoenix, and it will not be much cooler in the Usery Mountains. However, the walk up in the relatively cool midmorning is pleasant, thanks in part to the breeze sweeping the mountainside. The sky is a pure blue, a color that offers not the slightest prospect for winter rains in the near term.

The shrunken, folded leaves of the brittlebushes make it clear that the Userys have not had any real rain for a couple of months. The fall annuals that once enlivened the place have utterly disappeared except for a couple of silverleafs less than six inches tall. These plants still cling to life beside the trail to the top, albeit with just a few remaining leaves attached to their thin stems. The returning drought has swept the hillsides clean of most things lively, except the paloverdes, brave billows of greenness on a pale background of decomposed granite.

On top of the mountain a rock wren quickly ducks down behind a boulder. I am left behind as the only other visible vertebrate—except for a couple of ornate tree lizards pressed against the rocks scattered below the eastern end of the ridge. But we creatures with backbones are not the only animals on the hilltop, as I discover by finding a species of praying mantis that is new to me on top of a barrel cactus. Just an inch long with dark brown wings, the mantis looks like a bit of a twig fallen onto the cactus; it refuses to move unless touched, wisely staying within the confines of a protective bower of downcurved spines.

In addition, some late-season hilltopping insects provide some modest entertainments for a vertebrate observer. A male tachinid fly, all black and hairy, is hanging out in paloverde B. This male, a representative of the tachinid species *Leschenaultia adusta* that I studied extensively this past spring, confirms that these flies can appear on warmer days in any of at least seven months, which makes for a remarkably prolonged fall-winter-spring mating season. While I watch the big fly bumble about the paloverde, switching perches, a rival male flies in, and instantly the two flies switch into competitive flight mode. They race together, first this way and then back, over the outer surface of the tree. The flies move so quickly and are so alike in size that I cannot tell if one male consistently leads the other on the chase, or if the males take it in turns to force the opposition to keep pace, having to match the leader swerve for swerve, dive for dive, spin for spin. Whatever the rules of the game, they result in some impressive aerial maneuvers lasting for more than three minutes before one male hangs up his spurs and quits. The apparent winner returns to a perch high in paloverde B where he clings to a green twig.

Besides the tachinid, several species of syrphid flies, including *Palpada mexicana*, are also in the mating game today, as well as the big bot fly, *Cuterebra austeni*. The delicate tan syrphids look crisp and clean compared to the brutish bots, with their irregular splotches of gray on black cuticle. The male bot near paloverde B is either very old or very cold, because he can barely fly; a short flight to a new perch is preceded by several seconds in which the bot literally stumbles forward on uncertain legs before finally getting airborne. The fly cannot be long for this world.

Likewise, the dying saguaro below paloverde A appears, as it has for weeks, to be on its last legs. Although still upright, the unfortunate cactus looks yellower than ever. The fluid oozing from its rot spot high on the trunk has streaked the lower trunk in black lacquer. Its situation appears desperate. In contrast, when I check on the young saguaro whose fate I have been following for six years, I find a cactus that is the picture of health, although it is thinner now than just after the monsoon. The specimen has grown to be nearly a foot tall and seems to be stretching up toward the lower branches of the sheltering paloverde above. Here is a cactus with a future, a reason for optimism as the year draws to a close, testimony to the capacity of some living things to cope with the desert and its droughts.

November *The South Maricopa Wilderness*

Today, I decide to try something new on the hiking front for the end of the year. Instead of heading to the northern part of the Sonoran Desert National Monument with its formal trails and relatively familiar terrain, I opt for the South Maricopa Mountains where I have never been before. I reach the turnoff for the northern trailheads before 7:00 a.m., but instead of bumping my way north, I park the car near the highway and cross the road to walk south. The scene at this hour is positively spectral, with the sun yet to come up in the east, the desert washed in gray, and the cold night air draped over everything.

Even when daybreak occurs, the long line of mountains that runs from the southeast to the northwest screens the sunshine, and so, for a long time, I will march along in deep morning shadows. But first I must find a way through a fence beside the railway, climb up onto the elevated tracks, then down the other side, where I have to crawl under the parallel fence on the other side. From there I aim for the mountain wall close by, keeping the hills on my left while off to the right a vast plain stretches out for miles before the flats give way again to several ranges stacked up one behind the other to the horizon.

The mountains on my left rise almost straight out of the plain, so that the almost perfectly level ground becomes the South Maricopa Mountains with great abruptness. The mountains themselves are composed of a great jumble of brown boulders stacked precariously one atop another, a house of geologic cards that looks likely to collapse at any moment. The infrequent rains of the past have washed all the soil in the mountains down to the plain and carried it off along little gullies, most of which are only a few feet wide and just inches deep, conduits that spread dirt, fine gravel, and clay evenly over the land.

The summer monsoon was not kind to this chunk of the Sonoran Desert. One thing for sure: it hasn't rained here recently. I pass a great number of dead plants: skeletonized chain-fruit chollas and blackened teddy bear chollas, saguaros in all stages of decay, creosotebushes reduced to leafless brittle twigs, dead ironwoods that have been sculpted over the years into weird forms, some upright, others lying on their side. As the dead ironwood ages, wood flakes off the trunk and limbs in large pieces, giving the remains an angular look almost as if someone had taken an adze and plane to the wood. Salvador Dali would have been pleased with the product.

At about the time I have escaped from most of the signs of humans (the railroad line, telephone wires, tracks made by off-road vehicles), the sun finally begins to inch around the far southeastern corner of the Maricopas. The distant mountains to the west and north acquire a reddish purple cast, while long shafts of light stretch out across the plain, turning what had been a monochrome landscape into a far more colorful one, heavy on the yellow-green and red-brown.

With the coming of sunshine, a few birds come out of the rockwork to enliven the desert. A canyon wren bobs on a boulder top while piping out a weak alarm call, its white bib set off by the surrounding chestnut red plumage. It then flies on stubby wings to another rock pile a short distance away before ducking into a crack between two boulders. Far off a flicker produces its short sharp cry.

The sun gradually envelops the desert. At this time of year, the heat it supplies is a welcome antidote to the chilly breeze, which picks up as the morning progresses. A black-tailed jackrabbit, the first mammal seen today, bounds off through a colony of teddy bear chollas. Later I will see two more members of this species, each displaying his black-tailed behind for just a few seconds before disappearing behind desert shrubs and chollas.

The chollas aren't going anywhere. They remain anchored to the rocky ground in alcoves and bays formed by the projection of two parallel mountain ridges out into the plain. I imagine that the densely packed armies of cholla sometimes found in these protected bays are the clonal descendants of one or a few ancestors. These cacti may have benefited from conditions that were particularly conducive to the asexual brand of reproduction often practiced by teddy bear chollas. The ground here is littered with fat sausage-sized "joints" that have fallen from the limbs of the mature chollas growing in a dense grove. Each joint has the potential to take root, creating a ready-made baby cactus that will grow up next to its parent, if all goes well. In some places, however, it looks as if entire family groups, a tight cluster of several chollas, have died together, leaving behind a little stand of upright corpses clothed in blackish spines. In places, the spiny covering has peeled back, revealing the pale latticework within the limb, which constitutes its internal tubular skeleton but really seems more like botanical artwork than a functional skeleton.

Although teddy bear cholla are not immortal, they are nonetheless a quintessentially tough customer, at least when it comes to tolerating high temperatures. For one thing, their dense coat of pale spines reflects a considerable amount of the sunlight they are subjected to, so that the temperature of their cuticle is only fourteen degrees Fahrenheit (eight degrees centigrade) above air temperature. In contrast, the skin of the far less spiny barrel cactus can reach temperatures forty degrees Fahrenheit (twenty-two degrees centigrade) higher than that of ambient temperatures (26).

For another thing, teddy bear cholla can boost their heat tolerance as summer bears down on them by making biochemical adjustments of various sorts. In a laboratory study of the species, when cholla joints were given the chance to acclimate slowly to ever-higher temperatures over a period of weeks, many of the "subjects" were able to withstand an hour at 59 degrees centigrade (a staggering 138 degrees F.) and live to tell the tale. (If, however, the plant parts were first held at much lower temperatures for some time, raising the temperature to a "mere" 48 degrees centigrade led to their death (26)).

Today, the cholla have made it through a night when temperatures dropped pretty close to freezing. I suspect that they have been slowly acclimating to cooler nighttime temperatures ever since the end of the monsoon. But even acclimated teddy bear cholla are frost-sensitive, which may be why they grow so densely next to the mountains, where they are on slightly higher ground. Cold air spills downhill, drifting off to the low spots far out on the flat land, leaving the cacti slightly warmer, the better to live another winter day, while waiting for things to warm up again. As we might expect, a different cactus that makes its home in the Canadian prairie provinces has evolved special thermal adaptations to cold weather. This plant adjusts to freezing winters as the cold comes in with autumn; at first, its tissues can tolerate air that is only a few degrees below freezing, but by December, -50 degrees centigrade is not a problem. This tremendous cold tolerance makes sense given that in winter the cactus (the misnamed *Opuntia fragilis*) must endure natural temperatures as low as -30 degrees centigrade (42).

Having walked south long enough to suit me, I turn to trace a minimalist wash as it runs off to the west. The very occasional water supplied by this half-hearted watercourse, dry as a bone of course on this day, has made it possible for a small number of ironwoods, blue paloverdes, and saguaros to grow to adulthood with their roots underneath the gravel. On the flats between the little washes, only creosotebushes have the toughness to persist, and even they seem to have hunkered down, holding on for the winter rains, which show no sign of coming yet this November.

Gradually the little wash bends around to run more or less northward, and I accept its decision to do so because my car lies off in that direction. Coming around a living ironwood, I sense movement on my left in the creosote flat. When I focus on the area, I see a coyote and he sees me. We stare at one another. The coyote has on its winter coat, which it acquired in anticipation of the cold nighttimes at this time of year. As a result of its thermal adaptation, the animal bears little similarity to the almost painfully thin and scruffy creatures that I occasionally encounter in the late spring and summer. After a minute of reciprocal inspection, the coyote turns and lopes away rather than risk interacting with a human being. A smart animal.

December *The Cut Fence*

I continue my inspection of the southern part of the Sonoran Desert National Monument on the following weekend, after which I put in a call to the Bureau of Land Management. I report on the vandalism of a fence that is intended to keep unauthorized persons and livestock out of the southwestern part of the Monument. Someone had cut the wire strands in several places, creating an illegal opening wide enough to be driven through. The fence cutter or his accomplices had then done just that. After veering off the legal track just before a locked gate, they crossed over the cut barbed wire before bending back to regain the legitimate track on the other side.

I engaged in a little detective work to determine who the fence cutters might have been. By following the track to the west, I soon encountered abundant evidence that illegal aliens had been driven up this marginal road, while others had almost certainly hiked the route on their own. In the acacias and paloverdes near the track, empty water bottles manufactured in Sonoyta, Sonora, Mexico, and bearing the label "Agua Purificada" and the brand name "Thelma" lay where they had been casually discarded by their consumers. A smaller, more fragile plastic bottle once held a "solución esterilizada de electrolitos orales indicada para prevenir o tratar la deshidratación." The little jug, which once contained a fluid for the treatment of dehydration, fell apart in my hands, a sure indication that it had been lying out in the sun for some time. And in a narrow wash by the roadside, a sun-bleached backpack in pale blue with frayed straps provided yet another piece of evidence favoring the people-smuggling hypothesis for the cut fence at the border of Area A. Persons entering the United States from Mexico often carry small backpacks, sometimes to hold illegal drugs for sale, other times for their personal effects.

Farther along, I came across a pair of blue-gray trousers and a work shirt of the same color lying by the edge of the track. They were matted, dusty, and faded, but not torn or seriously stained. Someone had carried these clothes with them on their arduous journey into the United States, and yet that person had then thrown his possessions to one side before he even reached Gila Bend. Why would he have gone to the trouble of bringing shirt and trousers this far only to leave them in the desert? I wonder if he was suffering from extreme heat stress and dehydration; persons in this state not uncommonly remove their clothes as death approaches in an irrational response to their distress. Could I be looking at the clothes of a dead man? Or, much more probably, was he someone who had to lighten his load over the last and most trying stage of his journey to a place where he hoped he could get a decent job as a field hand, roofer, gardener, or what have you? Short of finding a skeleton, something that thank goodness I have never found on my desert walks, I had no way of knowing what happened to the man who left his clothes behind.

I placed the shirt and pants in the large black plastic trash bag that I had carried with me on my hike for just this purpose. The bag was already nearly filled with the glass bottles, aluminum cans, plastic containers, and shotgun shells that litter the roadside even in this extra-remote place.

In the winter, the risk of lethal dehydration for desperate desert travelers is low, especially when compared with the chance of getting into trouble in June or July. But at any time of year, persons entering this part of the Monument, legally or otherwise, would still be wise to bring some water with them given that the washes are usually completely waterless. I know of no springs or rock tanks with pools of stagnant water for miles around the former ranch, and it is a long ways to Gila Bend. I always carry plastic bottles filled with Tempe city water, potable, if well chlorinated. If the local plants were capable of envy, I suspect they would have experienced that emotion when they saw me drinking freely from my plastic water bottle. No winter rains have even dampened the soil here, let alone given the saguaros a chance to rehydrate.

On my way back to the car, I come across a massive saguaro leaning dangerously to one side. Five of its arms must have drooped downward decades ago because now the arm tips have turned and grown several feet upward after touching the ground. The saguaro's curled and twisted limbs look vaguely like a collection of cobras dancing to a snake charmer. The curled cactus stands frozen in the middle of its dance, waiting for rain.

December *Winter Ants*

Today I have time only for the quickest of visits to the top of Usery Mountain. It's the middle of the afternoon on a seasonably warm day with a temperature of about seventy. As I plod uphill, sweat soon dampens the area on my back that is in contact with my daypack. I am just about the only thing with moisture to spare in the Userys, which look as sun-dried as a desert can be.

I do not expect to see many animals at all, and my expectations are met. One canyon towhee slips off to the side as I start the climb up, and the odd grasshopper or two whirrs up out of my way to drop down again promptly on the hillside. Otherwise it is all blue sky, dry air, sunshine, and silence, an animal-free environment today—except for a column of tiny reddish ants hurrying straight across the hillside near the mountaintop. Normally insects so inconspicuously small as these would not slow my dogged walk uphill, but, because I am out of breath, I am happy to have an excuse to pause for a moment. During this time, I peer as closely as I can at the minute ants, which are even smaller than the *Pogonomyrmex pima* that came to the peak for their monsoon mating swarms. As best I can tell, every third or fourth ant is carrying something whitish, an object half or a third the size of a rice grain. I try to pick up one of these laden ants, but it's not easy. Eventually, however, I succeed, although in so doing, I mash the ant and its burden, which turns out to be the carcass of a tiny white termite. The ants apparently have found a termite colony and have raided the chambers where the recently hatched termite workers reside. These unlucky infants have been snatched from their home by the very small but effective carnivorous ants, which are carting their prey back to their nest.

I secure a trio of tiny workers for later identification by my colleague, Bob Johnson, who tells me that these are *Pheidole titanis*. The genus *Pheidole* is a huge one, with well over six hundred species known in the Western Hemisphere alone (106), of which about fifty have been recorded in Arizona. Not surprisingly, almost nothing has been written in the scientific literature about the vast majority of *Pheiodole* ants, but as it turns out, *P. titanis* is an exception to this rule, since Donald Feener has reported it to be a termite-hunting specialist (31). Feener learned that the species hunts for termite prey at night during the monsoon, but during the dry season raids occur in the early morning or late afternoon. The reason for this difference in timing has to do with a tiny parasitic fly, which is present during the summer rainy season but not at cooler, drier times of the year. The fly has the ability to zip down onto an unwary ant and insert an egg into the ant's abdomen in the blink of an eye. The parasitic egg then develops inside its victim, ultimately causing the death of the ant.

To avoid becoming an incubator for a parasitic fly larva, the ants stay safely inside their nests during the daytime in the rainy months. Then they forage for termite prey only at night. But when November and December come, the ants can go looking for termite nests during the day without risking the horrors of parasitization.

If the local *P. titanis* behaves similarly to the populations Feener studied, as I believe they do, I owe my brief encounter with them in the middle of the afternoon to the absence of the parasitic fly during the wintry dry spell we are having. I probably should have followed the column back to the ant nest, which was doubtless nearby, but I am eager to see what is happening on the ridgetop per se. Therefore, I proceed to the saddle and then inspect the trees and shrubs growing along the ridgeline trail. The fat black tachinid fly, *Leschenaultia adusta*, is once again on the lookout for mates in paloverdes B and L, which supply favorite perches for males of this species. A handful of syrphids, including the beelike *Eristalis tenax*, are distributed along the ridgeline, hovering briefly when disturbed, only to settle slowly onto rocks scattered in open areas. One dragonfly waits (hungrily?) in paloverde B. Nothing else. The winter lull in insect activity on the peak continues.

The dying saguaro on the southern hillside seems more askew than ever, a judgment that I confirm later by comparing photographs of the cactus taken about one month apart. Nonetheless, despite its listing to one side, the saguaro is still standing. I cannot imagine that it will remain erect for much longer. When and if it topples, slumps, or crashes onto the hillside, the saguaro will be the third of its kind to give up the ghost on Usery Peak during 2006, making this year a hard one for the local population. But for all I know, more than three tiny saguaro seedlings have popped out of the soil ready to take the place of the fallen. It is comforting to think so.

Having established that the unfortunate saguaro is still standing and that hilltopping insects are in short supply, I make my way downhill, stopping at the place where the line of foraging *titanis* crossed the trail. The diminutive ants have all returned home, their raid completed, their larder restocked with termite corpses. My encounter with them was highly fortuitous. I wonder how many other small insects I have not yet been privileged to meet on the mountain.

December *Winter "Rain"*

For some reason, the march up into the Userys today requires more exertion than I enjoy, particularly since I am quite certain that I will see nothing of note when I get to the top. Because it has not rained in over sixty days, desert life seems distilled almost to the point of nothingness. The plants are leafless. All the dead grasses have fragmented and blown away. The only birds I see are two ravens drifting by the peak. No rock wren, no black-throated sparrow. No lizards either. Not even one grasshopper flutters up and sails down again to the pale gravel on my way to the top. Although the temperature is in the comfortably low seventies, a thin overcast blocks the sun, creating a mildly foreboding sensation. Perhaps a weather change is on the way, which in fact is supposed to be the case what with cooler temperatures and a small, very small, chance of a shower or two tomorrow.

When I reach the saddle in the oppressive silence, I put down my backpack, take out my water bottle for a quick drink, and extract my camera. Leaving my pack behind, I walk toward paloverde B. On my way, I glance over toward the sick saguaro on the southern slope to check on its condition. Ten days ago, the saguaro's upper trunk was intact but was leaning more than ever to one side. Today that portion of the cactus is missing, having broken off and tumbled to the ground sometime during the past week or so.

The partial collapse of the infected cactus, although inevitable, still is somewhat upsetting. On my way to inspect the disaster, I pass paloverde B, which is currently hosting a great purple hairstreak. Paloverde B is otherwise quiet without other butterflies, or hover flies, or any other insects in its vicinity. Picking my way downslope from the ridgeline, I soon come to the unfortunate cactus. The remaining trunk, still at least fifteen or sixteen feet tall, has a ragged top where the upper section tore itself free, exposing a big rotten patch on the new crown. With its remaining arms dangling in contorted poses, the cactus looks a total wreck. Dark streaks of lacquer have oozed down the trunk from its new top to the base of the cactus. On the ground lies the fallen chunk of cactus, about eight feet of wrinkled, already partly dried upper trunk. It cannot be too long before the still standing portion joins the rest of the saguaro lying in a heap on the mountainside.

But for now, the lower trunk and one great curled arm are still defying gravity. And on the yellowed trunk with its decorative stripes of deep brown lacquer, I see some highly distinctive flies. These half-inch creatures have elongate bodies, oversized legs, and odd two-part antennae with a short flat basal section that terminates in a smaller, almost hairlike distal portion. The fore- and hindlegs have lines of short spines on the underside of the thickened segment closest to the fly's body. Are these adaptations for defense against predators? Or are the spiny parts of their legs somehow used in combat against their fellow flies?

The flies on the half-dead saguaro are called *Odontoloxozus longicornis* by entomologists, while everyone else settles for "cactus flies" because the adults of this species usually hang out on decaying cacti, the food source for the immature cactus flies. In the 1970s, Robert Mangan studied the fly in some detail, documenting that under some conditions, males attempt to hold territories around "good" rot spots. By excluding other males, successful territory holders monopolize access to females on the hunt for a suitable place in which to lay their eggs.

Before they oviposit, gravid females must mate with a territory-holder in order to gain permission to deposit their offspring in the rot held by their partner, a mercenary copulation indeed (47).

At eye level, only three *O. longicornis* are visible, and they are not doing much, certainly not mating or fighting, in keeping with the subdued nature of the day. There may well be more female and male cactus flies higher up near the amputation site, a place rich in rotting cactus, a desirable locale into which a female could drop her eggs and over which males could fight.

Before leaving the mountain, I make my way gingerly across the slippery gravelly slope to check on the smallest saguaro I have found yet in the Userys. Barely six inches in height, this specimen is dwarfed by its companion, a robust fifteen-footer with one substantial arm. The tiny cactus seems thin and stunted with discolored spines. Perhaps the competition for water provided by the much bigger neighboring cactus has made life difficult for the youngster. It looks as if junior will need more than a little luck if it is to ever take its place among the big boys on the hillside.

The gray clouds stretch out overhead, encouraging me to think of winter rains, gentle, persistent, soaking, which could give all the saguaros, large and small, many-armed and armless, an infusion of water that they would surely appreciate. True, the forecast gives us a mere 10 percent chance of a shower tomorrow. But we can dream, can't we?

///// By George, it does rain the next morning in Tempe. The shower is more drizzle than anything else, but what falls from the skies is unquestionably precipitation. Sure, the amount we are talking about is barely enough to wet the gravel in the front yard, but it is enough to contradict the thought that it will never rain again. The question is, will the showers reach the Userys as well?

Before it stops raining in Tempe, I hurry out to the mountains. On my way, the car enters and then leaves one shower after another. In the distance, a fine rain creates a gauzy white curtain that partly hides my destination. When I arrive, the Userys are enveloped in mist, and soon a real shower pelts down on me, my hat, and my poncho, which I wisely brought with me today. As I hike up a wash toward the hills, the rain comes down even more energetically, leading me to readjust my daypack, which had been outside the poncho but will be dryer beneath it. The sand and gravel of the wash are thoroughly wetted; a thousand silvery drops of water cling to the tangle of branches and twigs in every little paloverde along my route.

The rain stops. I take off my broad-brimmed hat, pull back the hood of my poncho, replace my hat, and carry on up the wash. After a while, I remove my poncho altogether and stuff it into my daypack. The only raindrops I will encounter from this time forward come in ones and twos at long intervals, lightly pinging my hat. But the clouds hang low over the mountains and surrounding desert and towns, with the sun breaking through only long enough to momentarily illuminate Red Mountain on the western side of the Salt River. For several seconds the red sandstone glows, and a double rainbow forms off to the right before gray shadows regain control of the mountain and the rainbows fade from view.

A couple of mountain bikers come charging along a bike trail that cuts across the wash. Their tires on the damp trail make an odd noise that startles me, although the riders themselves are dead silent, heads down, legs pumping, oblivious to all things even a few feet from their bicycles.

After letting the bikers go on their self-absorbed way, I continue up the wash toward the canyon, where I often see one or two great horned owls, a canyon that also serves as a gateway to Michael Johnson's fallen saguaro and other dead giants in the hidden basin beneath Usery Peak. Before reaching the narrow canyon with its jumbled walls, I march up a broad segment of the wash that is dotted with the foot-wide miniature volcanoes of gravel created by an ant, *Aphaenogaster cockerelli*, whose colonies reside in a network of tunnels and chambers under sand and gravel. I rarely pay much attention to these rather ordinary looking ants, in part because they are nocturnal for much of the year and therefore nowhere near as conspicuous as the more frequently diurnal *Pogonomyrmex* harvester ants. But today the ants cannot be missed because they have come up out of the ground to form dark pancakes the size of my hand around the entrances to their nests. The ants are piled three and four and five deep about their entryway. What on earth are they doing?

I get down on my hands and knees and peer at them closely. The ants are probably fairly cold and not very active, although they are not immobilized either. They seem profoundly uninterested in me. By peering at them closely, I see that many of the ants have small droplets of water adhering to their head, legs, or thorax, which supplies me with a hypothesis. Perhaps they have formed a rain-collecting brigade, using their bodies to intercept the droplets of drizzle before the water can reach the gravel.

This kind of behavior has been reported for several other desert creatures, including a few species of tenebrionid beetles that live in the water-deprived coastal sand dunes of the Namib Desert in southern Africa. When thirsty, the beetles climb to the top of a sand dune and stand on their heads, presenting their smooth hard wing covers to the occasional early morning fog rolling in from the nearby South Atlantic Ocean. The fog condenses on their back, and water droplets trickle down to the beetle's mouthparts (34, 79).

Much the same tactics have evolved closer to home in certain North American horned lizards, which flatten their bodies and arch their broad backs to intercept the raindrops when exposed to a shower following a period of drought. The skin of these water-collecting lizards possesses many tiny interconnected grooves that draw up water via capillary action, after which gravity guides the droplets downhill toward and into the animal's slightly open mouth (81, 82).

Unfortunately I cannot find any written account of rain interception by *A. cockerelli* or any other desert ant, although researchers have demonstrated that ants will sometimes remove *excess* water that has entered their nest chambers by drinking it and marching outside the nest to excrete the unwanted fluid (49), an ingenious solution to nest flooding. But it would not be surprising to learn that a light rain after several dry months could stimulate some desert ants to use their bodies as water collectors, especially since some desert ants do drink fluids when they are available. Indeed, the liquids that ooze from glands in the top of some barrel cacti appeal to ants, particularly during the summer (70).

Presumably the cacti take advantage of the water needs of ants in summer to encourage them to visit their fluid-dispensing glands; once on the cactus, the ants may discourage cactus-consuming herbivores from doing damage to the plant.

Even though I cannot solve the mystery of the *Aphaenogaster* aggregations, I am quite thrilled to have found yet another curious phenomenon unfamiliar to me, something that will send me searching through the scientific literature for clues, something that will cause me to pick the brains of biologists who study social insects. The Userys and their animals and plants are my University of the Desert.

December *Full Circle*

Last winter, I arrived at this trailhead in the Sonoran Desert National Monument before the rising sun had topped the line of mountains to the east. Today on Christmas Eve I get here a little later, and so the first rays of the sun are already reaching far across the creosote flats as I leave the car. Although the sunshine makes for a less somber landscape, I am mildly depressed because on my way to the trailhead I pass a small herd of cows feasting on paloverde twigs and the sparse remnants of dead grasses, most of which probably grew and died here more than a year ago. By the small sign announcing the southern boundary of the North Maricopa Mountains Wilderness Area, several cows have defiantly deposited some unusually large black cowpies. Smaller, less ostentatious cowpats litter the ground near the trailhead.

One would never know that two days ago a gentle winter rain drifted down from the northwestern part of Phoenix to the southeast, passing slowly over Tempe and Mesa. This rain was all the more welcome because it had not been forecast by the local weathermen. In between showers on this happy day, I eagerly collected rainwater for my garden in a large trash can strategically located by a rainspout. But as I kept an eye on the radar during the day, I could see that the green blob representing the moving mass of showers was not large and would almost certainly miss the Sonoran Desert National Monument. Which it evidently did.

Because the storm track had passed to the north of the Monument, the dust on the dirt road to the trailhead boiled up behind me on the way in, especially in spots where four-wheeler ATVs have been chewing up the track. Without even the briefest of showers, the desert plants too look as dry as the dust, the creosotes seeming to be more reddish brown than green, the bursages all stick and no leaf. The year is ending as it began here, with drought strangling the desert.

My hike begins with an initial haul northward across the desiccated flats to a large wash that serves as entryway into the North Maricopas. On my way, I encounter very few desert animals, just one black-tailed jackrabbit, which makes itself scarce in a hurry, and a kestrel perched on top of a saguaro, as well as a lone sage sparrow in a creosotebush. Many sage sparrows spend the winter in southern Arizona after leaving their breeding grounds within the Great Basin Desert of Utah and Nevada. Although sparrows are generally dismissed as drab brown things hardly worth identifying, let alone admiring, sage sparrows are well worth a second look. The sparrow's pure blue-gray head contrasts nicely with its clean white throat and streaked brown back, creating a color combination that is subtle but pleasing.

Although I am happy to have seen a sage sparrow, I am less enthusiastic about the little band of five cows that I come across near the mountains on the other side of the creosote plain. The cattle, a motley mix of red and black creatures, some with blanched white faces, stare at me with the slow puzzlement and concern of their breed. Each animal carries a Christmas ornament of sorts in the form of a bright red ear tag. After pausing to consider its next move, one cow resumes grazing, nipping off the few dried grasses that still can be found standing upright on the hard desert floor. But then others in the scattered group begin to move away ever more anxiously, trotting past the paloverdes, creosotes, and saguaros that constitute the cows' deficient pasture. The grazer joins its fellows as they depart, stumbling as it breaks into a rodent burrow before regaining its stride. The cows leave behind their hoofprints and their droppings, which are concentrated around the stunted ironwoods standing along the miniature washes that wander through the plain. I will learn later from Karen Kelleher of the Bureau of Land Management that the permit holder has the right to run as many as four hundred cows over a large part of the Sonoran Desert National Monument, but that at the moment nowhere near that number are left on his BLM grazing lease, a reflection of the fact that the cows have consumed all there is to consume here. In accordance with this reality of the range, the rancher has, according to Ms. Kelleher, been removing his animals steadily in recent weeks. He still has some work to do.

When I reach the broad wash that bisects a long valley between two curving lines of mountains, I continue north, sometimes walking on the loose gravel of the wash, sometimes on the firmer ground by the side of the open corridor. In places, the mountains seem to stack up one on top of the other, with the most distant ridge rising pale gray on the horizon above and behind its darker companions. The quiet is broken only twice, once by the piercing cry of a far-off flicker, and later by the scream of a red-tailed hawk.

After about an hour of walking, I am warm enough to remove my jacket. My water bottle stays within my backpack until I climb a low ridge at the end of a side valley. While removing the cap from my canteen, I look out from my elevated vantage point over another vast desert plain encircled by mountains. The zigzagging washes that wander into and across this landscape are lined in green, the product of paloverdes and ironwoods. At this distance, the rest of the desert looks virtually lifeless, a pale tan mosaic of sunbaked gravel dotted irregularly with slightly darker creosotebushes.

With the morning half gone, I circle around to walk back via the big central wash as it descends to the southern plain. A flock of black-throated sparrows on the border of the wash briefly interject their soft twitters and tinkles into the silence. Later, one cactus wren follows another into the crown of a paloverde. I stop to remove the fine gravel that has somehow insinuated itself into my boots, which are coming apart at the seams.

Eventually I leave the wash and make my way toward a small hill that looks over the creosote flat ahead. From there, I march for thirty minutes or so among the stressed bushes. Halfway across the seemingly empty plain, I flush the first members of a large and diffuse flock of sage sparrows. Every ten steps another bird or two slips out of the creosotes and flies far away, landing on the ground or ducking into distant shrubs. Some birds let me look at them for a few seconds through my binoculars. A sage sparrow nervously flips its tail up and down before scampering out of sight. The overwintering sparrows are here by the dozens, making a go of it, finding what they need in what seems the most unpromising of habitats.

Back at the trailhead, I turn to look at the spartan North Maricopa Mountains once again. Fortunately for them, they are unaware of the drought, the cattle, the ATVs, the vast new city of Maricopa a thirty-minute drive away. These hills and mountains are in it for the long haul. One more year down, one that ends more or less as it began with the creosotebushes apparently on the ropes, the foothill paloverdes nearly leafless, the brown and black rocks piled onto the slopes of the mountains on the horizon. Everything here takes the seasons as they come, perfecting the art of endurance, and I love them for it.

December *The End of a Year*

Today is the eighty-third time that I have visited the Usery Mountains in 2006. The large majority of these visits have involved a climb to the peak, and today is no exception. Although it is midafternoon and sunny with not a trace of cloud in the sky, the temperatures are cool in keeping with the season. In the last ten days, showers have touched down briefly in Tempe, and I am eager to see if the rain also reached the Userys, and if so, whether any annuals have germinated in response. At first, it appears that the recent showers have skipped the mountains altogether. When I kick the gravel away in sunny areas well downhill, the soil underneath is dry. Not surprisingly, no minute poppy or lupine has poked its nose out of the ground here. I tentatively conclude that the clouds must have passed without giving the area even a drop to drink.

But then as I ascend the shaded northeastern side of the mountain, I find a smattering of spike mosses with touches of green, generally on the north-facing edge of boulders and rocks, which would have channeled a bit of the drizzle down to the plants. The amount of rain cannot have been large since 90 percent of the plants are still brown and curled up in their dormant pose, although some of these individuals may have been greener immediately after the rain. Thanks to the protective shadows cast by the mountain, whatever moisture reached the shaded ground has not been evaporatively recycled into the air, so that the soil under the top layer of gravel is still dark and vaguely damp.

Even so, no spring annuals or introduced grasses have dared to present themselves even in this less-desiccated hillside, perhaps because not enough time has elapsed since the showers or because the amount of precipitation was insufficient to stimulate the seeds of annuals to germinate.

Once I near the top of the mountain, I pause to look up toward paloverde B and the saguaros growing on the western ridge before me. Although the scene looks static, I know that there have been significant changes here during the several decades that I have been making my uphill pilgrimages. For one thing, a young adult saguaro on the horizon that was a pure totem pole in the early 1990s has acquired an arm during the intervening years. On the other hand, some of the creamy white teddy bear chollas that once clung to the southern slope below paloverde B have expired, decayed, and disappeared during the same period.

As I proceed to the top of the peak, I review the changes that the seasons have brought to the Userys this year, starting with the major March storm that rescued the desert from the seemingly endless winter drought. The rain stimulated an exuberant response of long-repressed wolfberries, brittlebushes, and many others. This brief vegetative festival soon gave way to the typical summer drought of the premonsoon, a trying period when the climb to the peak in blast furnace heat was a recipe for dehydration. But after much teasing and tantalizing, the monsoon pulled itself together, and gorgeous white cumulus clouds mushroomed high in the sky before spilling their contents on the desert. Then the monsoon-responsive insects came into their own, including the mating harvester ants and desert termites, the alert male *Tachytes* wasps and hungry robber flies, each adding its own touch of life to the mountains. When the monsoon fizzled out in September, as is its custom, drought reasserted itself more vigorously than usual. The late summer's crop of baby paloverdes and ironwoods, which had come up so enthusiastically, began to succumb one by one; the summer hilltopping insects also became scarcer and scarcer, and then they too were gone.

Now at the end of the year, the Userys, like the Maricopa Mountains two hours' drive to the southeast, are pretty much back where they started at the beginning of 2006, bone dry, dead still, in the waiting mode. No substantial rains are forecast for anytime soon in what looks like a rerun of last year's December. Paloverde B is leafless and dusty, although the recent shower must have cleaned it up a bit. All or part of the three saguaros that died in 2006 lie about the peak, their cracked carcasses symbolizing the terminal season of the year. The half-trunk of the most recent dead specimen still stands upright downslope, although signs of its continuing decay are apparent in the trickles of dark fluid that have recently oozed their way down the trunk before drying in place. The vertical lines of black look like thin ribbons of shiny satin lying on the paler skin of the cactus. I expect to find most of the remaining exterior of the cactus on the ground before the winter is out.

Far below me, the master-planned community of Las Sendas is largely obscured by haze and smog, the product of a heat inversion of the sort that regularly afflicts Greater Phoenix at this time of year. As cool, polluted air fills the basin that is the Valley of the Sun, a warmer layer forms above the stagnant smog, holding the contaminated air in place until a windy cold front comes along to push the entire mess eastward.

I would like to believe that I am superior to the smog-inhaling inhabitants of Las Sendas, albeit superior only in the altitudinal sense of being higher up and therefore out of the worst of the trapped pollutants that the Las Sendans must breathe. But I suspect that the smog is up here with me too, with the haze merely invisible at close range.

A rock wren distracts me from my mildly gloomy thoughts by playing hide-and-seek behind a paloverde. It then ducks downhill for good. On my way back to the ridge, before turning downhill myself, I pass the young saguaro whose fortunes I have been following for nearly six years now. The juvenile may be less plump than it was at the end of the monsoon, but it is in no danger of dying, having already withstood in its relatively short life several episodes of months-long drought. This latest dry spell will end sometime this winter, probably well before March,

The southern slope of Usery Peak in the winter of 1991 (left) and winter 2006 (right). During these fifteen years, changes have occurred in the landscape here as some saguaros and barrel cacti have grown larger and changed form while some teddy bear cholla cacti have died and disappeared.

or so I hope. The baby saguaro will then harvest rainwater from the soil and invest in still more bulk and still more spines, which already form a nearly impenetrable thicket over its entire surface. No jackrabbit, no matter how desperate, would choose to gnaw on this cactus now.

I look forward to checking on the little saguaro and its companions on Usery Peak in the year 2007 and beyond. I am a privileged observer in these hills, wonderfully rich as they are in drought-adapted cacti, rock wrens, jojobas, and hilltopping insects. This island of naturalness feels as if it is a million miles from the less appealing urban environment below. Here real seasons come and go, red-tailed hawks and ravens cruise overhead, black and blue swallowtails swirl past at eye level, and rainfall really matters. When the next rain does come, I will take this as an excuse to come here again to find out how the plants and animals are responding to their good fortune, each visit to this mountain increasing my understanding and appreciation of an always changing but most excellent place.

REFERENCES

1. Alcock, J. 1989. The mating system of *Mydas ventralis* (Diptera: Mydidae). *Psyche* 96:167–176.

2. Alcock, J., and K. M. O'Neill. 1986. Density-dependent mating tactics in the gray hairstreak, *Strymon melinus* (Lepidoptera: Lycaenidae). *Journal of Zoology* 209:105–113.

3. Asner, G. P., A. J. Elmore, L. P. Olander, R. A. Martin, and A. T. Harris. 2004. Grazing systems, ecosystem responses, and global change. *Annual Review of Environment and Resources* 29:261–299.

4. Attiwill, P. M. 1994. Ecological disturbance and the conservative management of eucalypt forests in Australia. *Forest Ecology and Management* 63:301–346.

5. Axelrod, D. I. 1979. Age and origin of Sonoran Desert vegetation. *Occasional Papers of the California Academy of Sciences*, no. 132:1–74.

6. Barnosky, A. D., P. L. Koch, R. S. Feranec, S. L. Wing, and A. B. Shabel. 2004. Assessing the causes of Late Pleistocene extinctions on the continents. *Science* 306:70–75.

7. Bayman, J. A. 2001. The Hohokam of southwest North America. *Journal of World Prehistory* 15:257–311.

8. Bean, T. L., and J. L. Betancourt. 2006. Buffelgrass in the Sonoran Desert: Can we prevent the unhinging of a unique American ecosystem? *Plant Press* 30:4–5.

9. Betancourt, J. L., T. R. Van Devender, and P. S. Martin. 1990. *Packrat Middens: The Last 40,000 Years of Biotic Change.* University of Arizona Press, Tucson.

10. Bildstein, K. L. 2001. Raptors as vermin: A history of human attitudes toward Pennsylvania's birds of prey. *Endangered Species Update* 18:124–128.

11. Bixler R. D., M. F. Floyd, and W. E. Hammitt. 2002. Environmental socialization: Quantitative tests of the childhood play hypothesis. *Environment and Behavior* 34:795–818.

12. Bock, C. E., and J. H. Bock. 1999. Response of winter birds to drought and short-duration grazing in southeastern Arizona. *Conservation Biology* 13:1117–1125.

13. Bowers, J. E., and R. M. Turner. 2002. The influence of climatic variability on local population dynamics of *Cercidium microphyllum* (foothill paloverde). *Oecologia* 130:105–113.

14. Bowers, J. E., R. M. Turner, and T. L. Burgess. 2004. Temporal and spatial patterns in emergence and early survival of perennial plants in the Sonoran Desert. *Plant Ecology* 172:107–119.

15. Bowers, J. E. 2005. Effects of drought on shrub survival and longevity in the northern Sonoran Desert. *Journal of the Torrey Botanical Society* 132:421–431.

16. Boyd, R. S., and G. D. Brum. 1983. Predispersal reproductive attrition in a Mojave Desert population of *Larrea tridentata* (Zygophyllaceae). *American Midland Naturalist* 110:14–24.

17. Brazel, A., N. Selover, R. Vose, and G. Heisler. 2000. The tale of two climates—Baltimore and Phoenix urban LTER sites. *Climate Research* 15:123–135.

18. Brower, J.V.Z., and L. P. Brower. 1965. Experimental studies of mimicry. 8. Further investigations of honeybees (*Apis mellifera*) and their dronefly mimics (*Eristalis* spp.). *American Naturalist* 96:173–187.

19. Bryant, N. A., L. F. Johnson, A. J. Brazel, R. C. Balling, C. F. Hutchinson, and L. R. Beck. 1990. Measuring the effect of overgrazing in the Sonoran Desert. *Climate Change* 17:243–264.

20. Burney, D. A., and T. F. Flannery. 2005. Fifty millennia of catastrophic extinctions after human contact. *Trends in Ecology and Evolution* 20:395–401.

21. Burquez-Montijo, A., M. E. Miller, and A. Mártinez-Yrízar. 2002. Mexican grasslands, thornscrub, and the transformation of the Sonoran Desert by invasive exotic buffelgrass (*Pennisetum ciliare*). In: Tellman, B. (ed.), *Invasive Exotic Species in the Sonoran Region*. University of Arizona Press, Tucson, 126–146.

22. Cane, J. H., R. L. Minckley, L. J. Kervin, T. H. Roulston, and N. M. Williams. 2006. Complex responses within a desert bee guild (Hymenoptera: Apiformes) to urban habitat fragmentation. *Ecological Applications* 16:632–644.

23. Contreras-Ramos, A. 1999. Mating behavior of *Platyneuromus* (Megaloptera: Corydalidae), with life history notes on dobsonflies from Mexico and Costa Rica. *Entomological News* 110:125–135.

24. Cook, E. R., C. A. Woodhouse, C. M. Eakin, D. M. Meko, and D. W. Stahle. 2004. Long-term aridity changes in the western United States. *Science* 306:1015–1018.

25. Diamond, J. 2005. *Collapse: How Societies Choose to Fail or Succeed*. Viking Penguin, New York.

26. Didden-Zopfy, B., and P. S. Nobel. 1982. High temperature tolerance and heat acclimation of *Opuntia bigelovii*. *Oecologia* 52:176–180.

27. Drezner, T. D. 2003. A test of the relationship between seasonal rainfall and saguaro cacti branching patterns. *Ecography* 26:393–404.

28. Drezner, T. D. 2004. Saguaro recruitment over their American range: A separation and comparison of summer temperature and rainfall. *Journal of Arid Environments* 56:509–524.

29. Esque, T. C., and C. R. Schwalbe. 2002. Alien annual grasses and their relationships to fire and biotic change in Sonoran desertscrub. In: Tellman, B. (ed.), *Invasive Exotic Species in the Sonoran Region*. University of Arizona Press, Tucson, 165–194.

30. Faeth, S. H., P. S. Warren, E. Shochat, and W. A. Marussich. 2005. Trophic dynamics in urban communities. *BioScience* 55:399–407.

31. Feener, D. H., Jr. 1988. Effects of parasites on foraging and defense behavior of a termitophagous ant, *Pheidole titanis* Wheeler (Hymenoptera: Formicidae). *Behavioral Ecology and Sociobiology* 22:421–427.

32. Fleming, T. H., M. D. Tuttle, and M. A. Horner. 1996. Pollination biology and the relative importance of nocturnal and diurnal pollinators in three species of Sonoran Desert columnar cacti. *Southwestern Naturalist* 41:257–269.

33. Golding, Y., R. Ennos, M. Sullivan, and M. Edmunds. 2005. Hoverfly mimicry deceives humans. *Journal of Zoology* 266:395–399.

34. Hamilton, W. J., III, and M. K. Seely. 1976. Fog basking by the Namib Desert beetle, *Onymacris unguicularis*. *Nature* 262:284–285.

35. Hasting, J. R., and R. M. Turner. 1965. *The Changing Mile: An Ecological Study of Vegetation Change with Time in the Lower Mile of an Arid and Semiarid Region*. University of Arizona Press, Tucson.

36. Haverty, M. I. 2001. The role of toilet paper in studies of desert subterranean termites (Isoptera) in Arizona, USA: A substrate for nondestructive observations of foraging activity. *Sociobiology* 37:245–252.

37. Hawkes, C. V., I. F. Wren, D. J. Herman, and M. K. Fireston. 2005. Plant invasion alters nitrogen cycling by modifying the soil nitrifying community. *Ecology Letters* 8:976–985.

38. Hawkins, T. W., A. J. Brazel, W. L. Stefanov, W. Bigler, and E. M. Saffeil. 2004. The role of rural variability in urban heat island determination for Phoenix, Arizona. *Journal of Applied Meteorology* 43:476–486.

39. Hayashi, F. 1998. Multiple mating and lifetime reproductive output in female dobsonflies that receive nuptial gifts. *Ecological Research* 13:283–289.

40. Hölldobler, B., and E. O. Wilson. 1990. *The Ants*. Harvard University Press, Cambridge, MA.

41. Hunter, K. L., J. L. Betancourt, T. R. Van Devender, K. L. Cole, and W. G. Spaulding. 2001. Ploidy race distributions since the Last Glacial Maximum in the North American desert shrub, *Larrea tridentata*. *Global Ecology and Biogeography* 10:521–533.

42. Ishikawa, M., and L. V. Gusta. 1996. Freezing and heat tolerance of *Opuntia* cacti native to the Canadian prairie provinces. *Canadian Journal of Botany* 74:1890–1895.

43. Johnson, C. N. 2002. Determinants of loss of mammal species during the Late Quaternary "megafauna" extinctions: Life history and ecology, but not body size. *Proceedings of the Royal Society B* 269:2221–2227.

44. Kinzig, A. P., P. Warren, C. Martin, D. Hope, and M. Katti. 2005. The effects of human socioeconomic status and cultural characteristics on urban patterns of biodiversity. *Ecology and Society* 10 (June 2005). http://www.ecologyandsociety.org/vol10/iss1/art23/.

45. Krueper, D., J. Bart, and T. D. Rich. 2003. Response of vegetation and breeding birds to the removal of cattle on the San Pedro River, Arizona (U.S.A.). *Conservation Biology* 17:607–613.

46. Louv, R. 2005. *Last Child in the Woods: Saving Our Children from Nature-Deficit Disorder.* Algonquin Books, Chapel Hill, NC.

47. Mangan, R. L. 1979. Reproductive behavior of the cactus fly, *Odontoloxozus longicornis*, male territoriality and female guarding as adaptive strategies. *Behavioral Ecology and Sociobiology* 4:265–278.

48. Martin, B. E., and T. R. Van Devender. 2002. Seasonal diet changes of *Gopherus agassizii* (desert tortoise) in desert grassland of southern Arizona and its behavioral implications. *Herpetological Natural History* 9:31–42.

49. Maschwitz, U., and J. Moog. 2000. Communal "peeing": A new mode of flood control in ants. *Naturwissenschaften* 12:563–565.

50. McAuliffe, J. R. 1990. Paloverdes, pocket mice, and bruchid beetles: Interrelationships of seeds, dispersers, and seed predators. *Southwestern Naturalist* 35:329–337.

51. McAuliffe, J. R. 1995. The aftermath of wildfires in the Sonoran Desert. *Sonoran Quarterly* 49:4–8.

52. McAuliffe, J. R. 2002. Boom to bust and back again: Impacts of extreme droughts and floods in the desert. *Sonoran Quarterly* 56:4–9.

53. McAuliffe, J. R., E. P. Hamerlynck, and M. C. Eppes. 2007. Landscape dynamics fostering the development and persistence of long-lived creosotebush (*Larrea tridentata*) clones in the Mojave Desert. *Journal of Arid Environments* 69:96–126.

54. McAuliffe, J. R., P. C. Sundt, B. A. Valiente, A. Casas, and J. L. Viveros. 2001. Pre-Columbian soil erosion, persistent ecological changes, and collapse of a subsistence agricultural economy in the semi-arid Teohuacan Valley, Mexico's "Cradle of Maize." *Journal of Arid Environments* 47:47–75.

55. McAuliffe, J. R., and T. R. Van Devender. 1998. A 22,000-year record of vegetation change in the north-central Sonoran Desert. *Palaeogeography, Palaeoclimatology, Palaeoecology* 141:253–275.

56. McGregor, S. E., S. M. Alcorn, and G. Olin. 1962. Pollination and pollinating agents of the saguaro. *Ecology* 43:259–267.

57. McIntyre, N. E., and M. E. Hostetler. 2001. Effects of land use on pollinator (Hymenoptera: Apoidea) communities in a desert metropolis. *Basic and Applied Ecology* 2:209–218.

58. M'Closkey, R. T., R. J. Deslippe, C. P. Szpak, and K. A. Baia. 1990. Ecological correlates of the variable mating system of an iguanid lizard. *Oikos* 59:63–69.

59. Myles, T. G. 1986. Oviposition and development of *Volucella isabellina* (Diptera: Syrphidae) on saguaro cactus *Cereus giganteus*. *Entomological News* 97:104–108.

60. Novak, S. J., and R. N. Mack. 2001. Tracing plant introduction and spread: Genetic evidence from *Bromus tectorum* (cheatgrass). *BioScience* 51:114–122.

61. Nutting, W. L., M. I. Haverty, and J. P. Lafage. 1987. Physical and chemical alteration of soil by 2 subterranean termite species in Sonoran Desert grassland. *Journal of Arid Environments* 12:233–239.

62. O'Neill, K. M. 1992. Body size asymmetries in predatory interactions among robber flies (Diptera, Asilidae). *Annals of the Entomological Society of America* 85:34-38.

63. Parker, K. C. 1993. Climatic effects on regeneration trends for two columnar cacti in the northern Sonoran Desert. *Annals of the Association of American Geographers* 83:452-474.

64. Penn, D. J. 2003. The evolutionary roots of our environmental problems: Toward a Darwinian ecology. *Quarterly Review of Biology* 78:275-301.

65. Pierson, E. A., and R. M. Turner. 1998. An 85-year study of saguaro (*Carnegiea gigantea*) demography. *Ecology* 79:2676-2693.

66. Pimentel, D., R. Zuniga, and D. Morrison. 2004. Update on the environmental and economic costs associated with alien-invasive species in the United States. *Ecological Economics* 52:273-288.

67. Pitzl, M. J. 2005. Desert took worst of state's worst fire year. *Arizona Republic* (Phoenix), August 26.

68. Pyne, S. J. 1992. *Burning Bush: A Fire History of Australia*. Allen and Unwin, North Sydney, NSW.

69. Rost, T. L., A. D. Simper, P. Schell, and S. Allen. 1977. Anatomy of jojoba (*Simmondsia chinensis*) seed and the utilization of liquid wax during germination. *Economic Botany* 31:140-147.

70. Ruffner, G., and W. D. Clark. 1986. Extrafloral nectar of *Ferocactus acanthodes* (Cactaceae): Composition and its importance to ants. *American Journal of Botany* 73:185-189.

71. Sabo, J. L., R. Sponseller, M. Dixon, K. Gade, T. Harms, J. Heffernan, A. Jani, G. Katz, C. Soykan, J. Watts, and A. Welter. 2005. Riparian zones increase regional species richness by harboring different, not more, species. *Ecology* 86:56-62.

72. Salo, L. F. 2005. Red brome (*Bromus rubens* subsp. *madritensis*) in North America: Possible modes for early introductions, subsequent spread. *Biological Invasions* 7:165-180.

73. Salo, L. F., G. R. McPherson, and D. G. Williams. 2005. Sonoran Desert winter annuals affected by density of red brome and soil nitrogen. *American Midland Naturalist* 153:95-109.

74. Sanderson, E. W., M. Jaiteh, M. A. Levy, K. H. Redford, A. V. Wannebo, and G. Woolmer. 2002. The human footprint and the last of the wild. *BioScience* 52:891-904.

75. Savory, A. 1988 *Holistic Resource Management*. Island Press, Washington DC.

76. Schaefer, H. M., and N. Stobber. 2006. Disruptive coloration provides camouflage independent of background matching. *Proceedings of the Royal Society B* 273:2427-2432.

77. Schmidt, J. O., and S. L. Buchmann. 1986. Floral biology of the saguaro (*Cereus giganteus*). 1. Pollen harvest by *Apis mellifera*. *Oecologia* 69:491-498.

78. Schulte, L. A., A. M. Pidgeon, and D. J. Mladenoff. 2005. One hundred fifty years of change in forest bird breeding habitat: Estimates of species distributions. *Conservation Biology* 19:1944-1956.

79. Seely, M. K., C. J. Lewis, K. A. O'Brien, and A. E. Suttle. 1983. Fog response of tenebrionid beetles in the Namib Desert. *Journal of Arid Environments* 6:135-143.

80. Sels, R.V.C., and L. J. Vitt. 1984. Desert lizard reproduction: Seasonal and annual variation in *Urosaurus ornatus* (Iguanidae). *Canadian Journal of Zoology* 62:1779-1784.

81. Sherbrooke, W. C. 1990. Rain-harvesting in the lizard, *Phrynosoma cornutum*: Behavior and integumental morphology. *Journal of Herpetology* 24:302-308.

82. Sherbrooke, W. C. 2004. Integumental water movement and rate of water ingestion during rain harvesting in the Texas horned lizard, *Phrynosoma cornutum*. *Amphibia-Reptilia* 25:29-39.

83. Shoshat, E., W. L. Stevanov, M.E.A. Whitehouse, and S. H. Faeth. 2004. Urbanization and spider diversity: Influences of human habitat structure and modification. *Ecological Applications* 14:268-280.

84. Siemens, D. H. 1994. Factors affecting regulation of maternal investment in an indeterminate flowering plant (*Cercidium microphyllum*; Fabaceae). *American Journal of Botany* 81:1403–1409.

85. Smith, S. D., T. E. Huxman, S. F. Zitzer, T. N. Charlet, D. C. Housman, J. S. Coleman, L. K. Fenstermaker, J. R. Seeman, and R. S. Nowak. 2000. Elevated CO_2 increases productivity and invasive species success in an arid ecosystem. *Nature* 408:79–82.

86. Steenbergh, W. F., and C. H. Lowe. 1983. *Ecology of the Saguaro: III: Growth and Demography*. National Park Services Monographic Series, no. 17. National Park Service, Washington DC.

87. Stevens, M., I. C. Cuthill, A.M.M. Windsor, and H. J. Walker. 2006. Disruptive contrast in animal camouflage. *Proceedings of the Royal Society B* 273:2433–2438.

88. Terborgh, J. W. 1989. *Where Have All the Birds Gone?* Princeton University Press, Princeton, NJ.

89. Tevis, L., Jr., and I. M. Newell. 1962. Studies on the biology and seasonal cycle of the giant red velvet mite, *Dinothrombium pandorae* (Acari, Trombidiidae). *Ecology* 43:497–505.

90. Thompson, C. W., and M. C. Moore. 1991. Throat colour reliably signals status in male tree lizards, *Urosaurus ornatus*. *Animal Behaviour* 42:745–753.

91. Turner, R. M., R. H. Webb, J. E. Bowers, and J. R. Hastings. 2003. *The Changing Mile Revisited: An Ecological Study of Vegetation Change with Time in the Lower Mile of an Arid and Semiarid Region*. University of Arizona Press, Tucson.

92. Turner, W. R., T. Nakamura, and M. Dinetti. 2004. Global urbanization and the separation of humans from nature. *BioScience* 54:585–590.

93. Ulrich, R. S. 1993. Biophilia, biophobia, and natural landscapes. In: Kellert, S. R, and E. O. Wilson (eds.), *The Biophilia Hypothesis*, 73–137. Island Press, Washington DC.

94. Valone, T. J., M. Meyer, J. H. Brown, and R. M. Chew. 2002. Timescale of perennial grass recovery in desertified arid grasslands following livestock removal. *Conservation Biology* 16:995–1002.

95. Van Devender, T. R. 2000. The deep history of the Sonoran Desert. In: Phillips, S. J., and P. W. Comus (eds.), *The Natural History of the Sonoran Desert*, 61–69. University of California Press, Berkeley and Los Angeles.

96. Van Devender, T. R. 2001. Deep history and biogeography of La Frontera. In: Webster, G. L., and C. J. Bahre (eds.), *Changing Plant Life of La Frontera*, 56-66. University of New Mexico Press, Albuquerque.

97. Vasek, F. C. 1980. Creosote bush: Long-lived clones in the Mojave Desert. *American Journal of Botany* 67:246–255.

98. Vose, R. S., D. R. Easterling, and B. Gleason. 2005. Maximum and minimum temperature trends for the globe: An update through 2004. *Geophysical Research Letters* 32:L23822.

99. Waguespack, N. M. 2007. Why we're still arguing about the Pleistocene occupation of the Americas. *Evolutionary Anthropology* 16:63–74.

100. Ward, J. P., S. E. Smith, and M. P. McClaren. 2006. Water requirements for emergence of buffelgrass (*Pennisetum ciliare*). *Weed Science* 54:720–725.

101. Waters, M. R., and J. C. Ravesloot. 2001. Landscape change and the cultural evolution of the Hohokam along the Middle Gila River and other river valleys in south-central Arizona. *American Antiquity* 66:285–299.

102. Weiss, J. L., and J. T. Overpeck. 2005. Is the Sonoran Desert losing its cool? *Global Change Biology* 11:2065–2077.

103. Wells, N. M., and K. S. Lekies. 2006. Nature and the life course: Pathways from childhood nature experiences to adult environmentalism. *Children, Youth, and Environment* 16:1–24.

104. Wilcove, D. S., D. Rothstein, J. Dubow, A. Phillips, and E. Losos. 1998. Quantifying threats to imperiled species in the United States. *BioScience* 48:607–615.

105. Wilson, E. O. 1984. *Biophilia*. Harvard University Press, Cambridge, MA.

106. Wilson, E. O. 2003. *Pheidole in the New World: A Dominant, Hyperdiverse Ant Genus.* Harvard University Press, Cambridge, MA.

107. Wolf, B. O., and C. Martínez del Rio. 2003. How important are columnar cacti as sources of water and nutrients for desert consumers? A review. *Isotopes in Environmental and Health Studies* 39:53–67.

108. Woodhouse, C. A., K. E. Kunkel, D. R. Easterling, and E. R. Cook. 2005. The twentieth-century pluvial in the western United States. *Geophysical Research Letters* 32 (7): L07701.

INDEX

Page numbers in *italics* indicate illustrations.

A

acacias, 223

agriculture, 32; in Greater Phoenix area, 33, 129; Hohokam, 53–54; jojoba, 176–77

air-conditioning: Mesa area growth, 34

air pollution, 319

alfalfa fields: spiders in, 133

animals: urban, 130–31. *See also by type*

annuals, 63, 69, 289; spring, 7, 58, *114*

ants: *Aphaenogaster cockerelli*, 310–11; fluid collection by, 311–12; harvester (*Pogonomyrmex* spp.), 169, 184, 185, *186*, 188–90, *191*, 192, 193, 195, 196, 197, 199–200, 203, 211, 212, 318; leaf-cutter, 192; *Pheidole titanis*, 303–4

Apache Junction, 35

Apaches, 43

Aphaenogaster cockerelli, 310–11

archaeology: Hohokam, 43–46, 53–54; petroglyphs, 261, 262, 277

Arizona Department of Agriculture: buffelgrass as noxious weed, 71

artifacts: prehistoric, 44–45, *46. See also* trash

Aspidoscelis tigris, 146, 151, 170, 183

Atlides halesus, 100–102, 103, 272–73, 286, 308

avocets, *142*, 143

Axelrod, Daniel, 27

B

bacteria: in decaying saguaros, 287

Ballantine Trail, *107*

barrel cacti, *162*, 163; fluid-dispensing glands on, 311–12; spiny, 295; summer heat, 167, 295; and wildfire, 63, 179

bats: saguaro pollination by, 156

Battus philenor, 98–99, *101*, 103, 212, 258, 272, 284, 286

bees, 74; biodiversity of, 134–35; digger (*Centris pallida*), 124, 125. *See also* honey bees

beetles: bruchid, 82; tenebrionid, 311; wood-boring (*Trachyderes mandibularis*), 173

Bermuda grass, 246

Betancourt, Julio, 54

bighorn sheep, desert: petroglyphs of, *277*

bikers: mountain, 310

biodiversity, 71; in cities, 131, 132, 133–34, 135–36; in Gilbert Riparian Preserve, 140–44; and grazing, 249–50; human exposure to, 138–39

Biophilia (Wilson), 137

biophilia hypothesis, 137–38, 139, 140

birds: city, 130–32; at Gilbert Riparian Preserve (Water Ranch), 142–44; grazing impacts on, 251–52; and saguaro fruit, 157, 159–60; on San Pedro River, 250. *See also by type*

bird-watching, 143–44, 264–65

bittern: least, 143

bladderpod, 7

Blandford Homes, 35

blitzkrieg hypothesis, 29

Bock, Carl, 251

Bock, Jane, 251

bosques: mesquite, 32–33

bot flies (*Cuterebra austeni*), 96, *97*–98

Boulder Creek Trail, 254–56

Bowers, Janice, 258

brittlebushes, 166, 207, 273, 278; blooms of, 58, 117; in burn areas, 178, 179; after monsoon rains, 196, *198*, *200*

brome, red (*Bromus madritensis*; *B. rubens*), 19, 65, 67, 68, 69, *178*, 179; fire and, 70–71

Bromus: madritensis; *rubens*, 19, 65, 67, 68, 69, 70–71, *178*, 179; *tectorum*, 68, 69

Broun, Maurice, 264

bruchid beetles, 82

buffelgrass, 67–68, 73; and wildfires, 69–71

Bureau of Land Management, 128–29, 299–300, 315

burn areas: recovery of, 175–76, 177–79, *180*

bursage, 58, 273; in burn areas, 178, 179

Bush Highway, 32, 34

butterflies: California patch, 236; empress, 245; hairstreaks, 98, 99–100, *101*, 102, 103, 213, 272–73, 286, 308; lyside sulphurs, 224; skipper, *204*, 272; swallowtail, 98–99,

101, 103, 212, 258, 272, 284, 286; time partitioning by, 103–4; *Vanessa* spp., 100, 102

C

cacti, 28; and wildfires, 70. *See also by type*

camouflage, 213, *214*, 215

cannibalism: in robber flies, 184–85

carbon dioxide: exotic plants and, 68–69

Cardell, Bob, 111

caterpillars: fall, 236–37, 245; paloverde, 236–37

cats, 132

cattle, 67, 247, 249; ecological recovery from, 250–51; in Maricopa Mountains, 260, 313, 314–15

Cave Creek Complex fire, 61–62

Centris pallida, 124, 125

Cephenemyia sp., *97*

Chaco Canyon, 54

cheatgrass (*Bromus tectorum*), 68, 69

chia, 58

chicory: desert (*Rafinesquia neomexicana*), *115*

children: exposure to nature, 136–37, 138–39

chipmunk, cliff, 160

chollas: chain-fruit, 8, 63, 167; teddy bear, 167, 295–96, 318

cities: bees in, 134–35; biodiversity in, 135–36; birds in, 130–31; children raised in, 136–37; impacts of, 129–31; insects in, 132–33; spiders in, 133–34

citrus orchards: Phoenix area, 33, 129

climate, 27; reconstruction of past, 51–54; and urban development, 42–43

climate change: post-Pleistocene, 28, 42–43; saguaro distribution and, 27

Clinton, Bill: Sonoran Desert National Monument, 128

Clovis people, 29, 43

Coffee Flats Trail, 240, 244, 245–47

coloration: cryptic, *214*, 215, 267–68; disruptive, 265, 268–70

columnar cacti, 28. *See also* saguaros

conservation: water, 54

239–44, 253–54; in Usery Mountains, 9–10, 166–67

Hohokam, 33; artifacts, 43–*46*; climate and, 52–53; cultural collapse, 53–54; petroglyphs, 261, 262

honey bees, 124, 134, 184; mimics of, 271–72; saguaro pollination by, 154, 156

horned lizards, 199, 200, 215; rain collecting by, 311; regal, 265, *266*, 269

horses: in Usery Mountains, 283–84

Hostetler, Mark: bee study by, 134–35

housing developments, 39; in Maricopa, 127–28; in Mesa area, 34–38, *285*, 319

human footprint, 2–3

hummingbirds: Anna's, 131; Costa's, 131; as saguaro pollinators, 156

I

illegal aliens: in Sonoran Desert National Monument, 299–301

insects, 1; hilltopping, 87–88, 89, 91–104, 192, 202, 203–5, 211–12, 227–30, 235–36, 258, 263–64, 271–73, 284, 286, 290, 305, 319; monsoon-responsive, 244–45, 318; in Phoenix, 134–35; time partitioning of, 102–4. *See also by type*

ironwoods, 294; flowering and germination of, 122–24, 125; monsoon rains and, 231, 233, 318; seedlings of, 222–*23*, 283, 318

irrigation systems, 32; Hohokam, 33, 53

J

jackrabbit: black-tailed, 295

Janusia gracilis, 233

Johnson, Bob, 304

Johnson, Michael, 10–11, 12–13; saguaro, 9, *14*

jojobas, 178; agricultural production of, 176–77

Jones, Robert Trent: golf course design, 35

jumping beans, Mexican (*Sebastiania bilocularis*), 259

K

kangaroo rats, 282

katydids, 173, 268

Kelleher, Karen, 315

King Clone: age of, 41–42

Krameria grayi, 115

L

LaBarge Narrows, 254–55

larkspur: desert, 114

Larrea divaricata; L. tridentata, 40, 51, 63, 69, 135, 278; ages of, 41–43

Las Sendas development, 35, 36–*37*, 284, *285*, 319

learning: biophilic, 138

Leschenaultia adusta, 96, *97*, 286, 290, 305

Libellula saturata, 202, 203–4, 210, 235–36

limb autotomy: in chollas, 167; in paloverdes, 81–82

littering. *See* trash

livestock, 67; ecological restoration and, 250–51; grazing impacts of, 251–52; Maricopa Mountains, 260, 313, 314–15; water use by, 247, 249

lizards: ornate tree (*Urosaurus ornatus*), 146, 147–51, 172–73, 183, 273; side-blotched (*Uta stansburiana*), 146, 147, 151, 172–73, 273; tiger whiptail (*Aspidoscelis tigris*), 146, 151, 170, 183. *See also* horned lizards

Long-Term Ecological Research (LTER) project, 132–34

lupines, 58, 114

Lycium berlandieri, 11, 116, 179, 200, 224

M

Mangan, Robert, 308

Maricopa: housing developments in, 127–28

Maricopa Mountains, 41, 44, 49, 261–62; monsoon rainfall on, 259–60

marigolds: foetid, 278

Martin, Paul, 29

McAuliffe, Joe, 41

McIntyre, Nancy: bee study, 134–35

megafauna, Pleistocene, 28–30

Mesa: growth of, 33–38; winter rainfall, 313–14

mesquite forests: on Salt River, 32–33

mice, pocket, 82–83, 222

microbursts, 15

middens, packrat, 26–27, 42, 52

midges, 202, 236

migrations: bird, 143, 250, 264

milkweed (*Sarcostemma cynanchoides*), *214*, 215

milkweed bugs, *214*, 215

mimicry: drone fly, 271–72; robber fly, 229

mites: giant red velvet, 190

Mojave Desert, 41, 67, 69

monsoon, 1, 161, 318; dust storms, 171–72; hilltopping insects in, 211–12, 244–45, 318; rainfall, 183, 196–97, 222, 231, 233, 234, 259–60; storms, 13, 15, 161, 187–88, 207–8, 210–11, *232*

Moore, Michael: ornate tree lizard study, 149–50

Mormons: in Mesa, 33

mosses: spike, 163–64, 207, 273, 317–18

moths, 213, *214*; gelechiid, 121, 122

motorbikes, 175

mustard: bladderpod, 7; European, 33

Mydas ventralis, 172, 181, *204*

N

Namib Desert, 311

nature: human exposure to, 136–39

nature-deficit disorder, 137

Newton, Doug, 261

nitrogen cycling: exotic plants and, 68–69

North Maricopa Mountains Wilderness Area: foresummer, 119–25; winter, 313–16

noxious weeds: buffelgrass as, 71

O

ocotillos, 114, 116, 196, 259

Odontoloxozus longicornis, 308

offroad vehicles, 222

Opuntia fragilis, 296

orioles, 156; Scott's, 124–25; streak-backed, 143

overgrazing: ecological impacts of, 250–51

overpopulation, 140

P

packrats, white-throated: bot flies and, 97–98; middens, 26–27, 52; nests, *18*, 19; and paloverde seeds, 82–83

painted ladies, 100, 102

paleobotany/paleoecology, 26–27, 52

Palmodes praestans, 173

palms: South American, 129

paloverde #1, 81

paloverde #10, 74, 76–77, 78–*79*

paloverde #16, 80–81

paloverde #17, 77, 78–*79*, 181

ABOUT THE AUTHOR

John Alcock, a Regents' Professor of biology at Arizona State University, has been a natural historian of the Sonoran Desert in central Arizona for more than three decades. Although his academic research has focused on the reproductive behavior of a diversity of desert insects, ranging from tarantula hawk wasps to blister beetles, he has an interest in all creatures (and plants) great and small that live in this wonderful desert. When not visiting his primary field research site, the Usery Mountains near Phoenix, he can often be found walking in wild places like the Superstition Mountains and the Barry M. Goldwater Range. Over the years he has written ten books on subjects ranging from orchid biology to animal behavior. His books on the biology of desert life include *Sonoran Desert Spring*, *Sonoran Desert Summer*, and *In a Desert Garden*, all published by the University of Arizona Press.